ANDREA IMMER'S

WINE BUYING GUIDE

for Everyone

D0067571

ANDREA IMMER'S

WINE BUYING GUIDE

for Everyone

FEATURING MORE THAN 400 TOP WINES
AVAILABLE IN STORES AND RESTAURANTS

Andrea Immer

Edited by Anthony Giglio

Broadway Books / New York

BROADWAY

Broadway Books titles may be purchased for business or promo-tional use or for special sales. For information, please write to: Special Markets Department, Random House, Inc., 280 Park Avenue, New York, NY 10017.

PRINTED IN THE UNITED STATES OF AMERICA

BROADWAY BOOKS and its logo, a letter B bisected on the diag-onal, are trademarks of Broadway Books, a division of Random House, Inc.

Visit our website at www.broadwaybooks.com

Cataloging-in-Publication Data is on file with the Library of Congress.

FIRST EDITION

ISBN 0-7679-1184-9

10 9 8 7 6 5 4 3

CONTENTS

INTRODUCTION

Although enjoying a good glass of wine is easy, all the types, costs, and confusing labels can make *shopping* for a bottle pretty hard. For the typical wine consumer, buying guidance—in the form of critics' 100-point scores and elaborate tasting reports of rare and exclusive bottlings—isn't much help. That is why I wrote *Andrea Immer's Wine Buying Guide for Everyone*. It is your road map to the *real* world of wine buying—from restaurants and hotels to supermarkets, price clubs, wine shops, and websites. Here is what you'll find inside:

Real-World Wines
This guide showcases more than 400 of the most popular and available wines on the market. That includes everything from supermarket stalwarts to trade-up labels to superpremium "restaurant" brands (with plenty of boutique pedigree but without the you-can't-get-it frustration). Putting it plainly, if the wine is in your favorite neighborhood shops and eateries, at your supermarket or Costco, Olive Garden or Walt Disney World, Marriott or Carnival Cruises, Delta Airlines or wine.com, it's probably in this book.

Wine Reviews from the Trenches
I am indebted to the many consumers and wine pros who helped assess, for each of the wines in this book, what really matters to buyers at the point of purchase—taste and value for the money. For each wine, you'll also see their real-world reactions, as well as my impressions of how the wine stacks up in its grape or style category and in the marketplace overall. My tasters also contributed write-in candidates to the list of wines, and I've included those that received the highest number of positive mentions and have decent availability. There's also space in each listing for your notes, so you can keep track of the wines you

try. (I hope you'll share your impressions with me for the next edition—read on to see how.)

Other Helpful Buying Tools in the Guide

Throughout the *Immer Guide*, I've included simple tools to address just about every major wine buying question I've ever been asked. They are:

Best-Of Lists—A quick reference to the top-performing wines in each grape or style category.

Andrea's Kitchen Fridge Survivor™ and Kitchen Countertop Survivor™ grades—"How long will a wine keep after it's opened?" Having heard this question more than any other from my restaurant customers and wine students, I decided several years ago that it was time to find out, so I started putting every wine I taste professionally to the "fridge/countertop test." The resulting report card should help both home wine drinkers and restaurateurs who pour wine by the glass make the most of the leftovers, by simply recorking and storing red wine on the kitchen countertop and storing recorked sparkling, white, and pink wines in the fridge.

Immer Best Bets—This is the book's "search engine" of instant recommendations for every common wine occasion and buying dilemma, from Thanksgiving wines to restaurant wine list best bets, party-crowd pleasers, blue chip bottles to impress the client, and more.

Wine List Decoder—This handy cross-reference chart will help you crack the code of different wine list terms, so you can quickly and easily find the styles you like.

***Great Wine Made Simple* Mini-Course**—Mini-lessons covering wine styles, label terms, glassware, buying wine in stores and restaurants, and other housekeeping details to simplify buying and serving wine, so you can focus on enjoying it.

I had been in the restaurant wine business for more than a decade before I wrote my first book, *Great Wine Made Simple*. Having studied like crazy to pass the Master Sommelier exam (the hardest wine test you can imagine), I knew there were lots of great books out there. So why another? Because as I worked training waiters and budding sommeliers, I began to see that in practice those books weren't much help. Wine, like food, golf, the saxophone, and so many other sensory pursuits, is something you learn not by studying but by doing. So *Great Wine Made Simple* teaches wine not through memorization but the way I learned it—through tasting. It works, and it's fun, whether you are just a dabbler or a committed wine geek.

Similarly, I intend this guide to fill a gap. Most people around the country buy wine based on price and convenience. And whether it's restaurant guests, live callers on my Food Network and radio appearances, or e-mail from readers of my *Esquire* column, they all have the same questions: What are the good, cheap wines? And which wines are really worth the splurge? This buying guide is the first to answer those questions realistically, featuring wines and tastes in the broad marketplace, along with plenty of shrewd pro advice to help you make the most of every wine purchase. Food is one major way to do that, so as a professionally trained cook I've also included lots of pairing pointers.

HOW TO USE THIS
BUYING GUIDE

Here is everything you need to know to get instant buying power from the *Immer Guide*.

Looking Up Wine Recommendations— by Wine Category or Winery Name

Wine Category—Grape, Region, or Type
The wine reviews are grouped by major grape variety, region, or type. For example:

Reviews
section
headings
look like this

WHITE WINES
Sparkling/Champagne

You'll probably recognize some of the main grape and style categories, because they lead the wine market in both quality and sales. These include what I call the Big Six grapes (the white grapes Riesling, Sauvignon Blanc, and Chardonnay; and the reds Pinot Noir, Merlot, and Cabernet Sauvignon), plus Pinot Grigio, Italian reds, Syrah/Shiraz, and some other popular categories. This is also the way most wine lists and many shops are set up. The "Other Whites" and "Other Reds" sections are used for less common grapes and proprietary blends.

Helpful to know: I've arranged all the wine categories from lightest to fullest in body, as a quick reference for when you are shopping or perusing a wine list. More and more, restaurant wine lists are being arranged by body style, too, because it helps both the guest and the server quickly determine which wines are lightest or heaviest, so they can match their personal preference or food choice if they wish.

Winery Name—Alphabetical Wine Listings

The wines in each category are in alphabetical order by winery name, so you can easily find the specific wine you're looking for. For example:

Wine category heading

Alphabetical wine listings

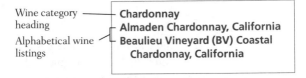

Chardonnay
Almaden Chardonnay, California
Beaulieu Vineyard (BV) Coastal
Chardonnay, California

Helpful to know: If you are looking for a specific winery name rather than a grape or style category, the Winery Index at the back of the book will show you which producers' wines were reviewed for the guide and the page number for each wine review.

Key to the Ratings and Symbols in Each Wine Entry

This sample entry identifies the components of each wine listing.

1. Wine name and provenance (country or state)
2. Price category
3. Taste and value ratings
4. Symbols: These identify wines rated as
   ✓ best-of (rated most popular in their category)
   ⚑ pro picks, or
   ✗ worthy write-ins in their respective categories.
   ♥ indicates an Immer "Top 50 Wines You're Not Drinking" selection.

---

❶ Chateau Andrea Rosé   **PC**   **T**   **V**
New York   **$$**   **26**   **28**

❷ ❸

❹ ♥ Tasters marvel at its "amazing quality for a ❺ bag-in-the-box." Pro buyers (including me) find it "every bit as good as the finest Cold Duck … and sometimes better!"

❻ *Kitchen Fridge Survivor™ Grade: A*

❼ Your notes: _____

---

5. Reviewers' commentary, in quotation marks, along with my notes on the wine
6. My Kitchen Fridge/Countertop Survivor™ Grade
7. Space for your wine notes.

Price Category

Prices for the same wine can vary widely across the country. Here's why: individual states regulate the sale and taxation of wine within their borders, and sometimes local municipalities have further regulations and taxes. That means the price for any particular wine depends very much on where you live and shop. In general, wines are cheapest in large urban areas, where there's lots of retail competition. They are usually most expensive in so-called "control states," where there is zero competition because the state acts as the sole retailer (Pennsylvania is one example). In addition, some of the wines in the survey are available in a different size or in more than one size (e.g., half-bottles, standard 750 ml bottles, magnums, jugs, and larger). The price categories here, based on a standard 750 ml bottle, are intended as a guideline to help you compare relative prices of the different wines in the survey:

$ = up to $12
$$ = $12.01 to $20
$$$ = 20.01 to $35
$$$$ = above $35

NA indicates a wine not available in 750 ml bottles (sold only in jugs or bag-in-box format; prices for these are quite low).

Note: These are retail store prices, not restaurant wine list prices.

Taste and Value Ratings

Tasters (no pro credentials necessary, just an opinion) were asked to assess any of the listed wines that they'd tried in the past year on the following criteria:

- *Taste*—What did you think of the wine's taste?
- *Value for the Money*—Were you happy with what you got for the price you paid?

I kept the rating criteria simple, with scores listed on a scale of 0 to 30:

  0–9 = Poor
 10–15 = Fair
 16–19 = Good
 20–25 = Very good
 26–30 = Outstanding
     X = No data available

Certainly everyone has an opinion based on his or her own preferences and experience, and that is precisely what I sought to capture with this simple scale. I have also come to believe, from my years in the restaurant business and teaching wine classes, that most consumers can recognize inherent wine quality, regardless of their level of wine sophistication. I am pleased to say that the responses bore that out. Specifically, the wines that are consistently recognized by experts as quality and value leaders in their category were standouts among my tasters, too. Similarly, wines that have slipped, or whose price has risen unduly, were for the most part assessed accordingly. Other provocative attributes that influenced commentary and ratings included extreme prices (either high or low), an extreme reputation (either good or bad), and substantial inconsistency in the taste from one year to the next.

Symbols

Worthy Write-In **X** —Denotes that a wine was added to the book listings by popular demand (as noted earlier, only those write-ins with decent availability were included). Because most tasters gave their write-ins verbal endorsements rather than scores, I haven't included scores here but will do so in future editions of the guide.

Pro Pick **⚑** —Indicates that a wine received consistently high praise from trade tasters.

Best-Of **✓**—Identifies the top-rated wines in each category. (Rated "most popular" in the category—an average of the taste and value scores.)

Top 50 WYND **♥** —Denotes an Immer "Top 50 Wines You're Not Drinking" selection. Since they are my write-ins and thus not assessed by my tasters, no scores are included.

Reviewers' Commentary and My Notes

Along with their taste and value assessments, reviewers were asked to include comments on the wines—not tasting descriptions per se but "buyers' notes" reflecting their gut reactions to the wine. If they felt a wine was overrated, underappreciated, delicious, awful, in a beautiful (or ugly) bottle, or whatever, I asked them to say so and have passed along those impressions, as well as my own based on working every day with myriad wines, wine servers, and wine drinkers.

Andrea's Kitchen Fridge Survivor™ and Kitchen Countertop Survivor™ Grades

I think a great many people hesitate to open wine for everyday meals because they won't know what to do with leftovers. No wonder! It's wildly expensive to pour out unfinished wine. And the frustration of wondering and worrying whether your wine's over the hill, *after* the intimidation of shopping for the wine, is more than most of us can be bothered with.

Since I couldn't stand the idea of people pretty much giving up on wine with dinner, and "How long will it keep after I open it?" is one of the most common wine questions I'm asked, I decided it was time to give some real answers.

I'm a bit embarrassed to admit that I began to test how long wines hold up in the everyday kitchen not because I was on a quest to answer these big-picture questions but because I kept tasting some impressive leftovers. In my sommelier and writing duties, I taste multiple wines often, and rarely with enough company to finish them the day they're opened, or even the next. In going back to the leftovers—to see if they were as good (or as disappointing) as I'd remembered—I got some amazing surprises. Far more often than you'd think, the good wines stayed that way for days. Even more astonishing, some of the wines that were initially underwhelming actually came around and started tasting better after being open for a while (in the same way that some cheeses need to sit out at room temperature to show their best flavor or a bowl of chili can taste better after a day or two in the fridge).

And thus were born the Kitchen Fridge Survivor™ and Kitchen Countertop Survivor™ experiments. I hope the grades will give you confidence to enjoy wine with dinner more often, or even multiple wines with one meal (I frequently do), knowing that you can have tastes or just a glass of many wines, over several days, without the wines going "bad."

To test the wines' open-bottle longevity, I handled them as follows:

Whites—Recorked with the original cork (whether natural or synthetic). Placed in the fridge.

Reds—Recorked with the original cork. Placed on the kitchen counter.

Sparkling wines—Opened carefully without popping (popping depletes carbonation faster). Closed with a "clamshell" stopper designed for sparkling wines—sold in housewares departments and sometimes wine stores. Placed in the fridge.

Bag-in-box wines—These were not tested, because the airtight bag inside keeps the wine from oxidizing as it's consumed—one of the major virtues of this type of packaging.

The same process was repeated after each daily retaste, until the wine's taste declined noticeably. As I said, some wines actually taste better after a day or two. They were handled the same way.

There's no science to this. My kitchen is just a regular kitchen, probably much like yours. Hopefully these grades, which showed the wines' staying power in an everyday setting, will give you the confidence to enjoy wine more often with your everyday meals:

Avg = a "one-day wine," which tastes noticeably less fresh the next day. This doesn't mean the wine is less worthy, just less sturdy— so plan accordingly by inviting someone to share it with you.

B = holds its freshness for 2–3 days after opening

B+ = holds *and gets better* over 2–3 days after opening

A = has a 3- to 4-day "freshness window"

A+ = holds *and gets better* over 3–4 days

To learn how to lengthen the survival rate of your wine leftovers, see "Handling Wine Leftovers" in the *Great Wine Made Simple* Mini-Course chapter of this book.

Your Notes

Would you join my tasting panel? Of course, I would love for you to record your wine impressions and share them with me for the next edition of the *Immer Guide* (please see the form at the back of the book to request a survey, or you may do so at *www. greatwinemadesimple.com*). But even if you are not the survey type, do it for yourself. Whether you're at home or in a restaurant, the guide is a handy place to keep notes on what you drank, what you paid, what food you had with it, and what you thought. Don't you hate it when you've enjoyed a wine, then can't remember the name when you want to buy it again?

A Few Questions About the Wine Entries

How Were Wines Chosen for Inclusion in the Book?

The wines represented are the top sellers in stores and restaurants nationally, in each style category. I featured mostly the top-selling premium, cork-finished wines because they outsell generics overall. However, I did include the dominant screw-top and bag-in-box wines, and my tasters did not ignore them. Don't see one of your favorite wines? Keep in mind that both popularity and availability of specific wines can vary a lot regionally, so a big brand in your area may not have the same sales and presence in other markets. This is especially true with local wines—for example, the Texas Chenin Blanc or New York Riesling that's on every table in your neck of the woods may not even be distributed in the next state. I also included worthy write-ins—those with decent availability that got the highest number of positive mentions from my tasters, although in some cases that availability may be skewed heavily to restaurants. Why? you ask. Many buyers have told me of their frustration at seeing the wines they'd like to purchase available only in restaurants. It's a phenomenon that has become increasingly common in the wine boom of the last few years. Simply put, wineries with a limited supply often concentrate on restaurant lists because of the image enhancement they can offer—good food, nice setting, and (usually) fewer competing selections than in a shop. Finally, I am constantly asked for specific wine recommendations, especially for the so-called "sleepers," the new-and-different, outstanding values, and up-and-coming regions. So I added my own list of "write-ins" which I've called the Top Fifty Wines You're *Not* Drinking. These nifty selections have good availability but aren't so well-known. I think they should be!

Why No Vintage Years?

This guide deals with the top-selling wines in the market, and so, for the most part, the year available in stores and restaurants is the winery's current release. But I am also making a philosophical statement about vintages for the wines in the guide, and it is this: I believe that the leading wines in the market *should* be fairly consistent from one year to the next so that consumers, and the retail and restaurant wine buyers who serve them, need not sweat the vintage, as long as it's current and fresh. There are certain wine categories where vintage is a bigger consideration—among them expensive California reds, French Bordeaux and Burgundy, and upscale Italian reds. But even with these, if you do not intend to cellar the wines (very few buyers do), vintage isn't so critical. A few of the tasters mentioned the vintage issue, but most were comfortable with my approach.

> **IMMER INSIGHT:** Ninety-five percent of the quality wines on the market are meant to be consumed within one to three years of the harvest (the vintage date on the label), while they are young, fresh, and in good condition. Most wines do not get better with age, so why wait?

Can You Really Define "Outstanding" Wine?

Indeed I can. We all can. Broadly, it is a wine that captures your attention. It could be the scent, the taste, the texture, or all three that make you say first, "Mmm. . . ," and then, "Wow" as your impressions register in the moment, in the context of all your prior experience and the price you paid. If it all sounds very personal and subjective, you're exactly right—it is. That is why I felt a guide like this, showcasing the impressions of real-world buyers, was so important. The fact that the wines herein are big sellers is already an endorsement. The details put each wine in context—of price, similar-style wines, occasion, and whatever else buyers feel is important. No other wine buying guide does that.

Who Were the Tasters?

Over a six-month period in 2001 I surveyed thousands of American wine buyers—trade colleagues (retail and restaurant buyers, sommeliers, hoteliers, chefs, waiters, importers, and distributors). The trade buyers included most major chain restaurants and stores, chefs, and my master sommelier colleagues, among others. I also surveyed consumers, recruited through my restaurant guests, the events and classes I conduct around the country, my website, and of course the friends and family network, including family members I didn't even know I had until I found them on the e-mail trail. I originally thought consumers would be less keen than trade to share their wine opinions, but I was wrong. Consumers account for more than half of the responses. Although I didn't purposely exclude anyone, I did review every survey returned for signs of ballot stuffing from winery companies and eliminated all suspicious responses (there were literally just a couple).

Why Do These Tasters' Opinions Matter?

Clearly, this guide for everyone takes an utterly populist perspective that's different from every other wine publication on the market—and that is exactly what I intended. I think the honest assessments and perspective of consumers who have to pay their own money for wine (while wine journalists rarely do), and the restaurateurs and retailers who serve them, are extremely important and helpful—because they're the real world. (With so little of that perspective in the marketplace, can it be any wonder that wine is barely a blip on Americans' cultural radar screen?) I am not dismissing the value of, and expertise behind, the leading critics' scoring reports. But I do think they often further the notion that there are haves and have-nots in the wine world: the 90+-rated "good stuff" that none of us can afford; and the rest—the wines we see every day whose lower scores seem bad by comparison. That perspective is perhaps valuable to a tiny, elite group of luxury wine buyers. But for what I call the OTC (other than collectors) market, which comprises the bulk of the nation's buyers (including just about everyone I know), this dichotomy leaves us feeling utterly insecure about our own taste and budget, skeptical about the quality of the selection at the stores and restaurants we frequent, and self-conscious about our (legitimate) desire for value for the money—in the vernacular, good, cheap wine. If I've achieved my goal, this guide's real-world information will give you a renewed sense of confidence in your own taste and some great word-of-mouth guidance on new wines to try that are actually available where you shop and dine. Enjoy!

MY GUEST INSIDERS' VIEW OF WINE MARKET TRENDS

By Brian Yost

VICE PRESIDENT, BEVERAGE
MARRIOTT INTERNATIONAL

An interesting phenomenon is taking shape across the country. Guests in the restaurants, bars, and ballrooms of our hotels are becoming increasingly knowledgeable about and interested in food and beverage, wine in particular. The impact of the Food Network, the multitude of wine-related consumer magazines, and the many well-written books on wine has been to enlighten and encourage wine fanciers to further explore the world of wine and all that it has to offer.

This newfound passion has been fueled by the fact that, in general, our guests are more traveled than ever before, expanding their wine horizons as they collect stamps in their passports. The combination of this passion and education is driving our guests to seek out new experiences, to try varietals that they have not tasted before, and to look for appellations that may represent new finds. While many travelers are still enjoying luxury wines like first-growth French Bordeaux and cult California Cabernets, just as many are seeking out the values (and quality) offered by a Syrah-based Crozes-Hermitage from France, a superripe Chilean Chardonnay, or an aromatic Argentine Malbec. And speaking of quality and value, the Australian portion of our portfolio continues to enjoy great success, with Shiraz and Merlot leading the wave of the wines from down under.

Having said all of this, American wines continue to dominate the sales landscape in our hotels. However, as already pointed out, here too guests are searching for a quality/value balance—not a low-cost alternative but a high-quality, perhaps lesser-known, better-value bottle. As might be expected, the core varietals (Chardonnay, Cabernet) still account for the majority of our American wine sales, but it is interesting to note a bit of a surge in Sauvignon Blanc, Pinot Noir, and Zinfandel as more adventurous consumers continue to experiment. Before leaving a discussion of American wines, I would be remiss not to mention what seems to be an increased thirst for wines from growing areas other than California, most notably Washington state, where again the quality is very high and there is still value to be found.

Finally, a quick look at the other categories on our wine list reveals the following. First, it seems that we've begun to drink more Champagne and other sparklers. This is particularly evidenced by a trend toward more sparkling wines by the glass and toward traditional bubbly-based cocktails as aperitifs. Second, Italy continues to play a growing role in our wine sales, led by the increase in the Pinot Grigio and Chianti categories. Finally, although still a relatively small proportion, we have begun to see some acceptance of Spanish Rioja and German Riesling—again, purchased primarily by the more adventurous guests.

I fully expect wine sales to continue to grow as an integral part of the dining/entertaining experience in our hotels. This will be aided by aggressive wine-by-the-glass programs, allowing guests to experiment at relatively low risk, continued focus on the selection of the products in our portfolio, and most important, by the ever-increasing interest and passion of you, our guests. Enjoy your adventure!

By Annette Alvarez
BUYER, SOUTHERN CALIFORNIA,
COSTCO WHOLESALE

AND

David Andrew
DIRECTOR OF WINE, COSTCO WHOLESALE

One advantage of buying for a national retailer is that we can sit at our desks and see at a glance what wine trends are taking place all over the country.

Perhaps the most striking trend is that consumers are "trading up;" they're buying better-quality and more expensive wines. Over the past several years price hasn't seemed to be an issue for our customers, but this may be changing. We're noticing that when wineries take a substantial price increase, say $2 or $3 per bottle, otherwise loyal customers will look elsewhere. Our members rely on us for value at every price point, but when they perceive that the value is no longer there, they move on.

Wine drinkers are definitely drinking more red wine than white. What's interesting is that it's not all Cabernet and Merlot as you might expect. We're seeing the strongest growth in Shiraz, Pinot Noir, and Zinfandel. Particular countries and regions are trending very strongly, too. Australia, Bordeaux, Burgundy, and the Rhône are doing very well for us. We really think that this is a clear indication of American wine drinkers becoming more adventurous and looking for something new.

This applies equally to whites. While Chardonnay is still a huge category, we're seeing much stronger growth in Sauvignon Blanc and Pinot Grigio. New Zealand Sauvignon Blanc is particularly popular, and it's not difficult to understand why.

The good news for wine consumers is that there has never been so much high-quality wine available in this country as there is now. Improvements in grape growing and winery technology around the world have helped wine regions maximize their potential, bringing better and better wine to market. This brings with it an increasingly wide range of choices for the consumer, too.

With today's wine drinker's thirst for adventure, there's never been a better time to go out and experiment with great value wines from around the world.

MOST POPULAR WINES—REFLECTING BOTH TASTE AND VALUE FOR THE MONEY

25 Most Popular Whites
Based on Taste and Value

Name Style Category	Wtd. Avg. T/V Score*	Price Cate- gory
Lucien Crochet Sancerre, France Sauvignon Blanc/Fumé Blanc	24	$$
Brancott Rsv. Sauv. Blanc., New Zealand Sauvignon Blanc/Fumé Blanc	24	$$
Trimbach Riesling, Alsace, France Riesling	24	$$
Jolivet Sancerre, France Sauvignon Blanc/Fumé Blanc	24	$$
Trimbach Pinot Gris, Alsace, France Pinot Gris/Pinot Grigio	24	$$
Leflaive (Domaine) Puligny-Montrachet, France Chardonnay	23	$$$$
Martin Codax Albariño, Spain Other White Wines	23	$$
Cloudy Bay Sauv. Blanc., New Zealand Sauvignon Blanc/Fumé Blanc	23	$$$
Hugel Pinot Blanc, Alsace, France Other White Wines	23	$
Chalone Central Coast Chard., Calif. Chardonnay	23	$$$
Honig Sauv. Blanc, Calif. Sauvignon Blanc/Fumé Blanc	23	$$

*Scores were rounded off. Wines are listed in order of actual score ranking. The number of wines in each "Most Popular" listing reflects the overall number of wines in the category. So our "Top Whites" list numbers 25, while the Top Rieslings ranking shows just five entries. It's also a fairly close reflection of each category's sales and prominence in the fine wine market overall.

Name Style Category	Wtd. Avg. T/V Score*	Price Cate- gory
Bernardus Chard., Calif. Chardonnay	23	$$$
Alois Lageder Pinot Grigio, Italy Pinot Gris/Pinot Grigio	23	$$
Hugel Gewürztraminer, Alsace, France Other White Wines	23	$$
Talbott (Robert) Sleepy Hollow Vineyard Chard., Calif. Chardonnay	22	$$$$
Leflaive (Olivier) Puligny-Montrachet, France Chardonnay	22	$$$$
Château Montelena Chard., Calif. Chardonnay	22	$$$$
Penfolds Semillon/Chardonnay, Australia Other White Wines	22	$
Didier Dagueneau Silex Pouilly-Fumé, France Sauvignon Blanc/Fumé Blanc	22	$$$
Dry Creek Fumé Blanc, Calif. Sauvignon Blanc/Fumé Blanc	22	$
La Crema Chard., Calif. Chardonnay	22	$$
Frog's Leap Sauv. Blanc, Calif. Sauvignon Blanc/Fumé Blanc	22	$$$
Cakebread Napa Chard., Calif. Chardonnay	22	$$$$
Kenwood Sauv. Blanc, Calif. Sauvignon Blanc/Fumé Blanc	22	$
Rosemount Diamond Label Chard., Australia Chardonnay	22	$

25 Most Popular Reds
Based on Taste and Value

Name Style Category	Wtd. Avg. T/V Score*	Price Cate- gory

Muga Rioja Reserva, Spain
    Rioja, Ribera del Duero, and Other
    Spanish Reds
	25	$$$

Willakenzie Willamette Valley Pinot Noir, Oregon Pinot Noir	24	$$$

Ridge Geyserville (Zin.), Calif.	24	$$$
Red Zinfandel		
Alvaro Palacios Les Terrasses Priorat, Spain	24	$$$
Rioja, Ribera del Duero, and Other Spanish Reds		
Etude Pinot Noir, Calif.	24	$$$$
Pinot Noir		
Chât. de Beaucastel Chât.-du-Pape, France	24	$$$$
Syrah/Shiraz and Other Rhône-Style Reds		
Joseph Phelps Napa Cab. Sauv., Calif.	24	$$$$
Cabernet Sauv. and Blends		
Rosemount Diamond Label Shiraz, Australia	24	$
Syrah/Shiraz and Other Rhône-Style Reds		
Shafer Merlot, Calif.	24	$$$$
Merlot		
Duckhorn Napa Merlot, Calif.	23	$$$$
Merlot		
Pesquera Ribera del Duero, Spain	23	$$$
Rioja, Ribera del Duero, and Other Spanish Reds		
Rosemount Diamond Label Shiraz/ Cab. Sauv., Australia	23	$
Syrah/Shiraz and Other Rhône-Style Reds		
Chateau Gruaud-Larose Bordeaux, France	23	$$$$
Cabernet Sauv. and Blends		
Antinori, Marchese Chianti Classico Riserva, Italy	23	$$$
Chianti and Sangiovese		
St. Francis Sonoma Merlot, Calif.	23	$$$
Merlot		
Stag's Leap Wine Cellars Napa Merlot, Calif.	23	$$$$
Merlot		
Morgan Pinot Noir, Calif.	23	$$
Pinot Noir		
St. Francis Sonoma Zin, Calif.	23	$$
Red Zinfandel		
Querciabella Chianti Classico Riserva, Italy	23	$$$
Chianti and Sangiovese		
Beringer Knights Valley Cab. Sauv., Calif.	23	$$$
Cabernet Sauv. and Blends		

*Scores were rounded off. Wines are listed in order of actual ranking.

Name Style Category	Wtd. Avg. T/V Score*	Price Category
Penfolds Bin 389 Cabernet/Shiraz, Australia Cabernet Sauv. and Blends	23	$$$
Château La Nerthe Chât.-du-Pape, France Syrah/Shiraz and Other Rhône-Style Reds	23	$$$
Selvapiana Chianti Rufina, Italy Chianti and Sangiovese	23	$$
Jaboulet Côtes-du-Rhône, France Syrah/Shiraz and Other Rhône-Style Reds	23	$
Groth Napa Cab. Sauv., Calif. Cabernet Sauv. and Blends	23	$$$$

Best of the Big 6 Grapes

Name	Wtd. Avg. T/V Score*	Price Category
5 Most Popular Rieslings		
Trimbach Riesling, Alsace, France	24	$$
Hogue Fruit Forward Johannisberg Riesling, Wash.	22	$
Château Ste. Michelle Riesling, Wash.	21	$
Bonny Doon Pacific Rim Riesling, USA/Germany	21	$
J. Lohr Bay Mist Riesling, Calif.	20	$
10 Most Popular Sauvignon/Fumé Blancs		
Lucien Crochet Sancerre, France	24	$$
Brancott Rsv. Sauv. Blanc., New Zealand	24	$$
Jolivet Sancerre, France	24	$$
Cloudy Bay Sauv. Blanc, New Zealand	23	$$$
Honig Sauv. Blanc, Calif.	23	$$
Didier Dagueneau Silex Pouilly-Fumé, France	22	$$$
Dry Creek Fumé Blanc, Calif.	22	$
Frog's Leap Sauv. Blanc, Calif.	22	$$$
Kenwood Sauv. Blanc, Calif.	22	$
Ferrari-Carano Fumé Blanc, Calif.	22	$$
30 Most Popular Chardonnays		
Leflaive (Domaine) Puligny-Montrachet, France	23	$$$$

Chalone Central Coast Chard., Calif.	23	$$$
Bernardus Chard., Calif.	23	$$$
Talbott (Robert) Sleepy Hollow Vineyard Chard., Calif.	22	$$$$
Leflaive (Olivier) Puligny-Montrachet, France	22	$$$$
Château Montelena Chard., Calif.	22	$$$$
La Crema Chard., Calif.	22	$$
Cakebread Napa Chard., Calif.	22	$$$$
Rosemount Diamond Label Chard., Australia	22	$
Ferrari-Carano Sonoma Chard., Calif.	22	$$$
Cambria Katherine's Vineyard Chard., Calif.	22	$$
Lindemans Bin 65 Chard., Australia	22	$
Château St. Jean Sonoma Chard., Calif.	22	$$
Chalk Hill Chard., Calif.	21	$$$$
Sonoma-Cutrer Russian River Ranches Chard., Calif.	21	$$
Gallo of Sonoma Chard., Calif.	21	$
Edna Valley Vineyard Chard., Calif.	21	$$
Grgich Hills Chard., Calif.	21	$$$
Chât. Ste. Michelle Columbia Valley Chard., Wash.	21	$$
Benziger Chard., Calif.	21	$$
J. Lohr Riverstone Chard., Calif.	21	$$
Beringer Napa Chard., Calif.	21	$$
Jacob's Creek Chard., Australia	21	$
St. Francis Sonoma Chard., Calif.	21	$
Beringer Founders' Estate Chard., Calif.	21	$
Columbia Crest Chard., Wash.	21	$
Sterling Vineyards North Coast Chard., Calif.	21	$$
Hess Select Chard., Calif.	21	$$
Penfolds Koonunga Hill Chard., Australia	21	$
Raymond Estates Napa Chard., Calif.	21	$$

10 Most Popular Pinot Noirs

Willakenzie Willamette Valley Pinot Noir, Oregon	24	$$$
Etude Pinot Noir, Calif.	24	$$$$
Morgan Pinot Noir, Calif.	23	$$
Cristom Willamette Pinot Noir, Oregon	23	$$$
Robert Sinskey Napa Pinot Noir, Calif.	23	$$$

*Scores were rounded off. Wines are listed in order of actual ranking.

Name	Wtd. Avg. T/V Score*	Price Category
Archery Summit Arcus Estate Pinot Noir, Oregon	23	$$$$
Byron Santa Maria Valley Pinot Noir, Calif.	22	$$
Dom. Drouhin Willamette Valley Pinot Noir, Oregon	22	$$$$
La Crema Pinot Noir, Calif.	22	$$
Elk Cove Pinot Noir, Oregon	22	$$

20 Most Popular Merlots

Name	Wtd. Avg. T/V Score*	Price Category
Shafer Merlot, Calif.	24	$$$$
Duckhorn Napa Merlot, Calif.	23	$$$$
St. Francis Sonoma Merlot, Calif.	23	$$$
Stag's Leap Wine Cellars Napa Merlot, Calif.	23	$$$$
Frog's Leap Merlot, Calif.	22	$$$
Sterling Vineyards Napa Merlot, Calif.	22	$$$
Casa Lapostolle Classic Merlot, Chile	22	$
Chât. Ste. Michelle Columbia Valley Merlot, Wash.	22	$$
Columbia Crest Merlot, Wash.	21	$
Carmenet Dynamite Merlot, Calif.	21	$$$
Rodney Strong Merlot, Calif.	21	$$
Franciscan Oakville Estate Merlot, Calif.	21	$$$
Montes Merlot, Chile	21	$
Ravenswood Vintners Blend Merlot, Calif.	21	$$
Clos du Bois Sonoma Merlot, Calif.	21	$$$
Pine Ridge Crimson Creek Merlot, Calif.	21	$$$$
Blackstone Merlot, Calif.	21	$$
Gallo of Sonoma Merlot, Calif.	21	$
Lindemans Bin 40 Merlot, Australia	21	$
Bogle Merlot, Calif.	20	$$

30 Most Popular Cabernet Sauvignons and Blends

Name	Wtd. Avg. T/V Score*	Price Category
Joseph Phelps Napa, Cab. Sauv., Calif.	24	$$$$
Château Gruaud-Larose Bordeaux, France	23	$$$$
Beringer Knights Valley Cab. Sauv., Calif.	23	$$$
Penfolds Bin 389 Cabernet/Shiraz, Australia	23	$$$
Groth Napa Cab. Sauv., Calif.	23	$$$$
Carmenet Dynamite Cab. Sauv., Calif.	23	$$$
Stag's Leap Wine Cellars Napa Cab. Sauv., Calif.	23	$$$$
Cain Cuvée Bordeaux Style Red, Calif.	23	$$$

Château Larose-Trintaudon Bordeaux, France	22	$$
Cakebread Napa Cab. Sauv., Calif.	22	$$$$
Hess Select Cab. Sauv., Calif	22	$$
Château Greysac Bordeaux, France	22	$$
Franciscan Napa Cab. Sauv., Calif.	22	$$
Château Gloria Bordeaux, France	22	$$$$
Raymond Napa Cab. Sauv., Calif.	22	$$
Mt. Veeder Napa Cab. Sauv., Calif.	22	$$$
Beaulieu Vineyard (BV) Rutherford Cab. Sauv., Calif.	22	$$$
Jordan Cab. Sauv., Calif.	22	$$$$
Heitz Napa Cab. Sauv., Calif.	22	$$$$
Rosemount Diamond Label Cab. Sauv./ Merlot Australia	22	$
Guenoc Cab. Sauv., Calif.	22	$$
J. Lohr 7 Oaks Cab. Sauv., Calif.	22	$$
Silver Oak Alexander Valley Cab. Sauv., Calif.	22	$$$$
Chât. Ste. Michelle Columbia Valley Cab. Sauv., Wash.	22	$$
Sterling Vineyards Napa Cab. Sauv., Calif.	22	$$$$
Gallo of Sonoma Cab. Sauv., Calif.	22	$
Clos du Bois Sonoma Cab. Sauv., Calif.	21	$$
Rosemount Diamond Label Cab. Sauv., Australia	21	$
Simi Sonoma Cab. Sauv., Calif.	21	$$
Jacob's Creek Cab. Sauv., Australia	21	$

Best of the Rest

Name	Wtd. Avg. T/V Score*	Price Category
5 Most Popular Champagnes and Sparkling Wines		
Roederer Estate Sparkling, Calif.	23	$$$
Veuve Clicquot Yellow Label NV Champ., France	23	$$$$
Taittinger Brut La Francaise NV Champ., France	23	$$$$
Perrier-Jouët Grand Brut NV Champagne, France	21	$$$$
Mumm Cuvée Napa Brut Prestige Sparkling, Calif.	21	$$

*Scores were rounded off. Wines are listed in order of actual ranking.

Name	Wtd. Avg. T/V Score*	Price Category
5 Most Popular Pinot Grigio/Gris		
Trimbach Pinot Gris, Alsace, France	24	$$
Alois Lageder Pinot Grigio, Italy	23	$$
Livio Felluga Pinot Grigio, Italy	21	$$
King Estate Pinot Gris, Oregon	21	$$
Cavit Pinot Grigio, Italy	18	$
5 Most Popular Other Whites		
Martin Codax Albariño, Spain	23	$$
Hugel Pinot Blanc, Alsace, France	23	$
Hugel Gewürztraminer, Alsace, France	23	$$
Penfolds Semillon/Chardonnay, Australia	22	$
Miguel Torres Viña Sol, Spain	21	$
10 Most Popular Italian and Spanish Reds		
Muga Rioja Reserva, Spain	25	$$$
Alvaro Palacios Les Terrasses Priorat, Spain	24	$$$
Pesquera Ribera del Duero, Spain	23	$$$
Antinori, Marchese Chianti Classico Riserva, Italy	23	$$$
Querciabella Chianti Classico Riserva, Italy	23	$$$
Selvapiana Chianti Rufina, Italy	23	$$
Santa Cristina Sangiovese, Antinori, Italy	23	$
Vega Sindoa Tempranillo/Merlot Navarra Tinto, Spain	23	$
Arzuaga Crianza Ribera del Duero, Spain	22	$$$
Marqués de Cáceres Rioja Crianza, Spain	22	$$
5 Most Popular Shiraz/Syrahs and Rhône-Style Reds		
Chât. de Beaucastel Chât.-du-Pape, France	24	$$$$
Rosemount Diamond Label Shiraz, Australia	24	$
Rosemount Diamond Label Shiraz/ Cab. Sauv., Aust.	23	$
Château La Nerthe Chât.-du-Pape, France	23	$$$
Jaboulet Côtes-du-Rhône, France	23	$
5 Most Popular Red Zinfandels		
Ridge Geyserville (Zin.), Calif.	24	$$$
St. Francis Sonoma Zin., Calif.	23	$$
Cline Zin., Calif.	23	$
Grgich Hills Sonoma Zin., Calif.	22	$$$
Seghesio Sonoma Zin., Calif.	22	$$

Top Taste Rankings

Top 30 White Wines by Taste

Name Wine Type	Taste Score*	Price Cate- gory
Leflaive (Domaine) Puligny-Montrachet, France Chardonnay	26	$$$$
Talbott (Robert) Sleepy Hollow Vineyard Chard., Calif. Chardonnay	25	$$$$
Chalone Central Coast Chard., Calif. Chardonnay	25	$$$
Didier Dagueneau Silex Pouilly-Fumé, France Sauvignon Blanc/Fumé Blanc	24	$$$
Château Montelena Chard., Calif. Chardonnay	24	$$$$
Cakebread Napa Chard., Calif. Chardonnay	24	$$$$
Trimbach Riesling, Alsace, France Riesling	24	$$
Bernardus Chard., Calif. Chardonnay	24	$$$
Trimbach Pinot Gris, Alsace, France Pinot Gris/Pinot Grigio	24	$$
Brancott Rsv. Sauv. Blanc., New Zealand Sauvignon Blanc/Fumé Blanc	24	$$
Grgich Hills Chard., Calif. Chardonnay	24	$$$
Leflaive (Olivier) Puligny-Montrachet, France Chardonnay	24	$$$$
Honig Sauv. Blanc, Calif. Sauvignon Blanc/Fumé Blanc	24	$$
Grgich Hills Fumé Blanc, Calif. Sauvignon Blanc/Fumé Blanc	23	$$$
Chalk Hill Chard., Calif. Chardonnay	23	$$$$

*Scores were rounded off. Wines are listed in order of actual ranking.

Name Wine Type	Taste Score*	Price Category
Ferrari-Carano Sonoma Chard., Calif. Chardonnay	23	$$$
Martin Codax Albariño, Spain Other White Wines	23	$$
Alois Lageder Pinot Grigio, Italy Pinot Gris/Pinot Grigio	23	$$
Hugel Pinot Blanc, Alsace, France Other White Wines	23	$
Duckhorn Sauv. Blanc, Calif. Sauvignon Blanc/Fumé Blanc	23	$$$
Sonoma-Cutrer Russian River Ranches Chard., Calif. Chardonnay	23	$$
Ferrari-Carano Fumé Blanc, Calif. Sauvignon Blanc/Fumé Blanc	23	$$
La Crema Chard., Calif. Chardonnay	23	$$
Cakebread Sauv. Blanc, Calif. Sauvignon Blanc/Fumé Blanc	23	$$$
Hugel Gewürztraminer, Alsace, France Other White Wines	23	$$
Frog's Leap Sauv. Blanc, Calif. Sauvignon Blanc/Fumé Blanc	23	$$$
Murphy-Goode Fumé Blanc, Calif. Sauvignon Blanc/Fumé Blanc	23	$$
Cambria Katherine's Vineyard Chard., Calif. Chardonnay	23	$$
Château St. Jean Sonoma Chard., Calif. Chardonnay	22	$$
Livio Felluga Pinot Grigio, Italy Pinot Gris/Pinot Grigio	22	$$

Top 30 Red Wines by Taste

Name Wine Type	Taste Score*	Price Category
Duckhorn Napa Merlot, Calif. Merlot	26	$$$$
Etude Pinot Noir, Calif. Pinot Noir	26	$$$$
Shafer Merlot, Calif. Merlot	26	$$$$
Chât. de Beaucastel Chât.-du-Pape, France Syrah/Shiraz and Other Rhône-Style Reds	26	$$$$

Willakenzie Willamette Valley Pinot Noir, Oregon	26	$$$
Pinot Noir		
Ridge Geyserville (Zin.), Calif.	26	$$$
Red Zinfandel		
Joseph Phelps Napa Cab. Sauv., Calif.	25	$$$$
Cabernet Sauv. and Blends		
Muga Rioja Reserva, Spain	25	$$$
Rioja, Ribera del Duero, and Other Spanish Reds		
Stag's Leap Wine Cellars Napa Merlot, Calif.	25	$$$$
Merlot		
Archery Summit Arcus Estate Pinot Noir, Oregon	25	$$$$
Pinot Noir		
Silver Oak Alexander Valley Cab. Sauv., Calif.	25	$$$$
Cabernet Sauv. and Blends		
Pesquera Ribera del Duero, Spain	25	$$$
Rioja, Ribera del Duero, and Other Spanish Reds		
Dom. Drouhin Willamette Valley Pinot Noir, Oregon	25	$$$$
Pinot Noir		
Cakebread Napa Cab. Sauv., Calif.	25	$$$$
Cabernet Sauv. and Blends		
Alvaro Palacios Les Terrasses Priorat, Spain	25	$$$
Rioja, Ribera del Duero, and Other Spanish Reds		
Château Gruaud-Larose Bordeaux, France	25	$$$$
Cabernet Sauv. and Blends		
Stag's Leap Wine Cellars Napa Cab. Sauv., Calif.	25	$$$$
Cabernet Sauv. and Blends		
Mt. Veeder Napa Cab. Sauv., Calif.	25	$$$
Cabernet Sauv. and Blends		
Groth Napa Cab. Sauv., Calif.	24	$$$$
Cabernet Sauv. and Blends		
Robert Sinskey Napa Pinot Noir, Calif.	24	$$$
Pinot Noir		
Heitz Napa Cab. Sauv., Calif.	24	$$$$
Cabernet Sauv. and Blends		
Antinori, Marchese Chianti Classico Riserva, Italy	24	$$$
Chianti and Sangiovese		

*Scores were rounded off. Wines are listed in order of actual ranking.

Name Wine Type	Taste Score*	Price Cate- gory

Château La Nerthe Chât.-du-Pape,
France
    Syrah/Shiraz and Other Rhône-Style
    Reds
	24	$$$

Jordan Cab. Sauv., Calif. Cabernet Sauv. and Blends	24	$$$$
Beringer Knights Valley Cab. Sauv., Calif. Cabernet Sauv. and Blends	24	$$$
Morgan Pinot Noir, Calif. Pinot Noir	24	$$
Byron Santa Maria Valley Pinot Noir, Calif. Pinot Noir	24	$$
Grgich Hills Sonoma Zin., Calif. Red Zinfandel	24	$$$
Cain Cuvée Bordeaux Style Red, Calif. Cabernet Sauv. and Blends	24	$$$
Querciabella Chianti Classico Riserva, Italy Chianti & Sangiovese	24	$$$

Best of the Big 6 Grapes

Name	Taste Score*	Price Cate- gory
Top 5 Rieslings by Taste		
Trimbach Riesling, Alsace, France	24	$$
Hogue Fruit Forward Johannisberg Riesling, Wash.	22	$
Château Ste. Michelle Riesling, Wash.	21	$
Bonny Doon Pacific Rim Riesling, USA/ Germany	21	$
J. Lohr Bay Mist Riesling, Calif.	20	$
Top 10 Sauvignon/Fumé Blancs by Taste		
Cloudy Bay Sauv. Blanc., New Zealand	26	$$$
Lucien Crochet Sancerre, France	25	$$
Jolivet Sancerre, France	25	$$
Didier Dagueneau Silex Pouilly-Fumé, France	24	$$$
Brancott Rsv. Sauv. Blanc., New Zealand	24	$$
Honig Sauv. Blanc, Calif.	24	$$
Grgich Hills Fumé Blanc, Calif.	23	$$$
Duckhorn Sauv. Blanc. Calif.	23	$$$
Ferrari-Carano Fumé Blanc, Calif.	23	$$
Cakebread Sauv. Blanc, Calif.	23	$$$

Top 30 Chardonnays by Taste

Leflaive (Domaine) Puligny-Montrachet, France	26	$$$$
Talbott (Robert) Sleepy Hollow Vineyard Chard., Calif.	25	$$$$
Chalone Central Coast Chard., Calif.	25	$$$
Château Montelena Chard., Calif.	24	$$$$
Cakebread Napa Chard., Calif.	24	$$$$
Bernardus Chard., Calif.	24	$$$
Grgich Hills Chard., Calif.	24	$$$
Leflaive (Olivier) Puligny-Montrachet, France	24	$$$$
Chalk Hill Chard., Calif.	23	$$$$
Ferrari-Carano Sonoma Chard., Calif.	23	$$$
Sonoma-Cutrer Russian River Ranches Chard., Calif.	23	$$
La Crema Chard., Calif.	23	$$
Cambria Katherine's Vineyard Chard., Calif.	23	$$
Château St. Jean Sonoma Chard., Calif.	22	$$
Kendall-Jackson Grand Rsv. Chard., Calif.	22	$$$
Jordan Chard., Calif.	22	$$$
Edna Valley Vineyard Chard., Calif.	22	$$
J. Lohr Riverstone Chard., Calif.	22	$$
Beringer Napa Chard., Calif.	22	$$
Benziger Chard., Calif.	22	$$
Rosemount Diamond Label Chard., Australia	21	$
Sterling Vineyards North Coast Chard., Calif.	21	$$
Raymond Estates Napa Chard., Calif.	21	$$
Beringer Founders' Estate Chard., Calif.	21	$
Louis Jadot Pouilly-Fuissé, France	21	$$$
Hess Select Chard., Calif.	21	$$
Kenwood Chard., Calif.	21	$$
St. Francis Sonoma Chard., Calif.	21	$
Labouré-Roi Puligny-Montrachet, France	21	$$$$
Joseph Drouhin Pouilly-Fuissé, France	21	$$

Top 10 Pinot Noirs by Taste

Etude Pinot Noir, Calif.	26	$$$$
Willakenzie Willamette Valley Pinot Noir, Oregon	26	$$$
Archery Summit Arcus Estate Pinot Noir, Oregon	25	$$$$

*Scores were rounded off. Wines are listed in order of actual ranking.

Name	Taste Score*	Price Category
Dom. Drouhin Willamette Valley Pinot Noir, Oregon	25	$$$$
Robert Sinskey Napa Pinot Noir, Calif.	24	$$$
Morgan Pinot Noir, Calif.	24	$$
Byron Santa Maria Valley Pinot Noir, Calif.	24	$$
Cristom Willamette Pinot Noir, Oregon	23	$$$
Elk Cove Pinot Noir, Oregon	23	$$
Wild Horse Pinot Noir, California	23	$$

Top 20 Merlots by Taste

Name	Taste Score*	Price Category
Duckhorn Napa Merlot, Calif.	26	$$$$
Shafer Merlot, Calif.	26	$$$$
Stag's Leap Wine Cellars Napa Merlot, Calif.	25	$$$$
Sterling Vineyards Napa Merlot, Napa	23	$$$
St. Francis Sonoma Merlot, Calif.	23	$$$
Frog's Leap Merlot, Calif.	23	$$$
Pine Ridge Crimson Creek Merlot, Calif.	23	$$$$
Carmenet Dynamite Merlot, Calif.	22	$$$
Franciscan Oakville Estate Merlot, Calif.	22	$$$
Chât. Ste. Michelle Columbia Valley Merlot, Wash.	22	$$
Rodney Strong Merlot, Calif.	22	$$
Casa Lapostolle Classic Merlot, Chile	22	$
Clos du Bois Sonoma Merlot, Calif.	21	$$$
Ravenswood Vintners Blend Merlot, Calif.	21	$$
Columbia Crest Merlot, Wash.	21	$
Château Simard Bordeaux, France	20	$$$
Bogle Merlot, Calif.	20	$$
Montes Merlot, Chile	20	$
Gallo of Sonoma Merlot, Calif.	20	$
Kendall-Jackson Vintner's Rsv. Merlot, Calif.	20	$$

Top 30 Cabernet Sauvignons and Blends by Taste

Name	Taste Score*	Price Category
Joseph Phelps Napa Cab. Sauv., Calif.	25	$$$$
Silver Oak Alexander Valley Cab. Sauv., Calif.	25	$$$$
Cakebread Napa Cab. Sauv., Calif.	25	$$$$
Château Gruaud-Larose Bordeaux, France	25	$$$$
Stag's Leap Wine Cellars Napa Cab. Sauv., Calif.	25	$$$$
Mt. Veeder Napa Cab. Sauv., Calif.	25	$$$

Groth Napa Cab. Sauv., Calif.	24	$$$$
Heitz Napa Cab. Sauv., Calif.	24	$$$$
Jordan Cab. Sauv., Calif.	24	$$$$
Beringer Knights Valley Cab. Sauv., Calif.	24	$$$
Cain Cuvée Bordeaux Style Red, Calif.	24	$$$
Penfolds Bin 389 Cabernet/Shiraz, Australia	23	$$$
Carmenet Dynamite Cab. Sauv., Calif.	23	$$$
Raymond Napa Cab. Sauv., Calif.	23	$$
Hess Select Cab. Sauv., Calif.	23	$$
Sterling Vineyards Napa Cab. Sauv., Calif.	23	$$$$
Franciscan Napa Cab. Sauv., Calif.	23	$$
Château Gloria Bordeaux, France	23	$$$$
Beaulieu Vineyard (BV) Rutherford Cab. Sauv., Calif.	22	$$$
Simi Sonoma Cab. Sauv., Calif.	22	$$
Guenoc Cab. Sauv., Calif.	22	$$
Château Larose-Trintaudon Bordeaux, France	22	$$
Château Greysac Bordeaux, France	22	$$
Robert Mondavi Napa Cab. Sauv., Calif.	22	$$$
J. Lohr 7 Oaks Cab. Sauv., Calif.	22	$$
Kenwood Cab. Sauv., Calif.	22	$$
Clos du Bois Sonoma Cab. Sauv., Calif.	22	$$
Chât. Ste. Michelle Columbia Valley Cab. Sauv., Wash.	22	$$
Gallo of Sonoma Cab. Sauv., Calif.	21	$
Rosemount Diamond Label Cab. Sauv./ Merlot Australia	21	$

Best of the Rest

Name	Taste Score*	Price Category

Top 5 Champagnes and Sparkling Wines by Taste

Taittinger Brut La Francaise NV Champ., France	25	$$$$
Veuve Clicquot Yellow Label NV Champ., France	25	$$$$
Roederer Estate Sparkling, Calif.	24	$$$
Perrier-Jouët Grand Brut NV Champagne, France	23	$$$$
Mumm Cuvée Napa Brut Prestige Sparkling, Calif.	21	$$

*Scores were rounded off. Wines are listed in order of actual ranking.

Name	Taste Score*	Price Category
Top 5 Pinot Grigio/Gris by Taste		
Trimbach Pinot Gris, Alsace, France	24	$$
Alois Lageder Pinot Grigio, Italy	23	$$
Livio Felluga Pinot Grigio, Italy	22	$$
King Estate Pinot Gris, Oregon	22	$$
Santa Margherita Pinot Grigio, Italy	18	$$$
Top 5 Other Whites by Taste		
Martin Codax Albariño, Spain	23	$$
Hugel Pinot Blanc, Alsace, France	23	$
Hugel Gewürztraminer, Alsace, France	23	$$
Penfolds Semillon/Chardonnay, Australia	22	$
Miguel Torres Viña Sol, Spain	20	$
Top 10 Italian and Spanish Reds by Taste		
Muga Rioja Reserva, Spain	25	$$$
Pesquera Ribera del Duero, Spain	25	$$$
Alvaro Palacios Les Terrasses Priorat, Spain	25	$$$
Antinori, Marchese Chianti Classico Riserva, Italy	24	$$$
Querciabella Chianti Classico Riserva, Italy	24	$$$
Felsina Chianti Classico, Italy	23	$$
Banfi Brunello di Montalcino, Italy	23	$$$$
Ruffino Chianti Classico Rsva. Ducale Gold Label, Italy	23	$$$$
Selvapiana Chianti Rufina, Italy	23	$$
Arzuaga Crianza Ribera del Duero, Spain	23	$$$
Top 5 Shiraz/Syrahs and Rhône-Style Reds by Taste		
Chât. de Beaucastel Chât.-du-Pape, France	26	$$$$
Château La Nerthe Chât.-du-Pape, France	24	$$$
Rosemount Diamond Label Shiraz, Australia	23	$
Rosemount Diamond Label Shiraz/ Cab. Sauv., Aust.	23	$
Jaboulet Côtes-du-Rhône, France	22	$
Top 5 Red Zinfandels by Taste		
Ridge Geyserville (Zin.), Calif.	26	$$$
Grgich Hills Sonoma Zin., Calif.	24	$$$
Cline Zin., Calif.	23	$
St. Francis Sonoma Zin., Calif.	23	$$
Ravenswood Vintners Blend Zin., Calif.	22	$$

BEST OF THE BARGAIN-PRICED WINES

Top 20 Budget Whites

Name	Taste Score*
Hugel Pinot Blanc, Alsace, France	23
Dry Creek Fumé Blanc, Calif.	22
Chât. Ste. Michelle Columbia Valley Sauv. Blanc, Wash.	22
Kenwood Sauv. Blanc, Calif.	22
Edna Valley Vineyard Chard., Calif.	22
Penfolds Semillon/Chardonnay, Australia	22
Rosemount Diamond Label Chard., Australia	21
Beringer Founders' Estate Chard., Calif.	21
Hess Select Chard., Calif.	21
St. Francis Sonoma Chard., Calif.	21
Hogue Fumé Blanc, Wash.	21
Château Ste. Michelle Johannisberg Riesling, Wash.	21
Penfolds Koonunga Hill Chard., Australia	21
Bonny Doon Pacific Rim Riesling, USA/Germany	21
Miguel Torres Viña Sol, Spain	20
Columbia Crest Chard., Wash.	20
Geyser Peak Sauv. Blanc, Calif.	20
Kendall-Jackson Vintner's Rsv. Sauv. Blanc, Calif.	20
Gallo of Sonoma Chard., Calif.	20
Beringer Founders' Estate Sauv. Blanc, Calif.	20

Top 20 Budget Reds

Cline Zin., Calif.	23
Raymond Napa Cab. Sauv., Calif.	23
Rosemount Diamond Label Shiraz, Australia	23

*Scores were rounded off. Wines are listed in order of actual ranking.

Name	Taste Score*
Rosemount Diamond Label Shiraz/Cab. Sauv., Australia	23
Vega Sindoa Tempranillo/Merlot Navarra Tinto, Spain	22
Santa Cristina Sangiovese, Antinori, Italy	22
Jaboulet Côtes-du-Rhône, France	22
E & M Guigal Côtes-du-Rhône, France	22
Marqués de Riscal Rioja Crianza, Spain	22
Casa Lapostolle Classic Merlot, Chile	22
Gallo of Sonoma Cab. Sauv., Calif.	21
Montecillo Rioja Crianza, Spain	21
Rosemount Diamond Label Cab. Sauv./Merlot Australia	21
Beringer Founders' Estate Cab. Sauv., Calif.	21
Louis Jadot Beaujolais-Villages, France	21
Jacob's Creek Shiraz/Cabernet Sauv., Australia	21
Columbia Crest Merlot, Wash.	21
Cecchi Chianti Classico, Italy	21
Lindemans Bin 59 Shiraz, Australia	21
Jacob's Creek Cab. Sauv., Australia	21
Firesteed Pinot Noir, Oregon	21

Best of the Big 6 Grapes

Name	Taste Score*
Top 5 Budget Rieslings	
Hogue Fruit Forward Riesling, Wash.	22
Château Ste. Michelle Johannisberg Riesling, Wash.	21
Bonny Doon Pacific Rim Riesling, USA/Germany	21
J. Lohr Bay Mist Riesling, Calif.	20
Columbia Winery Cellarmaster's Reserve Riesling, Wash.	20
Top 5 Budget Sauvignon Blancs	
Murphy-Goode Fumé Blanc, Calif.	23
Dry Creek Fumé Blanc, Calif.	22
Chât. Ste. Michelle Columbia Valley Sauv. Blanc, Wash.	22
Kenwood Sauv. Blanc, Calif.	22
Hogue Fumé Blanc, Wash.	21

Top 10 Budget Chardonnays

Rosemount Diamond Label Chard., Australia	21
Beringer Founders' Estate Chard., Calif.	21
Hess Select Chard., Calif.	21
St. Francis Sonoma Chard., Calif.	21
Penfolds Koonunga Hill Chard., Australia	21
Columbia Crest Chard., Washington	20
Gallo of Sonoma Chard., Calif.	20
Jacob's Creek Chard., Australia	20
Lindemans Bin 65 Chard., Australia	20
Camelot Chard., Calif.	19

Top 5 Budget Pinot Noirs

Firesteed Pinot Noir, Oregon	21
Gallo of Sonoma Pinot Noir, Calif.	20
Beringer Founders' Estate Pinot Noir, Calif.	19
Duck Pond Pinot Noir, Oregon	19
Meridian Pinot Noir, Calif.	19

Top 10 Budget Merlots

Casa Lapostolle Classic Merlot, Chile	22
Columbia Crest Merlot, Wash.	21
Montes Merlot, Chile	20
Gallo of Sonoma Merlot, Calif.	20
Lindemans Bin 40 Merlot, Australia	20
Christian Moueix Merlot, France	20
Beringer Founders' Estate Merlot, Calif.	19
Beaulieu Vineyard (BV) Coastal Merlot, Calif.	18
Fetzer Eagle Peak Merlot, Calif.	18
Concha y Toro Frontera Merlot, Chile	18

Top 10 Budget Cabernets and Blends

Gallo of Sonoma Cab. Sauv., Calif.	21
Rosemount Diamond Label Cab. Sauv./ Merlot Australia	21
Beringer Founders' Estate Cab. Sauv., Calif.	21
Jacob's Creek Cab. Sauv., Australia	21
Rosemount Diamond Label Cab. Sauv., Australia	21
Casa Lapostolle Classic Cab. Sauv., Chile	20
Columbia Crest Cab. Sauv., Wash.	20
Black Opal Cabernet/Merlot, Australia	20
Santa Rita 120 Cabernet Sauv., Chile	19
Black Opal Cab. Sauv., Australia	19

*Scores were rounded off. Wines are listed in order of actual ranking.

Best of the Rest

Top 5 Budget Other Whites (budget Pinot Grigios were included in this taste ranking, but none made the top 5)

Name	Taste Score*
Hugel Pinot Blanc, Alsace, France	23
Penfolds Semillon/Chardonnay, Australia	22
Miguel Torres Viña Sol, Spain	20
Ruffino Orvieto, Italy	19
Marqués de Riscal White Rueda, Spain	19

Top 5 Budget Italian and Spanish Reds

Vega Sindoa Tempranillo/Merlot Navarra Tinto, Spain	22
Santa Cristina Sangiovese, Antinori, Italy	22
Marqués de Riscal Rioja Crianza, Spain	22
Montecillo Rioja Crianza, Spain	21
Cecchi Chianti Classico, Italy	21

Top 5 Budget Shiraz/Syrahs and Rhône-Style Reds

Rosemount Diamond Label Shiraz, Australia	23
Rosemount Diamond Label Shiraz/Cab. Sauv., Australia	23
Jaboulet Côtes-du-Rhône, France	22
E & M Guigal Côtes-du-Rhône, France	22
Lindemans Bin 59 Shiraz, Australia	21

Top 5 Budget Red Zinfandels

Cline Zin., Calif.	23
Monteviña Amador Zin., Calif.	20
Beaulieu Vineyard (BV) Coastal Zin., Calif.	19
Robert Mondavi Coastal Zin., Calif.	18
Fetzer Valley Oaks Zin., Calif.	17

TOP VALUES FOR THE MONEY (ACROSS ALL PRICES)

Top 20 White Wine Values

Wine Name Wine Type	Value Score*	Price Category
Brancott Rsv. Sauv. Blanc., New Zealand Sauvignon Blanc/Fumé Blanc	24	$$
Martin Codax Albariño, Spain Other White Wines	24	$$
Hugel Pinot Blanc, Alsace, France Other White Wines	23	$
Lindemans Bin 65 Chard., Australia Chardonnay	23	$
Lucien Crochet Sancerre, France Sauvignon Blanc/Fumé Blanc	23	$$
Trimbach Pinot Gris, Alsace, France Pinot Gris/Pinot Grigio	23	$$
Trimbach Riesling, Alsace, France Riesling	23	$$
Gallo of Sonoma Chard., Calif. Chardonnay	23	$
Penfolds Semillon/Chardonnay, Australia Other White Wines	23	$
Honig Sauv. Blanc, Calif. Sauvignon Blanc/Fumé Blanc	22	$$
Hugel Gewürztraminer, Alsace, France Other White Wines	22	$$
Alois Lageder Pinot Grigio, Italy Pinot Gris/Pinot Grigio	22	$$
Rosemount Diamond Label Chard., Australia Chardonnay	22	$
Jolivet Sancerre, France Sauvignon Blanc/Fumé Blanc	22	$$

*Scores were rounded off. Wines are listed in order of actual ranking.

Wine Name Wine Type	Value Score*	Price Cate- gory
Dry Creek Fumé Blanc, Calif. Sauvignon Blanc/Fumé Blanc	22	$
Jacob's Creek Chard., Australia Chardonnay	22	$
Hogue Fruit Forward Johannisberg Riesling, Wash. Riesling	22	$
Bernardus Chard., Calif. Chardonnay	22	$$$
Chat. Ste. Michelle Columbia Valley Chard., Wash.	22	$$
Kenwood Sauv. Blanc, Calif. Sauvignon Blanc/Fumé Blanc	22	$

Top 20 Red Wine Values

Wine Name Wine Type	Value Score*	Price Cate- gory

Rosemount Diamond Label Shiraz,
Australia
   Syrah/Shiraz and Other Rhône-Style
   Reds
	24	$

Muga Rioja Reserva, Spain
   Rioja, Ribera del Duero, and Other
   Spanish Reds
	24	$$$

Rosemount Diamond Label Shiraz/Cab.
Sauv., Aust.
   Syrah/Shiraz and Other Rhône-Style
   Reds
	24	$

Jaboulet Côtes-du-Rhône, France
   Syrah/Shiraz and Other Rhône-Style
   Reds
	23	$

Alvaro Palacios Les Terrasses Priorat, Spain
   Rioja, Ribera del Duero, and Other
   Spanish Reds
	23	$$$

Marqués de Cáceres Rioja Crianza,
Spain
   Rioja, Ribera del Duero, and Other
   Spanish Reds
	23	$$

Santa Cristina Sangiovese, Antinori, Italy Chianti and Sangiovese	23	$
Willakenzie Willamette Valley Pinot Noir, Oregon Pinot Noir	23	$$$
Selvapiana Chianti Rufina, Italy Chianti and Sangiovese	23	$$

Wine Name	Value Score	Price Category
Vega Sindoa Tempranillo/Merlot Navarra Tinto, Spain	23	$
Rioja, Ribera del Duero, and Other Spanish Reds		
St. Francis Sonoma Merlot, Calif. Merlot	23	$$$
St. Francis Sonoma Zin., Calif.	23	$$
Red Zinfandel		
Château Larose-Trintaudon Bordeaux, France	23	$$
Cabernet Sauv. and Cabernet Blends		
Ridge Geyserville (Zin.), Calif.	23	$$$
Red Zinfandel		
Casa Lapostolle Classic Merlot, Chile	22	$
Merlot		
Penfolds Bin 389 Cabernet/Shiraz, Australia	22	$$$
Cabernet Sauv. and Cabernet Blends		
Château Greysac Bordeaux, France	22	$$
Cabernet Sauv. and Cabernet Blends		
Marqués de Riscal Rioja Crianza, Spain	22	$
Rioja, Ribera del Duero, and Other Spanish Reds		
Rosemount Diamond Label Cab. Sauv./ Merlot, Australia	22	$
Cabernet Sauv. and Cabernet Blends		
Casa Lapostolle Classic Cab. Sauv., Chile	22	$
Cabernet Sauv. and Cabernet Blends		

Top 20 Chardonnay Values

Wine Name	Value Score*	Price Category
Lindemans Bin 65 Chard., Australia	23	$
Gallo of Sonoma Chard., Calif.	23	$
Rosemount Diamond Label Chard., Australia	22	$
Jacob's Creek Chard., Australia	22	$
Bernardus Chard., Calif.	22	$$$
Chât. Ste. Michelle Columbia Valley Chard., Wash.	22	$$
Columbia Crest Chard., Washington	21	$
Chalone Central Coast Chard., Calif.	21	$$$
La Crema Chard., Calif.	21	$$
Leflaive (Olivier) Puligny-Montrachet, France	21	$$$$
Edna Valley Vineyard Chard., Calif.	21	$$

*Scores were rounded off. Wines are listed in order of actual ranking.

Wine Name	Value Score*	Price Category
St. Francis Sonoma Chard., Calif.	21	$
Château St. Jean Sonoma Chard., Calif.	21	$$
Leflaive (Domaine) Puligny-Montrachet, France	21	$$$$
Cambria Katherine's Vineyard Chard., Calif.	21	$$$
Benziger Chard., Calif.	21	$$
Penfolds Koonunga Hill Chard., Australia	21	$
Mâcon-Lugny Les Charmes, France	21	$
Beringer Founders' Estate Chard., Calif.	21	$
Beringer Napa Chard., Calif.	21	$$

Top 20 Cabernet Values

Wine Name	Value Score*	Price Category
Chateau Larose-Trintaudon Bordeaux, France	23	$$
Penfolds Bin 389 Cabernet/Shiraz, Australia	22	$$$
Château Greysac Bordeaux, France	22	$$
Rosemount Diamond Label Cab. Sauv./Merlot, Australia	22	$
Casa Lapostolle Classic Cab. Sauv., Calif.	22	$
Rosemount Diamond Label Cab. Sauv., Australia	22	$
Joseph Phelps Napa Cab. Sauv., Calif.	22	$$$$
Carmenet Dynamite Cab. Sauv., Calif.	22	$$$
Estancia Cab. Sauv., Calif.	22	$$
Château Gruaud-Larose Bordeaux, France	22	$$$$
Jacob's Creek Cab. Sauv., Australia	22	$
Beringer Knights Valley Cab. Sauv., Calif.	22	$$$
Château Ste. Michelle Columbia Valley Cab. Sauv., Wash.	22	$$
Gallo of Sonoma Cab. Sauv., Calif.	22	$
Château Gloria Bordeaux, France	22	$$$$
J. Lohr 7 Oaks Cab. Sauv., Calif.	22	$$
Franciscan Napa Cab. Sauv., Calif.	22	$$
Beaulieu Vineyard (BV) Rutherford Cab. Sauv., Calif.	22	$$$
Cain Cuvée Bordeaux Style Red, Calif.	21	$$$
Beringer Founders' Estate Cab. Sav., Calif.	21	$

THE TOP 50 WINES
YOU'RE *NOT* DRINKING

My write-in candidates—wines with good availability and great taste for the money in their categories. Enjoy!

Sparkling
Bouvet Brut NV, Loire Valley, France
Domaine Carneros Brut, California
Domaine Chandon Brut Fresco NV, Argentina
Freixenet Brut de Noirs NV Cava Rosé, Spain
Gosset Brut Rosé NV, France
Iron Horse Wedding Cuvée Brut, California
Mionetto DOC Prosecco, Veneto, Italy
Pol Roger Blanc de Chardonnay Champagne
    Brut NV, France
Pommery Brut Royal NV, France
Segura Viudas Aria Estate Extra Dry Cava,
    Spain

White (*tasting notes are found in the grape or style category as noted*)
Artesa Carneros Estate Chardonnay, California
Burgess Chardonnay, California
Canyon Road Sauvignon Blanc, California
Columbia Crest Semillon/Chardonnay,
    Washington (Other Whites)
Concha y Toro Casillero del Diablo Sauvignon
    Blanc, Chile
Gunderloch Riesling Kabinett Jean Baptiste,
    Germany
Kendall-Jackson Great Estates Monterey
    Chardonnay, California
Michel Laroche Chablis St. Martin, France
    (Chardonnay)
Pepperwood Grove Viognier, California (Other
    Whites)
Pierre Sparr Pinot Blanc, France (Other Whites)
R.H. Phillips Sauvignon Blanc, California

Sokol-Blosser Evolution, Oregon (a multigrape blend, listed under Other Whites)

"TJ" Riesling Selbach-Oster, Germany

Weingartner Gruner Veltliner Federspiel, Austria (Other Whites)

Wente Riesling, California

Rosé

Bonny Doon Vin Gris de Cigare Pink Wine, California

Marqués de Cáceres Rioja Rosado, Spain

McDowell Grenache Rosé, California

Regaleali Rosato, Tasca D'Almerita, Italy

René Barbier, Mediterranean Rosado, Spain

Red

Buena Vista Carneros Pinot Noir, California

Casa Lapostolle Cuvée Alexandre Cabernet Sauvignon, Chile

Concannon Petite Syrah, California (Other Reds)

Concha y Toro Terrunyo Carmenere, Chile (Other Reds)

Clos du Bois Pinot Noir, California

Dry Creek Reserve Zinfandel, California

Escudo Rojo Cabernet Blend, Baron Philippe de Rothschild, Chile (Cabernet Sauvignon and Cabernet Blends)

Falesco Vitiano, Italy (Italian Regional Reds)

Frei Brothers Reserve Merlot, California

Greg Norman Cabernet/Merlot, Australia

Hill of Content Grenache/Shiraz, Australia (Syrah/Shiraz and Other Rhone-Style Reds)

Navarro Correas Malbec, Argentina (Other Reds)

Seven Peaks Cabernet Sauvignon, California

Stonestreet Alexander Valley Cabernet Sauvignon, California

Veramonte Primus, Chile (Other Reds)

Dessert Wines

Baron Philippe de Rothschild Sauternes, France

Blandy's 10-Year-Old Malmsey Madeira, Portugal

Ferreira Doña Antonia Port NV, Portugal

Ficklin Tinta "Port" NV, California

Michele Chiarlo Nivole (Clouds) Moscato d'Asti, Italy

THE REVIEWS

WHITE WINES
Sparkling/Champagne

Style Profile: Although all the world's bubblies are modeled on Champagne, only the genuine article from the Champagne *region* of France is properly called *Champagne*. *Sparkling wine* is the proper term for the other bubblies, some of which can be just as good as the real thing. Limited supply and high demand—plus a labor-intensive production process—make Champagne expensive compared to other sparklers but still an affordable luxury in comparison to other world-class wine categories, like top French Burgundy or California Cabernet estates. The other sparklers, especially Cava from Spain and Italian Prosecco (see the list of "Top 50 Wines You're Not Drinking" for my picks), are affordable for everyday drinking. *Brut* (rhymes with *root*) on the label means the wine is utterly dry, with no perceptible sweetness. But that *doesn't* mean they all taste the same. In fact, each French Champagne house is known for a signature style, which can range from delicate and elegant to rich, full, and toasty—meaning there's something for every taste and food partner.

Serve: Well chilled; young and fresh (only the rare luxury French Champagnes improve with age). Open with utmost care: flying corks can be dangerous.

When: Anytime! It's not just for special occasions, and it's great with meals.

With: Anything and anyone, but especially sushi and shellfish.

In: A narrow tulip- or flute-type glass; the narrow opening preserves the bubbles.

Kitchen Fridge Survival Tip for bubbly wine: Kitchenware shops and wine stores often sell "clamshell" stoppers specially designed to close Champagnes and sparkling wines if you don't finish the bottle. I've found that if you open the bottle carefully in the first place (avoid "popping" the cork, which is also the safest technique), a stoppered sparkling wine will keep its fizz for at least three days in the fridge, often longer. Having a hard time thinking of something else to toast? How about, "Here's to [insert day of week]." That's usually good enough for me!

Bouvet Brut (*boo-VAY broot*) NV	PC	T	V
Loire Valley, France	$$	X	X

♥ This, the first *real* sparkling wine I ever tasted, cleared up some early confusion in my wine life—namely, that there was no such thing as good, affordable bubbly. Thanks to a bum recommendation from my wine shop, my reference point up to that moment had been Cold Duck(!). Bouvet changed all that. It was (and still is) affordable but also fantastic, with a very complex scent of wilted blossoms and sweet hay, a crisp apple-quince flavor, and creamy texture. If you, too, thought there was no such thing as worthy, well-priced bubbly, try this.
Kitchen Fridge Survivor™ Grade: B+
Your notes:_____

Domaine Carneros Brut	PC	T	V
California	$$$	X	X

♥ It is impossible for me to choose a favorite California sparkling wine, because there are so many good styles and wineries. But this one's definitely on my "short list." It has very ripe pineapple fruit, expertly balanced between generous juiciness and elegant restraint. It is one of my very favorite wines for food, because it enhances intricate flavors without competing.
Kitchen Fridge Survivor™ Grade: B
Your notes:_____

Domaine Chandon (*shahn-DOHN*)   **PC**   **T**   **V**
Extra Brut Classic Sparkling, California $$ **20**   **21**

Fans—myself among them—"love" and "adore" this
American sparkler sibling of France's famous Moët &
Chandon, in part because it's one of the best bubblies
for the price. While a few Francophiles among my
trade tasters think that it doesn't pack "enough fruit
flavor," I don't find this a negative: I like the more
yeasty, creamy style that the majority of buyers agree
is a "great everyday sparkler."

Kitchen Fridge Survivor™ Grade: B+
Your notes:_____

Domaine Chandon (*dough-MAIN*   **PC**   **T**   **V**
***shahn-DOHN*) Brut Fresco NV**   **$**   **X**   **X**
Argentina

♥ This is the Argentinean sister sparkler from Moët &
Chandon, makers of White Star and Dom Perignon.
It has Chandon-style intensity, with tangy acidity and
very concentrated apple flavor that's like high gear for
your taste buds. For this high quality, the price is great.

Kitchen Fridge Survivor™ Grade: Avg
Your notes:_____

Domaine Ste. Michelle Cuvée Brut   **PC**   **T**   **V**
Sparkling, Washington   **$**   **18**   **21**

This is "the one bottle of bubbly to have when you're
having more than one," advised one festive-but-frugal
host, and consumers and trade alike agree: "you can't
beat the price" of this nicely balanced, fruity sparkler
made in the Champagne method. I've been serving
this wine for years by the glass and as my ultimate
smooth-move wedding bubbly (brides can handle the
taste and parents the price).

Kitchen Fridge Survivor™ Grade: B
Your notes:_____

Price Ranges: **$** = $12 or less; **$$** = 12.01–20; **$$$** = 20.01–35;
$$$$ = > $35
Kitchen Countertop Survivor™ Grades: **Avg.** = a "one-day wine,"
tastes noticeably less fresh the next day; **B** = holds its freshness for
2–3 days after opening; **B+** = holds *and gets better* over 2–3 days
after opening; **A** = a 3- to 4-day "freshness window"; **A+** = holds *and
gets better* over 3–4 days

Freixenet (*freh-shuh-NETT*) Brut PC T V
de Noirs NV, Cava Rosé, Spain $ X X

♥ Sometimes "yummy" is really the right word for a wine. This is one of those. It has a gorgeous pale watermelon color, a mouthwatering taste of tangy strawberries, and thirst-quenching juiciness that makes it great with fried foods, spicy foods . . . any foods. At this price, it's a gift. This actually held up for *weeks* in the fridge (I forgot it was in there).
Kitchen Fridge Survivor™ Grade: A+
Your notes:_____

_____

Gosset (*go-SAY*) Brut Rosé NV PC T V
France $$$$ X X

♥ Perhaps memories of those candy-sweet rosés we all drank in the seventies are to blame, but my experience is that when it comes to rosé Champagne, most people need convincing. This wine will do it. Despite being one of the lowest-priced of the French rosé Champagnes, it's an amazing one. The scent and flavors, of dried cherries, exotic spices and toasted nuts, would please any serious still wine drinker with their complexity and depth. Yet it retains the graceful texture and festive sparkle that is Champagne.
Kitchen Fridge Survivor™ Grade: A
Your notes:_____

_____

Iron Horse Wedding Cuvée PC T V
(*coo-VAY*) Brut, California $$ X X

♥ Brides, of course, love the romantic name of this vibrant bottling. It is my choice for receptions, having inspired more "What was the name of that wine?" reactions than any other in the history of my wine career. Its breathtaking acidity and concentrated tangerine and green apple flavors make it a great choice for sushi, and I love it with egg dishes for brunch.
Kitchen Fridge Survivor™ Grade: B
Your notes:_____

_____

Korbel Brut Sparkling   **PC**   **T**   **V**
California   **$$**   **14**   **17**

This light, crisp sparkler is, quite possibly, used to celebrate more weddings, anniversaries, and New Year's countdowns than any other bubbly in America. Though some in the trade wish it had "more fruit," my biggest beef is Korbel's use of the name "Champagne" on the label, which furthers consumer confusion over the term and devalues the important category in which Korbel is a leading brand: namely, sparkling wines that *don't* carry French Champagne price tags but *do* offer good value for the money.
Kitchen Fridge Survivor™ Grade: Avg
Your notes:_____

Mionetto DOC Prosecco (*me-oh-*   **PC**   **T**   **V**
***NETT-oh pro-SECK-oh*), Veneto, Italy**   **$$**   **X**   **X**

♥ Why has this classic Italian sparkler lately become the talk of trend watchers and restaurant buyers nationwide? Two reasons, I think. First, it's dry, refreshing, and sophisticated but also affordable. Second, it's Italian, an attribute that of course confers instant chic. Prosecco is the grape name, and the wine can range from just lightly sparkling to fully *spumante* (the Italian word for "sparkling"). It's also the traditional bubbly mixed with peach puree to make the Bellini, Venice's signature cocktail.
Kitchen Fridge Survivor™ Grade: B
Your notes:_____

Moët & Chandon (*MWETT eh*   **PC**   **T**   **V**
***shahn-DONH*)—White Star**   **$$$$**   **21**   **19**
Champagne, France

🍶 Famous pedigree, flower and biscuit scents, and a peachy finish—what's not to love? Seriously, trade and consumer tasters alike touted this as "fantastic

---

Price Ranges: **$** = $12 or less; **$$** = 12.01–20; **$$$** = 20.01–35; **$$$$** = > $35
Kitchen Countertop Survivor™ Grades: ***Avg.*** = a "one-day wine," tastes noticeably less fresh the next day; ***B*** = holds its freshness for 2–3 days after opening; ***B+*** = holds *and gets better* over 2–3 days after opening; ***A*** = a 3- to 4-day "freshness window"; ***A+*** = holds *and gets better* over 3–4 days

Champagne," and I feel the quality has leapt to a better-than-ever level in the last few years. Pros point out that the "reliable, crowd-pleasing style" is owed to the dollop of sweetness used to round out the taste of the finished product. That taste twist makes it a great complement to spicy foods and brunch (*sans* the OJ, which masks the Champagne taste and bubbles you're paying extra for).

Kitchen Fridge Survivor™ Grade: A

Your notes:_____

_____

Mumm Cuvée Napa Brut	PC	T	V
Prestige Sparkling, California	$$	21	21

Though it's popular among consumers, pros are more blasé, saying it's "fine for the price," and I agree. I think it underperforms its potential—"pleasant bubbles," in a price point that's a leap for most of the drinking public. But I am hopeful this will soon change, as this property was split from its French parent in the latest round of beverage industry mergers and acquisitions and the new owners have the chance to give the brand more focus. Buyers should note that the name definitely will change sometime in the next few years.

Kitchen Fridge Survivor™ Grade: B

Your notes:_____

_____

Perrier-Jouët (*PEAR-ee-ay JHWETT*)	PC	T	V
Grand Brut NV Champagne	$$$$	23	20
France			

Fans call it "PJ," and it's definitely a favorite among the lighter-bodied Champagne styles, offering a fresh and lively bouquet and subtle-but-complex flavors. Serving it for years as the Rainbow Room's house bubbly revealed to me one of this wine's greatest virtues: it's a stellar survivor in the fridge, especially if you don't "pop" the cork when opening. And even when the bubbles do dissipate, the flavors remain delicious, more like complex white wine than like "flat Champagne."

Kitchen Fridge Survivor™ Grade: A+

Your notes:_____

_____

Pol Roger (*paul row-JHAY*)   PC   T   V
Blanc de Chardonnay Champagne $$$$ X   X
Brut, France

♥ I love this wine, and you will too. It's got real-Champagne sophistication, and the style is unique, combining my two favorite Champagne taste qualities. On the one hand, there's the toasted hazelnut scent that I'd normally associate with richer Champagne styles; while the flavor has the tangy acidity and delicacy of blanc-de-blancs-style Champagnes (meaning they're made solely from Chardonnay as opposed to the traditional blend that includes the red grapes Pinot Noir and Pinot Meunier). The open bottle just gets better and better in the fridge, even as the bubbles fade.

Kitchen Fridge Survivor™ Grade: A

Your notes:_____

_____

Pommery (*POMM-er-ee*) Brut   PC   T   V
Royal, NV, France $$$ X   X

♥ Pommery, one of France's classic Champagne houses, is just becoming known in the U.S. It's a beautiful, elegant style with a creamy-rich scent that reminds me of malted milk from my childhood. The texture is delicate, and the Asian pear flavor is both subtle and exotic.

Kitchen Fridge Survivor™ Grade: A

Your notes:_____

_____

Roederer Estate Sparkling   PC   T   V
California $$$ 24   23

⚓ ✓ Pros rave that they "can't believe" Roederer's "amazing flavors and wonderful integration." Trade and consumers alike say it's about as close to Champagne as you can get without buying French, and I find the full, toasty style to be right in keeping with the house style of its French counterpart (they make

Price Ranges: **$** = $12 or less; **$$** = 12.01–20; **$$$** = 20.01–35; **$$$$** = > $35

Kitchen Countertop Survivor™ Grades: ***Avg.*** = a "one-day wine," tastes noticeably less fresh the next day; ***B*** = holds its freshness for 2–3 days after opening; ***B+*** = holds *and gets better* over 2–3 days after opening; ***A*** = a 3- to 4-day "freshness window"; ***A+*** = holds *and gets better* over 3–4 days

Cristal). One prosaic retailer writes, "On the way to Mendocino—in the middle of nowhere—they've found a tiny bit of Reims" (Champagne's HQ town). For bubbly lovers, this is the best of both worlds: although "reasonably priced," it offers the taste of "a special occasion wine."

Kitchen Fridge Survivor™ Grade: A
Your notes:_____

Segura Viudas (*seh-GUHR-uh vee-YOU-duss*) Aria Estate Extra Dry Cava, Spain

	PC	T	V
	$	X	X

♥ For the money, this is one of the most unabashedly delicious sparklers I have ever drunk—it wasn't enough just to taste it; I had to pour a whole glass to enjoy (and restrain myself from a second in order to leave leftovers for the survivor test). Although Segura Viudas is Freixenet's upmarket cava brand, it remains an amazing price for what you get—ripe, vibrant pear fruit, creamy texture. If you like to entertain, the beautiful bottle brings an elegant look to the gathering.

Kitchen Fridge Survivor™ Grade: A
Your notes:_____

Taittinger (*TAIT-in-jur*) Brut La Française NV Champagne , France

	PC	T	V
	$$$$	25	20

This is one of my favorites among the subtle, delicate house-style Champagnes. Pros like its distinctive style, pointing to the generous proportion of Chardonnay in its blend, which lends it finesse and delicacy. Fans say it's all about its fragrant fruit aromas and toastiness, balanced with refreshing acidity that makes it "simply dance across the tongue."

Kitchen Fridge Survivor™ Grade: A
Your notes:_____

Veuve Clicquot (*voov klee-COH*) Yellow Label NV Champagne France

	PC	T	V
	$$$$	25	21

⚜ Both pro and consumer devotees of Clicquot's "benchmark" quality and "impress your friends" yellow label utterly outcheer the few sour-grapes complaints that it's "overrated." Whatever your own taste, expect a full-bodied style. As the first Champagne I ever opened tableside for a guest (and boy, was I nervous!), this wine is both a sentimental and taste favorite of mine. Having served, over the years, literally thousands of cases of it by the glass in my restaurants, I can honestly say I never had one customer *not* like it.

Kitchen Fridge Survivor™ Grade: B+

Your notes:_____

Pinot Gris/Pinot Grigio

Grape Profile: Pinot Gris (*pee-no GREE*) is the French and Grigio (*GREE-jee-oh*) the Italian spelling for this crisp, delicate, very popular white wine grape. The French and American versions tend to be a bit more intensely flavored than the Italians (which are refreshing and noncerebral). To many of my trade tasters it's "the quintessential quaffing wine" and "a real winner by the glass" in restaurants. Both my trade and consumer tasters noted that many of the cheapest Pinot Grigios were among the best. I couldn't put it better than the taster who wrote, "If it doesn't *taste* a lot better, why should I *pay* a lot more?" As the Italians would say, *Ecco!*

Serve: Well chilled; young and fresh (as one of my wine buying buddies says to the waiters *she* teaches: "The best vintage for Pinot Grigio? As close to yesterday as possible!").

When: Anytime, but ideal with cocktails, outdoor occasions, lunch, big gatherings (a crowd-pleaser).

With: Very versatile, but perfect with hors d'oeuvres, salads, salty foods, and fried foods.

In: An all-purpose wine stem is fine.

Price Ranges: **$** = $12 or less; **$$** = 12.01–20; **$$$** = 20.01–35; **$$$$** = > $35

Kitchen Countertop Survivor™ Grades: *Avg.* = a "one-day wine," tastes noticeably less fresh the next day; *B* = holds its freshness for 2–3 days after opening; *B+* = holds *and gets better* over 2–3 days after opening; *A* = a 3- to 4-day "freshness window"; *A+* = holds *and gets better* over 3–4 days

Alois Lageder (*la-GAY-der—*	PC	T	V
no one says the first part)	$$	23	22
Pinot Grigio, Italy			

Though many fans understandably have trouble
pronouncing the maker (please see above), it would
seem they know plenty well what they like about this
"flowery" and "spicy" Pinot Grigio. Indeed, unlike
many of its lightweight contemporaries, this PG has
a smoky finish and complexity that few expect from
Pinot Grigio.

Kitchen Fridge Survivor™ Grade: B

Your notes:_____

_____

Bolla Pinot Grigio	PC	T	V
Italy	$	16	17

The Bolla name sells it, but it offers less flavor for
the money than its competitors at the same price
level. Fans say it's an "unassuming" wine with a
"no-nonsense" personality, while detractors say it
has "no personality at all." Still, for the price many
consider it a safe choice for a big cocktail party.

Kitchen Fridge Survivor™ Grade: Avg

Your notes:_____

_____

CAVIT (*CAV-it; rhymes with have-it*)	PC	T	V
Pinot Grigio , Italy	$	16	19

Though fans say this wine's "a nice summertime
sipper," I think it's great by the glass anytime and *the*
cocktail party choice. Yes, it's light, but entirely
pleasant, and that's what I want in Pinot Grigio. It's
light on the damage (as in wallet), too.

Kitchen Fridge Survivor™ Grade: B

Your notes:_____

_____

Ecco Domani (*ECK-oh dough-*	PC	T	V
MAH-nee) **Pinot Grigio, Italy**	$	16	19

"Tastes clean and refreshing," say fans of Gallo's
Italian offspring that smells like spice and pear. Pros
point out that, as a value, it's "pretty impressive for
the money." I concur.

Kitchen Countertop Survivor™ Grade: Avg

Your notes:_____

_____

Folonari (*foe-luh-NAH-ree*)   PC   T   V
Pinot Grigio, Italy $ 14   17

While many Pinot Grigio prices crept (and sometimes leapt) up during the "wine boom," this one held pretty steady on both the price and flavor fronts. That may explain its standing with some trade buyers as the "underrated overachiever"—definitely worth a look when you're seeking Italian, white, value, or any combination of the three.

Kitchen Fridge Survivor™ Grade: Avg
Your notes:_____

_____

King Estate Pinot Gris   PC   T   V
Oregon $$ 22   21

You really can't compare the style of Oregon Pinot Gris to that of Italian Pinot Grigio, as illustrated dramatically by the "cornucopia of tropical fruit aromas" in this mouthwatering "Carmen Miranda's hat of a wine." I share the concern of some pros that the price has risen quickly—and in stride—with its popularity. At present I still think there's nice quality for the money, and I'm keeping my fingers crossed that it holds.

Kitchen Fridge Survivor™ Grade: A
Your notes:_____

_____

Livio Felluga (*LIV-ee-oh fuh-LOO-*   PC   T   V
***guh*) Pinot Grigio, Italy** $$ 22   21

♵ "Lean," "stylish" and "exciting" are words pros use to describe this standout Pinot Grigio with the cool map label. I too fancy the pretty floral nose, ripe apricot flavors and fruity richness; that make it "definitely not your typical Pinot Grigio."

Kitchen Fridge Survivor™ Grade: B
Your notes:_____

_____

Price Ranges: **$** = $12 or less; **$$** = 12.01–20; **$$$** = 20.01–35; **$$$$** = > $35
Kitchen Countertop Survivor™ Grades: ***Avg.*** = a "one-day wine," tastes noticeably less fresh the next day; ***B*** = holds its freshness for 2–3 days after opening; ***B+*** = holds *and gets better* over 2–3 days after opening; ***A*** = a 3- to 4-day "freshness window"; ***A+*** = holds *and gets better* over 3–4 days

MezzaCorona (*METT-suh* *coh-ROH-nuh*) Pinot Grigio Italy	PC	T	V
	$	15	16

"A nice staple" and "great everyday wine," say pros, who depend on MezzaCorona to be consistent in flavor, though it's not necessarily dazzling when it comes to delivering on fruit—but that's not what we expect from Pinot Grigio anyway. What we do expect is delivered: "decent value" in a "mouthwatering" and "refreshing" crowd pleaser.

Kitchen Fridge Survivor™ Grade: B

Your notes:_____

_____

Santa Margherita Pinot Grigio Italy	PC	T	V
	$$$	18	15

I knew I'd uncork controversy with this one, as no other wine in the book evokes more conflicted reactions than this Pinot Grigio. While some consumers joined the majority of trade tasters in appraising Santa Margherita as "overrated" and "way overpriced" for the quality, some tasters say it's a "favorite" that will "impress your friends." As a trade buyer, I have a hard time seeing simple Pinot Grigio, which should be a value category, frequently priced in the same league as French Chablis and other world-class whites. Yet the numbers don't lie: we Americans managed to buy hundreds of thousands of cases of the stuff last year, perhaps because it's a "comfort zone" wine. Clearly, in the overwhelming world of wine, legions of consumers find that a known name is worth paying up for.

Kitchen Fridge Survivor™ Grade: Avg

Your notes:_____

_____

Trimbach (*TRIM-bock*) Pinot Gris Alsace, France	PC	T	V
	$$	24	23

✔ Here to join Italy and Oregon is this completely different French riff that provides further proof that the PG category is more exciting than it gets credit for, especially the Alsace versions. It's got the richer body that, as pros say, is perfect for people looking for alternatives to Chardonnay and Sauvignon Blanc, because it's fruity yet dry. It's also great with food, due to its crisp acidity and not-too-tart flavor profile.

Kitchen Fridge Survivor™ Grade: B+

Your notes:_____

Turning Leaf Pinot Grigio	PC	T	V
California	**$**	**13**	**15**

The reviews are mixed on this light quaffing wine. While fans say it's "fine on its own" and "an inexpensive crowd pleaser," many pros think the Gallo family is "more than capable of making a wine that is more exciting than this."

Kitchen Fridge Survivor™ Grade: Avg

Your notes:_____

Riesling

Grape Profile: Take note of two great things about the Riesling (*REES-ling*) category. The first is not a lot of dollar signs (so lots of value prices). Second, check out all the high survivor grades. Thanks to their tangy, crisp acidity, Riesling wines really hold up in the fridge. That makes them very practical for lots of everyday dining situations—you want a glass of white with your takeout sushi, but your dinner mate wants red with the beef teriyaki. At home I sometimes want to start with a glass of white while I'm cooking and then switch to red with the meal. It's nice to know that I can go back to the wine over several days, and every glass will taste as good as the first one.

Many tasters wondered "Where are the Germans?" in this survey, because classic Riesling hails from Germany. Sadly, they're not such big sellers—yet. I'm hopeful that after you taste a few of these you'll see that the grape is deliciously worth "rooting" out on its home turf—look for German Rieslings from the Mosel, Rheingau, Pfalz, and Nahe regions.

Price Ranges: **$** = $12 or less; **$$** = 12.01–20; **$$$** = 20.01–35; **$$$$** = > $35

Kitchen Countertop Survivor™ Grades: ***Avg.*** = a "one-day wine," tastes noticeably less fresh the next day; ***B*** = holds its freshness for 2–3 days after opening; ***B+*** = holds *and gets better* over 2–3 days after opening; ***A*** = a 3- to 4-day "freshness window"; ***A+*** = holds *and gets better* over 3–4 days

Want to know about the style before you dive into these? Rieslings are light-bodied but loaded with fruit flavor (which is what you're looking for in wine, right?), balanced with tangy acidity. It's my favorite white grape.

Serve: Lightly chilled is fine (the aromas really shine when it's not ice-cold); it's good young and fresh, but the French and German versions can evolve nicely for up to five years.

When: Every day (OK, my personal taste there); classy enough for "important" meals and occasions.

With: Outstanding with shrimp cocktail and other cold seafood, as well as ethnic foods with a "kick" (think Asian, sushi, Indian, Mexican).

In: An all-purpose wineglass.

Beringer Johannisberg Riesling	PC	T	V
California	$	18	19

Although this wine is a bit more difficult to find than the heavier hitters in the Beringer stable, the fruit-salad-in-a-glass flavor is worth the search. In my earliest days of writing wine lists, I found the notoriety of the Beringer name made it easier to get my guests to try Riesling. I still think it's one of the best values in their portfolio.
Kitchen Fridge Survivor™ Grade: B+
Your notes:_____

_____

Bonny Doon Pacific Rim Riesling	PC	T	V
USA/Germany	$	21	21

⚓ "Pacific Rim" is the winery's shorthand for "Drink this with Asian foods"—in case you didn't already get it from the random constellation of sushi morsels that serve as a pretty cool label. I join large numbers of both trade and consumers who love its "fruity yet dry" flavor profile and "great quality" for the money. Interestingly, and "true to the eclectic Bonny Doon style" as one taster put it, the grapes come from California, Washington, and Germany.
Kitchen Fridge Survivor™ Grade: A
Your notes:_____

_____

Château Ste. Michelle Johannisberg Riesling, Washington

	PC	T	V
	$	21	21

This is indeed a "tutti-frutti" Riesling, as one taster put it, with honeysuckle floral aromas and peaches and apricot flavor, with some crisp, lively acidity to give it the balance that is the hallmark of well-made Riesling. I often serve this wine in basic tasting seminars as an example of "textbook" Riesling.

Kitchen Fridge Survivor™ Grade: A

Your notes:_____

Columbia Crest Johannisberg Riesling, Washington

	PC	T	V
	$	19	19

Like all the varietals from Columbia Crest, this wine is of consistent quality, true to type, and a great value. It's got all the requisite peach, apricot, and honeysuckle aromas and flavors—with just a touch of sweetness. I completely agree with the taster who recommends it "with shucked oysters." At this price you can afford a whole mess of them.

Kitchen Fridge Survivor™ Grade: A

Your notes:_____

Columbia Winery Cellarmaster's Reserve Riesling, Washington

	PC	T	V
	$	20	18

Allow me to gush: this wine is a real gift to wine lovers, one of *the* great Rieslings made in North America. Fans say it's "dripping" with ripe peaches, apricots, "a drizzle of honey," and a long, "crisp, clean finish." I think it's great at any price, though it happens to be a major bargain.

Kitchen Fridge Survivor™ Grade: A+

Your notes:_____

Price Ranges: **$** = $12 or less; **$$** = 12.01–20; **$$$** = 20.01–35; **$$$$** = > $35

Kitchen Countertop Survivor™ Grades: *Avg.* = a "one-day wine," tastes noticeably less fresh the next day; *B* = holds its freshness for 2–3 days after opening; *B+* = holds *and gets better* over 2–3 days after opening; *A* = a 3- to 4-day "freshness window"; *A+* = holds *and gets better* over 3–4 days

Covey Run Riesling	PC	T	V
Washington	$	19	19

A nice touch of lemon distinguishes this Washington Riesling, which delivers a pleasant aroma of nectarine and peaches and a nice balance between sweetness and acidity. Fans say that "for the price, it simply can't be beat."

Kitchen Fridge Survivor™ *Grade: B*

Your notes:_____

_____

Fetzer Echo Ridge Johannisberg	PC	T	V
Riesling, California	$	15	17

Fans describe this wine as a "bold" Riesling, with "huge fruit" by way of "superripe pears" and apricots. Pros say it's skewed on the sweet side, which can make it "challenging to pair with food," but I disagree: I think the boldness and hint of sweetness are ideal for foods with a little bit of chile heat—Thai, Indian, and southwestern for example.

Kitchen Fridge Survivor™ *Grade: B+*

Your notes:_____

_____

Gunderloch Riesling Kabinett	PC	T	V
Jean Baptiste, Germany	$$	X	X

♥ This is the kind of wine I would drink every single day if it weren't my job (and lots of fun) always to try new things. It is a perfect rendition of what great German Riesling is about—so classy yet so approachable. By "classy" I mean amazing complexity and detail to the scent and flavor—flowers, chamomile tea, fresh cream, white peach . . . I could go on and on. Its utterly fresh, drink-me appeal, unencumbered by oak and alcohol, makes it approachable and magical with food.

Kitchen Fridge Survivor™ *Grade: A*

Your notes:_____

_____

Hogue Fruit Forward Johannisberg	PC	T	V
Riesling, Washington	$	22	22

Attention all white Zinfandel fans: here's a great alternative that's a little on the sweet side, with ripe, peachy fruit flavor and a candied orange finish.

I find that Hogue is always consistent with quality and value.

Kitchen Fridge Survivor™ Grade: B

Your notes:_____

J. Lohr Bay Mist White Riesling
California

PC	T	V
$	20	20

This wine's enticing floral aromas, along with apricot and apple fruit, draw fans to this "eminently quaffable" Riesling. I agree with pros who say that its "impression of sweetness"—balanced by crisp acidity—make it a stand-alone wine that's perfect as an aperitif.

Kitchen Fridge Survivor™ Grade: B+

Your notes:_____

Jekel Riesling
California

PC	T	V
$	19	20

I love this wine, and so do fans who describe it as "perfectly pleasant" Riesling, with a lovely floral nose and juicy, ripe peaches on the palate. A touch of sweetness on the finish makes it a perfect partner for spicy foods.

Kitchen Fridge Survivor™ Grade: B+

Your notes:_____

Kendall-Jackson Vintner's Reserve
Riesling, California

PC	T	V
$	19	18

For tasters new to Riesling, I often recommend this one, because it is a textbook "tasting lesson" for the Riesling style from a blue chip winery. Fans are attracted to its lush peach, pear, apricot, and tangerine flavors, which come at a great price, too.

Kitchen Fridge Survivor™ Grade: A+

Your notes:_____

Price Ranges: **$** = $12 or less; **$$** = 12.01–20; **$$$** = 20.01–35; **$$$$** = > $35

Kitchen Countertop Survivor™ Grades: *Avg.* = a "one-day wine," tastes noticeably less fresh the next day; *B* = holds its freshness for 2–3 days after opening; *B+* = holds *and gets better* over 2–3 days after opening; *A* = a 3- to 4-day "freshness window"; *A+* = holds *and gets better* over 3–4 days

Schmitt Söhne (*SHMITT ZOHN-uh*,	PC	T	V
Söhne is German for "sons")	$	17	18
Riesling Kabinett, Germany			

German Rieslings, especially at the value end of the price spectrum, are hard to come by. Luckily, my pro tasters recommend this wine as a "solid bet for the money." Fans like its tart, Granny Smith apple flavors and crisp and lively texture. And because it's lighter in body and alcohol than many of its American counterparts, it's a good summertime/picnic quaff.

Kitchen Fridge Survivor™ Grade: A

Your notes:_____

Trimbach Riesling	PC	T	V
Alsace, France	$$	24	23

✓ They might need to start a fan club for this wine (with our annual conventions in Alsace? This could be good!). It is indeed a "hell of a food wine" (tasters recommended "Chinese food," but I even tried it with lamb chops). And it is classically Alsace Riesling—bone dry, with an amazing balance of "both delicate and intense fruit" flavors and "mouthwatering acidity." I credit that acidity for its amazing survivor potential. The wine blossomed and evolved beautifully after opening for *ten* days, by which time I had run out anyway.

Kitchen Fridge Survivor™ Grade: A+

Your notes:_____

"TJ" Riesling Selbach-Oster	PC	T	V
(*ZELL-bock OH-stir*), Germany	$	X	X

♥ Since this wine has none of the image problems saddling many German Rieslings (tongue-twister name, cryptic label, flabby-sweet taste), you're free to just groove on its virtues. Foremost is the classic German Riesling character, including a delicate peaches-and-cream scent with a hint of fresh almond, and fruit flavors of tangerine and peach. It may sound odd, but really good yogurt or crème fraîche is an apt comparison because the flavor is at once creamy-soft and tangy, the finish rich and lingering. All of this with an easy name (TJ) and at a great price.

Kitchen Fridge Survivor™ Grade: A

Your notes:_____

Wente (*WEN-tee*) Riesling	PC	T	V
California	$	X	X

♥ This is truly a one-of-a-kind wine. It is the first California Riesling I have ever tasted that possesses the aromatic character we Riesling fanatics look for and love. The English describe said smell as "petrol," which sounds negative but is precisely the opposite. It reminds me of the scent of lanolin, and when I find it, along with gorgeous mandarin orange and peach fruit, I know I've got the real thing. This is also one of the only wines I've ever had that perfectly complemented the briny, fishy flavors of seaweed salad and sea urchin. But you don't have to eat such extreme food to love it. It will go with anything, and for the price you can afford to drink it often.

Kitchen Fridge Survivor™ Grade: A

Your notes:_____

_____

Sauvignon Blanc/Fumé Blanc

Grape Profile: Sauvignon Blanc (*soh-veen-yoan BLAHNK*) is one of my favorite everyday white wine grapes. Truly great ones are still available for under $10, which is something you can't say about many wine categories these days. Depending on whether it's grown in cool, moderate, or warm conditions, the exotically pungent scent and taste range from zesty and herbaceous to tangy lime-grapefruit to juicy peach and melon. All of the styles share vibrant acidity and growing admiration in the marketplace, as my tasters' comments and assessments made clear. The grape's home base is France's Loire Valley and Bordeaux regions. California and Washington state make excellent versions, sometimes labeled Fumé Blanc (*FOO-may BLAHNK*). In the Southern Hemisphere, Chile makes tasty examples, but it's the New Zealand Sauvignon Blanc category that garnered the most

Price Ranges: **$** = $12 or less; **$$** = 12.01–20; **$$$** = 20.01–35; **$$$$** = > $35

Kitchen Countertop Survivor™ Grades: *Avg.* = a "one-day wine," tastes noticeably less fresh the next day; *B* = holds its freshness for 2–3 days after opening; *B+* = holds *and gets better* over 2–3 days after opening; *A* = a 3- to 4-day "freshness window"; *A+* = holds *and gets better* over 3–4 days

impassioned raves from professionals and consumers alike, and I have to agree. Another of Sauvignon Blanc's major virtues is its food versatility: it goes so well with the foods many people eat regularly (especially those following a less-red-meat regimen), like chicken and turkey, salads, sushi, Mexican, and vegetarian.

Serve: Chilled but not ice-cold.

When: An amazing food partner, but the following notes spotlight specific styles that are good on their own, as an aperitif.

With: As noted, great with most everyday eats, as well as popular ethnic tastes like Mexican food.

In: An all-purpose wineglass.

Barnard Griffin Fumé Blanc Washington	PC	T	V
	$	20	18

This is classic Columbia Valley Fumé, balancing upfront flavors of pear, apple, and tropical fruit, steely, flinty notes, and a distinct grassiness that's typical of the grape—in short, lots of flavor and character for the price.
Kitchen Fridge Survivor™ Grade: B
Your notes:_____

_____

Beaulieu Vineyard (BV) Coastal Sauvignon Blanc, California	PC	T	V
	$	17	18

One of my favorite of the coastal Sauvignon Blancs and "great for a hot day," as tasters commented. The fruity, crisp citrus flavors balanced with a zestiness that some call herbal and others "spicy jalapeño" make it a great choice for appetizers and spicy food.
Kitchen Fridge Survivor™ Grade: B
Your notes:_____

_____

Benziger Sonoma Fumé Blanc California	PC	T	V
	$$	21	21

A "great wine list buy," say fans, citing the bright citrus, apple, and melon aromas and clean, crisp acidity that make it extremely versatile with a wide range of foods.

Kitchen Fridge Survivor™ Grade: B+

Your notes:_____

_____

Beringer Founders' Estate	PC	T	V
Sauvignon Blanc, California	$	20	20

I was blown away by the flavor depth and true-to-the-grape character of this wine—melon and grapefruit in luscious profusion, but not at all heavy. The "can't go wrong price" is a gift, and the open bottle stays fresh for days.

Kitchen Fridge Survivor™ Grade: A+

Your notes:_____

_____

Beringer Napa Sauvignon Blanc	PC	T	V
California	$$	20	19

Pros who like this wine cite "layers of stone fruit flavors," especially apricots, citrus, and quince,

Price Ranges: **$** = $12 or less; **$$** = 12.01–20; **$$$** = 20.01–35; **$$$$** = > $35

Kitchen Countertop Survivor™ Grades: *Avg.* = a "one-day wine," tastes noticeably less fresh the next day; *B* = holds its freshness for 2–3 days after opening; *B+* = holds *and gets better* over 2–3 days after opening; *A* = a 3- to 4-day "freshness window"; *A+* = holds *and gets better* over 3–4 days

though some say it's "trying to be Chardonnay" with its rich and creamy finish. Fans, however, don't mind the oaky vanilla at all—and it costs less than most Chardonnays.

Kitchen Fridge Survivor™ Grade: B

Your notes:_____

_____

Brancott Reserve Sauvignon Blanc	PC	T	V
New Zealand	$$	24	24

🍷 I've been serving this by the bottle and glass since it first came to these shores, so I'm happy to see that so many *Immer Guide* respondents love its "truly unique and refreshing taste." Lots of pros find it's "as good as Cloudy Bay" (the standard-bearer in NZ Sauvignon Blancs) at a fraction of the price. The English describe New Zealand SB character as "gooseberry"—something few Americans have ever tasted. So think of lime, crushed green herbs, a bit of grapefruit . . . but the easiest way is just to try a bottle.

Kitchen Fridge Survivor™ Grade: A+

Your notes:_____

_____

Buena Vista Sauvignon Blanc	PC	T	V
California	$	19	21

Yes, it's a "great summer sipper," but I fondly remember it selling like hotcakes by the glass to my Rockefeller Center rinkside guests in the dead of winter, too. The juicy nectarine and lime flavors are still every bit as good, and "always a good value," as retailers point out, and their customers "buy it by the case." One happy host suggests pouring it for an open house: "You won't drop a wad of cash, and you'll be happy to have the leftovers."

Kitchen Fridge Survivor™ Grade: A

Your notes:_____

_____

Cakebread Sauvignon Blanc	PC	T	V
California	$$$	23	19

Fans of Cakebread's full-bodied, sophisticated Chardonnay are rewarded with this similarly structured Sauvignon Blanc, with intense grapefruit aromas and a hint of fig and vanilla. Some pros say it's "a bit overblown" in style, but that makes it a good bet for Chardonnay drinkers who want to branch out.

Kitchen Fridge Survivor™ Grade: A

Your notes:_____

Canyon Road Sauvignon Blanc

	PC	T	V
California	$	X	X

♥ This is more proof that California's best white wine values are its Sauvignon Blancs, which exhibit the fruit ripeness and vibrancy Americans love, while retaining the true character of the grape. That character includes a hint of grassiness and grapefruit pungency, with lots of melon and peach fruit courtesy of the California sun. A streak of lively acidity makes this a wonderful food partner.

Kitchen Fridge Survivor™ Grade: A

Your notes:_____

Chât. Ste. Michelle Columbia Valley

	PC	T	V
Sauvignon Blanc, Washington	$	22	21

Considering the very high taste rank of this wine for the price, it's no wonder East Coast fans bemoan, "It's hard to find." In addition to being consistent and dependable, it is truly distinctive, with piquant aromas of grapefruit zest and lemongrass tea, a hint of ginger flavor, and wonderfully creamy texture.

Kitchen Fridge Survivor™ Grade: B

Your notes:_____

Chateau St. Jean Fumé Blanc

	PC	T	V
California	$$	21	22

This wine is aged, in part, in French and American oak barrels, which explains the creamy vanilla oak

---

Price Ranges: **$** = $12 or less; **$$** = 12.01–20; **$$$** = 20.01–35; **$$$$** = > $35

Kitchen Countertop Survivor™ Grades: *Avg.* = a "one-day wine," tastes noticeably less fresh the next day; *B* = holds its freshness for 2–3 days after opening; *B+* = holds *and gets better* over 2–3 days after opening; *A* = a 3- to 4-day "freshness window"; *A+* = holds *and gets better* over 3–4 days

aromas. That richness is balanced by its forward fruit
flavors of grapefruit, melon, and fig, plus a healthy
dose of tangy acidity at the end. Its track record for
consistency, year after year, is exemplary.
Kitchen Fridge Survivor™ Grade: B+
Your notes:_____

_____

Clos du Bois (*Cloh-dew-BWAH*)	PC	T	V
Sauvignon Blanc, California	$	20	20

The dollop of Semillon and oak barrel aging add richness and a touch of vanilla to this otherwise crisp,
grapefruit-scented wine that many pros point out is
well priced for the quality. Fans like its refreshing,
light flavor and say it's a great buy. I agree.
Kitchen Fridge Survivor™ Grade: B
Your notes:_____

_____

Cloudy Bay Sauvignon Blanc	PC	T	V
New Zealand	$$$	26	21

This, in my opinion, is *the* standard-bearer in NZ
Sauvignon Blancs—and I'm not alone. Pros wax
amorous about its "multiplicity of aromas" and a
taste that covers the full spectrum—from lean tastes
like lime to lush flavors like kiwi. Many buyers noted
that the wine is "hard to find outside restaurants" and
that "it just keeps getting more and more expensive,"
both of which are true.
Kitchen Fridge Survivor™ Grade: A
Your notes:_____

_____

Columbia Crest Sauvignon Blanc	PC	T	V
Washington	$	20	20

Pros admire this round, crisp wine for its no-
nonsense, classic profile of melon, herbal, and flinty
aromas—without the fat. It's got clean honey and
melon flavors and an "oyster-friendly finish." Everyone agrees that the price is right.
Kitchen Fridge Survivor™ Grade: A
Your notes:_____

_____

Concha y Toro Casillero del Diablo   PC   T   V
(cah-see-YAIR-oh dell dee-AH-blo) $ X   X
Sauvignon Blanc, Chile

♥ Although Chardonnay is the bigger seller, I think the Sauvignon Blanc grape is Chile's best foot forward for whites, giving much better character and balance for the money. This is a perfect example of what Chile can achieve, for cheap, with Sauvignon Blanc. It has lots of ripe kiwi and honeydew fruit flavor yet keeps the grape's signature tangy zestiness. A real "wow" wine for the money.

Kitchen Fridge Survivor™ Grade: B

Your notes:_____

_____

Corbett Canyon Sauvignon Blanc   PC   T   V
California $ 13   13

Retail pros describe this wine as "plain and simple," though there's an interesting twist in that it's blended with Viognier and Colombard grapes. Although they give it an unusual green tea and gooseberry aroma, I wish more came through in the flavor, which is light.

Kitchen Fridge Survivor™ Grade: Avg

Your notes:_____

_____

Covey Run Fumé Blanc   PC   T   V
Washington $ 18   18

Another super example of how Washington Fumé can balance a clean, refreshing, and crisp taste profile without being light and boring. Its lovely bouquet of lemongrass and pink grapefruit seem to make tasters yearn for seafood. As one buyer noted, "It's bracing enough for oysters but has enough substance to handle a big halibut steak."

Kitchen Fridge Survivor™ Grade: Avg

Your notes:_____

_____

Price Ranges: **$** = $12 or less; **$$** = 12.01–20; **$$$** = 20.01–35; **$$$$** = > $35

Kitchen Countertop Survivor™ Grades: *Avg.* = a "one-day wine," tastes noticeably less fresh the next day; *B* = holds its freshness for 2–3 days after opening; *B+* = holds *and gets better* over 2–3 days after opening; *A* = a 3- to 4-day "freshness window"; *A+* = holds *and gets better* over 3–4 days

Didier Dagueneau Silex Pouilly Fumé **PC** **T** **V**
(DID-ee-yay DAG-uh-no poo-YEE **$$$** **24** **20**
foo-MAY), France

While some in the trade complain that the utterly
original wines from this "idiosyncratic" winemaker are
overpriced, the majority agree that they are for the
most part exceptional in their complexity, expression
of Pouilly-Fumé regional character, and ageability.
The combination of creamy, earthy, exotic, tropical,
and herbal characters, all in one bottle, makes a truly
unique and worthy drinking experience. I think it
might be one of the only wines in the world that
works with sea urchin!

Kitchen Fridge Survivor™ Grade: A+

Your notes:_____

_____

Dry Creek Fumé Blanc **PC** **T** **V**
California **$** **22** **22**

Part of me selfishly wishes this would remain a
"sleeper" winery, because the quality really does
equate to luxury flavor at everyday prices. Pros give
this always dependable Sonoma Fumé high marks
for its wonderfully tart taste that's balanced with
melon and peach flavors. It was a winner with
guacamole and Mexican food and everything else I
tried it with over several days; in fact it kept getting
better and better. Look also for Dry Creek's reds—
especially the Zinfandels and Reserve Cabernet.

Kitchen Fridge Survivor™ Grade: A+

Your notes:_____

_____

Duckhorn Sauvignon Blanc **PC** **T** **V**
California **$$$** **23** **20**

Some pros question whether the flavor is "worth the
price," which indeed reflects a premium for the Duckhorn name, made famous by its benchmark Merlot.
While the quality languished for a few years, I think
it's back on form—tangerine fruit, nice balance, and
good length.

Kitchen Fridge Survivor™ Grade: A

Your notes:_____

_____

Ernest & Julio Gallo Twin Valley PC T V
Sauvignon Blanc, California $ 17 18

Pros are quick to point out the Gallo winery's split personality. On the one hand it's proven it can make serious, world-class wines. In addition, its "enormous portfolio" features plenty of "no-frills" wines like this Twin Valley Sauvignon Blanc. It's light and soft, for pleasant everyday drinking on a budget.

Kitchen Fridge Survivor™ Grade: Avg

Your notes:_____

_____

Ferrari-Carano Fumé Blanc PC T V
California $$ 23 20

Professional buyers rave, "Ferrari-Carano *defines* style" in winemaking, especially with this excellent, almost too good Fumé Blanc, which has enough body to please Chardonnay lovers, too. Indeed, it's well balanced and crisp, with ripe melon, fig, and honeysuckle flavors and an extra layer of richness in the scent, taste, and body due to the oak barrel aging.

Kitchen Fridge Survivor™ Grade: B+

Your notes:_____

_____

Fetzer Echo Ridge Sauvignon Blanc PC T V
California $ 16 17

The praise for offering a lot of varietal character without breaking the bank is well deserved. The pretty aromas and flavors of apples, grass, and citrus are lively, easy to drink, and great with so many foods. And the strong survivor grade makes it great for by-the-glass and everyday drinking.

Kitchen Fridge Survivor™ Grade: B

Your notes:_____

_____

Price Ranges: **$** = $12 or less; **$$** = 12.01–20; **$$$** = 20.01–35; **$$$$** = > $35

Kitchen Countertop Survivor™ Grades: *Avg.* = a "one-day wine," tastes noticeably less fresh the next day; *B* = holds its freshness for 2–3 days after opening; *B+* = holds *and gets better* over 2–3 days after opening; *A* = a 3- to 4-day "freshness window"; *A+* = holds *and gets better* over 3–4 days

Frog's Leap Sauvignon Blanc	PC	T	V
California	$$$	23	21

Every fine dining wine list that I have ever written and served from featured this wine, whose name recognition and "Napa" pedigree pushed its price into the luxury range for Sauvignon Blancs in the last few years. I'm sure that is why some pros say it "could deliver more for the money." It certainly does fearlessly deliver the 100 percent Sauvignon Blanc character of gooseberries, white grapefruit, and flinty, penetrating citrus flavors that I wish more could afford to enjoy.

Kitchen Fridge Survivor™ Grade: A
Your notes:_____
_____

Geyser Peak Sauvignon Blanc	PC	T	V
California	$	20	21

Trade buyers laud this "great wine for an even better price," because it "tastes expensive" and "makes almost any food taste better." It is lovely, classic California Sauvignon Blanc, combining the crisp tang of citrus with the juicier taste of kiwi. Look also for Geyser Peak's voluptuous California Shiraz.

Kitchen Fridge Survivor™ Grade: B+
Your notes:_____
_____

Glen Ellen Proprietor's Reserve	PC	T	V
Sauvignon Blanc, California	$	14	15

Pro buyers recommend this wine if you're having an intimate gathering of, say, a few hundred people, as it's "OK for a big party on a small budget." Other varietals in the Glen Ellen line fare better than this Sauvignon Blanc (check the Chardonnay, for example), which to me tastes pretty plain. Even at this price, there are Sauvignon Blancs with more flavor.

Kitchen Fridge Survivor™ Grade: Avg.
Your notes:_____
_____

Grgich (*GER-gich; both are hard*	PC	T	V
"g" like girl) Hills Fumé Blanc	$$$	23	20
California			

I credit Grgich Hills for consistent quality and for keeping true to its distinct Fumé style: crisp and clean, with scents of fresh herbs and citrus and flavors of tangy grapefruit and melon. Pros acknowledge it's the "standard quality expected from Mike Grgich"—meaning high—but note that the blue chip name exacts a premium price. Consumers also give high marks to the taste but are flummoxed by the "hard-to-pronounce name" (see above).

Kitchen Fridge Survivor™ Grade: B

Your notes:_____

_____

| **Guenoc Sauvignon Blanc** | **PC** | **T** | **V** |
| **California** | **$$** | **19** | **18** |

Often when consumers say "easygoing crowd pleaser," you could translate that as "ho-hum" taste, but not here. It's got impeccable balance and lots of inter-esting flavors—vanilla, orange, peaches, and lime. The finish is long, but the wine is not at all heavy. A lot of stylish flavor for the price.

Kitchen Fridge Survivor™ Grade: B

Your notes:_____

_____

| **Henri Bourgeois (*ahn-REE buh-*** | **PC** | **T** | **V** |
| ***JWAH*) Pouilly Fumé, France** | **$$** | **22** | **20** |

While many French classic whites have gotten out of budget reach for all but splurge occasions, the Loire Valley's twin Sauvignon Blanc regions, Pouilly-Fumé and Sancerre, are exceptions. This Loire Valley clas-sicist winemaker is considered "one of the best" by pros. Indeed the wine offers excellent balance and classic French subtlety and complexity, with floral and smoky scents, bracing acidity, and an elegant tanginess that's true to the Sauvignon Blanc grape.

Kitchen Fridge Survivor™ Grade: B+

Your notes:_____

_____

Price Ranges: **$** = $12 or less; **$$** = 12.01–20; **$$$** = 20.01–35; **$$$$** = > $35

Kitchen Countertop Survivor™ Grades: *Avg.* = a "one-day wine," tastes noticeably less fresh the next day; *B* = holds its freshness for 2–3 days after opening; *B+* = holds *and gets better* over 2–3 days after opening; *A* = a 3- to 4-day "freshness window"; *A+* = holds *and gets better* over 3–4 days

Hogue Fumé Blanc   PC   T   V
Washington $ 21   21

The great acid and bright fruit make this wine an amazing partner for food. "A very good wine at a very good price," say trade buyers, and I have to agree. It is rare to find this level of complexity—fresh ginger spice, crushed herbs, citrus peel, plus a juicy mouth-feel, in an under-ten-dollars wine. It also holds beautifully for days in the fridge, but you probably won't let it last that long. Bravo!

Kitchen Fridge Survivor™ Grade: A+

Your notes:_____

_____

Honig Sauvignon Blanc   PC   T   V
California $$ 24   22

"My favorite all-around California Sauvignon" sums up the consensus among trade, who credit Honig for knowing how to make Sauvignon Blanc in a classic style. That means flinty, grassy, and balanced with delicate herb and spice notes (like French Loire Valley Sauvignon Blancs), along with the plumped-up, succulent fruit character coming from its sunny California climate.

Kitchen Fridge Survivor™ Grade: B+

Your notes:_____

_____

Jolivet (Pascal) Sancerre   PC   T   V
(*jhoe-lee-VAY sahn-SAIR*), France $$ 25   22

"Oh, Sancerre!" wrote one ardent *Immer Guide* taster, adding, "What else can be said?" His comments reflect the consensus of both trade and consumers, and I share the love, especially for this producer, whose entire stable of Loire wines is worth searching out. This Sancerre, in particular, has for years been one of my go-to wines with restaurant guests, because it's a fail-safe. The elegant, well-balanced, and utterly "alive" taste and scent (lemongrass, lime cream, and even a hint of honey) never fails to blow people away, especially for the price. Add to that the great survivor performance, which I discovered from offering it by the glass, and you've got an amazing package.

Kitchen Fridge Survivor™ Grade: A+

Your notes:_____

_____

Kendall-Jackson Vintner's Reserve Sauvignon Blanc, California	PC $	T 20	V 19

As pros point out, "you get more bang for the buck" buying this not-too-distant cousin to the Chardonnay on which K-J stakes its reputation, because this wine offers comparable quality but at a cheaper price because the grape is less well known. Although it's Sauvignon Blanc in the richer style, it is still true to the grape, with flavors of melon, kiwi, and tangerine. A good bet for people who prefer a white that's less heavy than Chardonnay.

Kitchen Fridge Survivor™ Grade: B+

Your notes:_____

Kenwood Sauvignon Blanc California	PC $	T 22	V 22

"Always a favorite," commented my pro tasters, who note that it "used to be a Sonoma appellation" and now is labeled "North Coast," a turn of events that sometimes accompanies a quality decline, but not in this case. Frankly, I think this Sauvignon Blanc is better than ever. The taste reminds me of a summer melon salad with lime, honey, and mint. And it has amazing kitchen countertop staying power, to boot.

Kitchen Fridge Survivor™ Grade: A+

Your notes:_____

Lucien Crochet (*loo-SYEN crow-SHAY*) Sancerre, France	PC $$	T 25	V 23

✓ "Definitive Sauvignon Blanc" captures the consensus from tasters on this wine, who rated it very high for both taste and value. The gorgeous, floral-herbaceous nose, creamy-but-not-heavy texture, crisp citrus and lemon pie flavor, and overall finesse were also cited as "a huge relief for the oak-weary." I'll drink to that!

Kitchen Fridge Survivor™ Grade: B+

Your notes:_____

Price Ranges: **$** = $12 or less; **$$** = 12.01–20; **$$$** = 20.01–35; **$$$$** = > $35
Kitchen Countertop Survivor™ Grades: *Avg.* = a "one-day wine," tastes noticeably less fresh the next day; *B* = holds its freshness for 2–3 days after opening; *B+* = holds *and gets better* over 2–3 days after opening; *A* = a 3- to 4-day "freshness window"; *A+* = holds *and gets better* over 3–4 days

Meridian Sauvignon Blanc   PC   T   V
California $ 18   19

For the money, I've always found this wine high on the yum factor. Just juicy, forward honeydew melon flavor, a kiss of subtle oak that gives it roundness, and a whiff of just-cut grass in the scent.

Kitchen Fridge Survivor™ Grade: B

Your notes:_____

_____

Michel Redde Pouilly Fumé   PC   T   V
France $$ 21   21

Trade buyers call this Loire Valley classic "a winner" and "a great value." I, too, give it high marks for classic Pouilly-Fumé character—smoky gunflint and herbal scents, elegant structure, and clean-as-a-whistle acidity that carries the finish on for a long time. Try it with fresh goat cheese for a classic combination.

Kitchen Fridge Survivor™ Grade: B

Your notes:_____

_____

Murphy-Goode Fumé Blanc   PC   T   V
California $$ 23   21

While some call it "too Chardonnay-like," many tasters considered that a virtue. I, too, enjoy the less herbaceous, passion fruit and tropical flavor profile that some consumers said "tastes more expensive than it is."

Kitchen Fridge Survivor™ Grade: Avg

Your notes:_____

_____

R.H. Phillips Dunnigan Hills   PC   T   V
Sauvignon Blanc, California $ X   X

♥ If you've tasted only R.H. Phillips Chardonnays, you are missing out. The taste of this wine reminds me of one of the great Latin-inspired flavor tricks: eating ripe tropical fruits like mango, guava, and papaya with a squeeze of lime. The citrus kick gears up the intensity of the fruit flavors, all of which complement the vibrant food flavors in pan-Latin cooking. Delicious wine, great price.

Kitchen Fridge Survivor™ Grade: B+

Your notes:_____

_____

Robert Mondavi Coastal	PC	T	V
Sauvignon Blanc, California	**$**	**16**	**16**

Although this has been among my favorite varietals in Mondavi's coastal line, I've noticed bottle-to-bottle variation of late—with some bottles seeming fine and others tasting a bit off. At its best, the green apple and citrus fruit make it an easy-drinking match with spicy foods and salads.

Kitchen Fridge Survivor™ *Grade: B*

Your notes:_____

_____

Robert Mondavi Napa Fumé Blanc	PC	T	V
California	**$$**	**20**	**18**

Robert Mondavi pioneered the use of the name Fumé Blanc for SB, and this one remains a classic. It's layered with fruit, spice, and lemongrass and crisp, vivid citrus notes, all coming together in a richly tex-tured and well-balanced whole. The complexity of flavor makes it very food-versatile and thus a good wine list choice when the table's ordering a schizo range of dishes and you don't know what to do.

Kitchen Fridge Survivor™ *Grade: Avg.*

Your notes:_____

_____

Rodney Strong Charlotte's Home	PC	T	V
Sauvignon Blanc, California	**$$**	**19**	**19**

For oak fans, this Sauvignon Blanc delivers plenty, plus loads of tropical fruit, banana and apricot flavor, and a very full-bodied, creamy mouthfeel. It might overpower delicate flavors such as shellfish but would match up to bolder dishes and even meat.

Kitchen Fridge Survivor™ *Grade: Avg.*

Your notes:_____

_____

Price Ranges: **$** = $12 or less; **$$** = 12.01–20; **$$$** = 20.01–35; **$$$$** = > $35

Kitchen Countertop Survivor™ Grades: *Avg.* = a "one-day wine," tastes noticeably less fresh the next day; *B* = holds its freshness for 2–3 days after opening; *B+* = holds *and gets better* over 2–3 days after opening; *A* = a 3- to 4-day "freshness window"; *A+* = holds *and gets better* over 3–4 days

Silverado Sauvignon Blanc   PC   T   V
California $$ 22   20

On California's oak-lavished landscape, Silverado's enduring commitment to the stainless-steel style offers an alternative that's widely appreciated by both pros and consumers. The clean, crisp apple and grapefruit character and medium body are great with minimalist, natural food flavors—raw bar, fresh salads, and the like.

Kitchen Fridge Survivor™ Grade: B

Your notes:_____

_____

Simi Sauvignon Blanc   PC   T   V
California $$ 21   20

While many California wineries with blue chip reps and great track records have ridden a wave of rising prices, Simi has kept the magic combination—high quality yet still fair prices. This Sauvignon Blanc in the rich style, given creamy roundness by a dose of Semillon, and well-integrated oak, has nice tangy-apple flavors to balance it. It's among my favorites of all the Simi wines, but try the Cabernet and Chardonnay, too.

Kitchen Fridge Survivor™ Grade: B+

Your notes:_____

_____

Sterling Vineyards North Coast   PC   T   V
Sauvignon Blanc, California $$ 20   20

Yes, it's gotten slightly expensive as some tasters pointed out, but the blue chip name keeps it selling well. I've been using it on wine lists for years, and it remains true to its style—vibrant with grapefruit, nectarines, and even key lime flavors and scents.

Kitchen Fridge Survivor™ Grade: B

Your notes:_____

_____

Sutter Home Sauvignon Blanc   PC   T   V
California $ 14   14

Sutter Home wines are, across the board, some of the best at this easy-does-it price point. This is easy drinking, with light, fresh grapefruit, lime, and apple flavors that go very well with Tex-Mex and other spicy dishes. Holds well in the fridge after opening, too.

Kitchen Fridge Survivor™ Grade: B

Your notes:_____

_____

Villa Maria Private Bin Sauvignon	**PC**	**T**	**V**
Blanc, New Zealand	**$**	**X**	**X**

✗ "How could you not include Villa Maria?" one taster wrote, reflecting the consensus among respondents that it's one of the great New Zealand Sauvignon Blancs for the money. It's a nice balance between the grassy/herbal style in the scent but passion fruit-melon in the taste, with a green-apple tanginess that I love. The Reserve bottling shows the family resemblance, with a little more complexity— worth seeking out.

Kitchen Fridge Survivor™ Grade: B+

Your notes:_____

_____

Woodbridge (Robert Mondavi)	**PC**	**T**	**V**
Sauvignon Blanc, California	**$**	**15**	**15**

Among my favorites in the Woodbridge family of wines. Lively citrus character that's refreshing, crisp, and enjoyable, especially for the price.

Kitchen Fridge Survivor™ Grade: B

Your notes:_____

_____

Chardonnay

Grape Profile: Chardonnay is the top-selling white varietal wine in this country, and the fullest-bodied of the market-dominant white grapes. That rich body, along with Chardonnay's signature fruit intensity, could explain its extraordinary popularity with Americans,

Price Ranges: **$** = $12 or less; **$$** = 12.01–20; **$$$** = 20.01–35; **$$$$** = > $35

Kitchen Countertop Survivor™ Grades: *Avg.* = a "one-day wine," tastes noticeably less fresh the next day; *B* = holds its freshness for 2–3 days after opening; *B+* = holds *and gets better* over 2–3 days after opening; *A* = a 3- to 4-day "freshness window"; *A+* = holds *and gets better* over 3–4 days

although in truth this grape's style is pretty chameleonlike. It can yield wines of legendary quality, ranging from crisp and austere to soft and juicy to utterly lush and exotic (and very often oaky), depending on whether it's grown in a cool, moderate, or warm climate. I am pleased to say that, as these notes indicate, buyers find all of these styles worthy, perhaps offering some hope to pros who bemoan a so-called "style homogenization" of the Chardonnay category. "DO I REALLY HAVE TO RATE CHARDONNAYS???" is how one retailer in the trenches put it, rhetorically, of course, since they "fly out the door" at every price point. One taster commented: "French Chardonnay has a complexity and ageability not often found in California Chardonnays," and this is true for the world-class versions from Burgundy in France. The rest, like their non-French counterparts in the $ and $$ price categories, are pleasant styles meant for current drinking. California Chardonnays by far dominate store and restaurant sales, but the quality and value of both Washington State's and Australia's are considered as good and sometimes better. Although no New Zealand or Oregon offerings made the survey due to limited production, they're worth trying. Chile's big-brand Chardonnays sell a lot, but in my opinion they compete based more on price than quality, at least so far.

Serve: Chilled; however, extreme cold mutes the complexity of the top bottlings. Pull them off the ice if they get too cold.

When: There's no occasion where Chardonnay *isn't* welcomed by the majority of wine lovers; the grape's abundant fruit makes it great on its own, as an aperitif or a cocktail alternative.

With: Some sommeliers carp that Chardonnay "doesn't go well with food," but I don't think most consumers agree. Maybe they have a point that it "overpowers" some delicate culinary creations in luxury restaurants, but for those of us doing most of our eating and drinking in less-rarefied circumstances, it's a great partner for all kinds of food. The decadent, oaky/buttery styles that are California's calling card can even handle steak.

In: An all-purpose wineglass.

Almaden Chardonnay	PC	T	V
California	$	9	11

"Only half the party," jokes one sommelier, referring to Almaden's "Party in a Box," which contains two bags in the box, one this "tutti-frutti" Chardonnay, the other a white Zinfandel. It's light and simple, but as box Chardonnays go, one of the better ones.

Kitchen Fridge Survivor™ Grade: NA—bag-in-box package
Your notes:_____

Artesa Carneros Estate Chardonnay	PC	T	V
California	$$$	X	X

♥ Lush fruit and lavish oak are, I think, what defines great California Chardonnay for most people. But the "If some is good, then more must be better" attitude (very American) leads to wines that are sometimes so huge they're like a hostile takeover of both your taste buds and your dinner table. This wine could be your "white knight." Yes, it is plush with rich pear and pineapple fruit, but the acidity keeps it lively and inviting, so your palate doesn't feel numb after a few sips. The oak is sweet and toasty but supports the fruit rather than overwhelming it. Best of all, however, was the wine's enduring balance. I actually forgot to refrigerate it—for days. When I returned from a trip, and the bottle reemerged from behind some empty cereal boxes, it was simply amazing.

Kitchen Fridge Survivor™ Grade: A+
Your notes:_____

Beaulieu Vineyard (BV) Coastal	PC	T	V
Chardonnay, California	$	17	17

Like the entire BV Coastal line, this Chardonnay is a solid performer, with consistently good feedback from the widest range of tasters—novice to collector. It's textbook apple-pear Chardonnay in the not-too-heavy

---

Price Ranges: **$** = $12 or less; **$$** = 12.01–20; **$$$** = 20.01–35; **$$$$** = > $35
Kitchen Countertop Survivor™ Grades: *Avg.* = a "one-day wine," tastes noticeably less fresh the next day; *B* = holds its freshness for 2–3 days after opening; *B+* = holds *and gets better* over 2–3 days after opening; *A* = a 3- to 4-day "freshness window"; *A+* = holds *and gets better* over 3–4 days

style. It gets extra points from me for being among the best of all the "coastal" Chardonnays, yet one of the cheapest.

Kitchen Fridge Survivor™ Grade: Avg

Your notes:_____

_____

Beaulieu Vineyard (BV) Carneros	PC	T	V
Chardonnay, California	$$	21	20

If you want to taste "buttery" Chardonnay done right, this is it. Not at all heavy, and beautifully balanced, with both "lemony crisp" and apple notes balancing the richness. The price is right, too, and the quality consistency over the last few years exemplary.

Kitchen Fridge Survivor™ Grade: B+

Your notes:_____

_____

Benziger Chardonnay	PC	T	V
California	$$	22	21

Though some tasters find the prominent oak a bit overpowering compared to the fruit, plenty are pleased with the buttery vanilla scents and fruity citrus flavors.

Kitchen Fridge Survivor™ Grade: Avg.

Your notes:_____

_____

Beringer Founders' Estate	PC	T	V
Chardonnay, California	$	21	21

A great many pros rave about this "super bargain" Beringer Chard, in the "pretty," fruit-forward style that's so popular in the broad market. Citrus/tropical fruit, a whiff of vanilla-scented oak, and a juicy mouthfeel put this in the top budget Chardonnay ranks with my tasters. A lot of pleasure for the price.

Kitchen Fridge Survivor™ Grade: A

Your notes:_____

_____

Beringer Napa Chardonnay	PC	T	V
California	$$	22	21

I consider this wine to be benchmark Napa Valley Chardonnay—rich baked apple fruit, creamy texture, toasty oak. The dead-on consistency of quality and style is also amazing, as is the value for money in a California marketplace where so many well-known wineries raised prices willy-nilly. For a special splurge, the Private Reserve Chardonnay definitely rewards the premium.

Kitchen Fridge Survivor™ Grade: Avg.

Your notes:_____

_____

Bernardus Chardonnay   **PC**   **T**   **V**
California   **$$$**   **24**   **22**

For both taste and value, this Chardonnay is considered a "big kahuna" by trade and consumers alike. Few match its incredible complexity-for-the-money: enticing layers of flavor, including pear, pineapple, fig, honey, even butterscotch, enveloped in a beautiful, creamy texture. "Wow" taste for a doable price.

Kitchen Fridge Survivor™ Grade: B

Your notes:_____

_____

Buena Vista Chardonnay   **PC**   **T**   **V**
California   **$**   **18**   **18**

Pros call this wine "dramatically improved" after some time out of focus. It's a medium-bodied, modest Chardonnay, with delicate aromas of pear, vanilla, and pleasant citrus.

Kitchen Fridge Survivor™ Grade: B

Your notes:_____

_____

Burgess Chardonnay   **PC**   **T**   **V**
California   **$$$**   **X**   **X**

♥ Although Napa's Burgess Winery seems to have been around forever, I have to call it a "sleeper," quietly making stylish, quality Chardonnay year in and year out, while out of the California Chardonnay spotlight, which seems forever trained on fruit- and oak-bomb styles. This elegant Chardonnay is anything but. Yes, there is fruit. But it is subtle and touched

Price Ranges: **$** = $12 or less; **$$** = 12.01–20; **$$$** = 20.01–35; **$$$$** = > $35

Kitchen Countertop Survivor™ Grades: *Avg.* = a "one-day wine," tastes noticeably less fresh the next day; *B* = holds its freshness for 2–3 days after opening; *B+* = holds *and gets better* over 2–3 days after opening; *A* = a 3- to 4-day "freshness window"; *A+* = holds *and gets better* over 3–4 days

with a toasty nuttiness, like the classic French pear tart with almond cream. There is oak, too, but it's softly toasty in a style similar to French Meursault. Also like white Burgundy, the wine is restrained on opening and actually needs time and air to blossom—hence the A+ survivor grade.

Kitchen Fridge Survivor™ Grade: A+

Your notes:_____

_____

CK Mondavi Chardonnay	PC	T	V
California	$	16	17

Some confuse the name with Robert Mondavi, but it's a different winery (his brother's). Regardless, it's a solid crowd pleaser, with soft fruit and a "bargain price."

Kitchen Fridge Survivor™ Grade: Avg

Your notes:_____

_____

Cakebread Napa Chardonnay	PC	T	V
California	$$$$	24	19

"The best Chard I can *never* find," wrote one taster, with many others echoing the frustration of trying to find this longtime favorite Napa Chardonnay that I consider to be a classic in the category. Its heady aromas and flavors of ripe pears, green apples, and subtle oak, and its exceptional quality, are constants. No wonder the high demand keeps its availability limited largely to fine restaurants and boutique shops. A large number of tasters, both trade and consumer, ranked it their favorite of all the Chardonnays in the book.

Kitchen Fridge Survivor™ Grade: B

Your notes:_____

_____

Caliterra Chardonnay	PC	T	V
Chile	$	18	19

"Always a favorite," say fans of this medium-bodied, great-with-anything Chilean charmer, especially at this price. Considering the distinctive layers of vanilla and spice notes, I'd have to agree with them.

Kitchen Fridge Survivor™ Grade: Avg

Your notes:_____

_____

Callaway Coastal Chardonnay	PC	T	V
California	$	17	17

Since its vineyards in southern California's Temecula region were seriously damaged by a vine ailment called Pierce's disease, Callaway has gone "coastal," sourcing grapes for all its varietals from a range of California's best coastal wine districts. The results in this Chardonnay bottling are nice, especially for the money. The mouthwatering citrus, pear, and apple fruit and crisp acidity make it a delicious quaff on its own. The balance also makes it a great food partner, particularly for Asian flavors, fresh vegetables, and seafood.

Kitchen Fridge Survivor™ Grade: B

Your notes:_____

Cambria Katherine's Vineyard	PC	T	V
Chardonnay, California	$$	23	21

Both retail and restaurant buyers call this wine a "big seller," and it's no wonder: you get the big oaky California Chardonnay style that's popular with many consumers, for under $20 retail in most markets. The style is rich and mouth filling, plump with tropical fruit, a whiff of buttery scent, and the signature toasty oakiness. Nice.

Kitchen Fridge Survivor™ Grade: Avg

Your notes:_____

Camelot Chardonnay	PC	T	V
California	$	19	19

As pros note, this Chardonnay from the Kendall-Jackson family "isn't anything out of the ordinary, but just darn good for the price." K-J fans flock to it for its crowd-pleaser characteristics—buttery aromas and flavors and creamy finish.

Kitchen Fridge Survivor™ Grade: Avg

Your notes:_____

Price Ranges: **$** = $12 or less; **$$** = 12.01–20; **$$$** = 20.01–35; **$$$$** = > $35

Kitchen Countertop Survivor™ Grades: *Avg.* = a "one-day wine," tastes noticeably less fresh the next day; *B* = holds its freshness for 2–3 days after opening; *B+* = holds *and gets better* over 2–3 days after opening; *A* = a 3- to 4-day "freshness window"; *A+* = holds *and gets better* over 3–4 days

Chalk Hill Chardonnay	PC	T	V
California	$$$$	23	20

"Consistently good," say restaurant pros of this classy Chardonnay, whose rich oak and luscious tropical fruit flavor give it enough body to pair it even with steak. Tasters point out that it's gotten "pricey," but it's a quality leader whose premium price nevertheless remains reasonable compared to the overall category of luxury California Chardonnays. I often recommend it to guests as an impress-the-client wine, and have also found it to be one of the few big California Chardonnays that rewards a few years' cellaring.

Kitchen Fridge Survivor™ Grade: B

Your notes:_____

_____

Chalone Central Coast Chardonnay	PC	T	V
California	$$$	25	21

Since the early days of my career, this pioneering Central Coast Chardonnay has been a favorite of wine lovers, though many tasters noted they "hate how pricey it's getting." Pros cite this wine's "unique mineral quality" among its primary draws, which they astutely note is a Chalone signature, as well as the elegant, restrained style and "beautiful stone fruit" flavor medley of peaches and apricots. In my experience it gains in complexity with bottle age, if you've got the patience to wait.

Kitchen Fridge Survivor™ Grade: B+

Your notes:_____

_____

Château Montelena Chardonnay	PC	T	V
California	$$$$	24	20

"Worth every penny," say both pros and consumers of Montelena's restrained, understated, and elegant Chardonnay that features flinty-spicy aromas, firm, crisp apple fruit, and a subtle, long finish. The wine sells out so quickly that I fear most wine lovers never experience its greatest virtue—the wine gains extraordinary complexity with age.

Kitchen Fridge Survivor™ Grade: A

Your notes:_____

_____

Château Ste. Michelle Columbia | **PC** | **T** | **V**
Valley Chardonnay, Washington | **$$** | **21** | **22**

"Even when it doesn't bowl me over, it's still good," says a taster who sounds remarkably like Yogi Berra. But I get the point: this Columbia Valley Chardonnay offers amazingly consistent quality. The style of late has grown gradually more buttery, forsaking the clean citrus notes of old. Whether that's a good thing or not depends on your taste.

Kitchen Fridge Survivor™ *Grade: B*

Your notes:_____

Château St. Jean Sonoma | **PC** | **T** | **V**
Chardonnay, California | **$$** | **22** | **21**

Pros say you get "tremendous quality for the price," a consistent virtue of St. Jean Chardonnay since my career began more than ten years ago. The name recognition really sells this wine, and then the taste delivers. It is creamy and complex, rich with tropical fruit and ripe pear and an elegant, restrained touch of oak.

Kitchen Fridge Survivor™ *Grade: B*

Your notes:_____

Clos du Bois Sonoma Chardonnay | **PC** | **T** | **V**
California | **$$** | **20** | **20**

This wine surprised me with better-than-ever balance and quality in a category—California Chardonnay—where too often the biggest names have slipped in quality while prices have climbed. Not here, where along with (really) "good value for the money" as my trade tasters noticed, there's real excitement in the bottle. Lots of citrus, peach, and melon fruit, subtly framed in oak, cuts a stylish profile. Now the kicker: the open bottle lasts and lasts, getting better and better, in the fridge.

Kitchen Fridge Survivor™ *Grade: A+*

Your notes:_____

Price Ranges: **$** = $12 or less; **$$** = 12.01–20; **$$$** = 20.01–35; **$$$$** = > $35

Kitchen Countertop Survivor™ Grades: *Avg.* = a "one-day wine," tastes noticeably less fresh the next day; *B* = holds its freshness for 2–3 days after opening; *B+* = holds *and gets better* over 2–3 days after opening; *A* = a 3- to 4-day "freshness window"; *A+* = holds *and gets better* over 3–4 days

Columbia Crest Chardonnay   PC   T   V
Washington $ 20   21

"Great value" and "consistently good" pretty much capture the consensus among buyers of every stripe. I find that to be true of Columbia Crest varietals across the board. It's got precisely what most American Chardonnay drinkers look for: sweet spices, baked apple fruit, and a hint of butter in the taste and scent; all in balance and not too heavy.

Kitchen Fridge Survivor™ Grade: B+

Your notes:_____

_____

Concha y Toro Sunrise Chardonnay   PC   T   V
Chile $ 16   18

This "bargain-priced" Chilean Chardonnay has plumped up of late, toward a medium-bodied—and more oaky—wine. But tasters note that it's still "light enough to be your house white" and easy to pair with food.

Kitchen Fridge Survivor™ Grade: Avg.

Your notes:_____

_____

DeLoach Chardonnay   PC   T   V
California $$ X   X

✗ This is a tasty, balanced "classy Chardonnay for the money" that many buyers agree is "almost as good as their pricier Chardonnays." I, too, like several sommelier respondents, have served this one, which is redolent with peach and melon flavors, as a very successful premium by-the-glass offering that often elicits a second-glass sale.

Kitchen Fridge Survivor™ Grade: A

Your notes:_____

_____

Edna Valley Vineyard Chardonnay   PC   T   V
California $$ 22   21

Although "outstanding quality and taste" and "nice price tag" reflect the consensus among tasters of every stripe, they don't quite do the wine justice. It has an amazing balance between Burgundian subtlety and complexity in the scent—cream, pear, toasted nuts, and smoke—and vibrant fruit in the taste. It ages extremely well, too.

Kitchen Countertop Survivor™ *Grade: A*

Your notes:_____

_____

Ernest & Julio Gallo Twin Valley Chardonnay, California	PC $	T 16	V 18

I agree with tasters who say this wine delivers well-made, soft, and easy Chardonnay at the budget price point. Period.

Kitchen Fridge Survivor™ *Grade: Avg*

Your notes:_____

_____

Estancia Pinnacles Chardonnay California	PC $$	T 20	V 20

Although the price is inching up, this Chardonnay remains good for the money. It's also stayed true to the bold but balanced Monterey style. It's always been one of my favorites to offer by the glass, because the vibrant acidity makes it great with food, while the soft tropical fruit tastes delicious on its own.

Kitchen Fridge Survivor™ *Grade: A*

Your notes:_____

_____

Ferrari-Carano Sonoma Chardonnay California	PC $$$	T 23	V 20

"Excellent value if you can afford it" is how one taster summed up the fact that, while the price of entry into the luxury Chardonnay category is higher than ever, this wine is among the most accessible. I think its quality easily matches that of many others at twice the price or more. So if you like the neat package of spicy fruit and oak, and luscious citrus and honey flavors, as so many do, this splurge is totally worth it.

Kitchen Fridge Survivor™ *Grade: B*

Your notes:_____

_____

Price Ranges: **$** = $12 or less; **$$** = 12.01–20; **$$$** = 20.01–35; **$$$$** = > $35

Kitchen Countertop Survivor™ Grades: *Avg.* = a "one-day wine," tastes noticeably less fresh the next day; *B* = holds its freshness for 2–3 days after opening; *B+* = holds *and gets better* over 2–3 days after opening; *A* = a 3- to 4-day "freshness window"; *A+* = holds *and gets better* over 3–4 days

Fetzer Barrel Select Chardonnay   PC   T   V
California $$ 18   19

This wine, a pioneer in the category of big-fruit
Chardonnay at everyday prices, remains a classic,
managing to offer a lot of consistency and juicy drink-
ability for the money. As those in the trade point out,
the "bright flavors" and light toastiness make it an
"easy by-the-glass choice."

Kitchen Fridge Survivor™ Grade: B

Your notes:_____

_____

Fetzer Sundial Chardonnay   PC   T   V
California $ 16   19

A great sipping wine that's always dependable. The
cheap price and enticing aromas and flavors of fresh
pears and apples make it a fail-safe crowd pleaser.

Kitchen Fridge Survivor™ Grade: B

Your notes:_____

_____

Forest Glen Chardonnay   PC   T   V
California $ 16   18

"I can't believe it's not butter," quip more than a few
pros, citing "lots of oak" and "lots of toast and butter"
that's "omnipresent" in this 100 percent barrel-
fermented Chard. Fans call it a nice "by-the-glass
choice."

Kitchen Fridge Survivor™ Grade: Avg

Your notes:_____

_____

Franzia Chardonnay   PC   T   V
California $ 10   11

Franzia is one of the best-selling wines in America. Obvi-
ously this no-nonsense, supercheap, no-corkscrew-
needed white fills the bill for a lot of buyers.

Kitchen Fridge Survivor™ Grade: NA

Your notes:_____

_____

Gallo of Sonoma Chardonnay   PC   T   V
California $ 20   23

⚱ Restaurant buyers call this Chardonnay "outstand-
ing wine for the price." It offers both ripe, intense
flavors of pineapples, pears, and apples, and crispness

plus great balance. Like other varietals in the Gallo of Sonoma line, it prompts restaurant buyers especially to "hope the Gallo jug stigma doesn't prevail" with guests, because it's among the greatest by-the-glass options currently on the market. Keep that in mind next time you see it offered in a restaurant. And when you're buying for *your* house, don't worry about it, remember it's flavor you're paying for.

Kitchen Fridge Survivor™ *Grade: A*

Your notes:_____

Geyser Peak Chardonnay	PC	T	V
California	**$$**	**19**	**19**

This fresh, complex wine exhibits a perfect balance of apple, pear, and melon fruit, augmented by well-balanced nuances of smoky oak and a soft, creamy finish.

Kitchen Fridge Survivor™ *Grade: B*

Your notes:_____

Glen Ellen Proprietor's Reserve	PC	T	V
Chardonnay, California	**$**	**14**	**14**

Pros say, "you can always count on" this pleasant Chard to be well made and a consistent bargain. The clean apple flavor makes it "a perfect party wine."

Kitchen Fridge Survivor™ *Grade: B*

Your notes:_____

Gossamer Bay Chardonnay	PC	T	V
California	**$**	**11**	**12**

Wide availability has prompted many to try this wine, but reactions are disappointing. There are better choices at this price.

Kitchen Fridge Survivor™ *Grade: Avg*

Your notes:_____

Price Ranges: **$** = $12 or less; **$$** = 12.01–20; **$$$** = 20.01–35; **$$$$** = > $35

Kitchen Countertop Survivor™ Grades: ***Avg.*** = a "one-day wine," tastes noticeably less fresh the next day; ***B*** = holds its freshness for 2–3 days after opening; ***B+*** = holds *and gets better* over 2–3 days after opening; ***A*** = a 3- to 4-day "freshness window"; ***A+*** = holds *and gets better* over 3–4 days

Grgich Hills Chardonnay	PC	T	V
California	$$$	24	19

Though many reviewers asked how to pronounce
the producer's name (answer: "GER-gich"), none of
them seemed to have trouble praising this exceptional
Napa Chard, many calling it, unequivocally, "the
best." I think it's made in a complex, focused style
that's packed with fruit yet balanced with elegance.
Kitchen Fridge Survivor™ Grade: A
Your notes:_____

_____

Hess Select Chardonnay	PC	T	V
California	$$	21	20

Consumers and trade alike agree that this "crisp,
clean Chard is a great value for the money"; layered
with a full spectrum of fruits, from pineapple and
mango to banana, pear, and lemon.
Kitchen Fridge Survivor™ Grade: B
Your notes:_____

_____

Inglenook Chardonnay	PC	T	V
California	$	11	12

Like all leading names in the formerly dominant jug
market, Inglenook joined the varietal business, and its
Chardonnay is a big seller with consumers because it
gets decent taste marks for the price.
Kitchen Fridge Survivor™ Grade: Avg
Your notes:_____

_____

J. Lohr Riverstone Chardonnay	PC	T	V
California	$$	22	20

An "excellent," "full-bodied" Chardonnay, say J. Lohr
fans. Indeed it's a great value for the price, made in
the big buttery style, with flavors and scents of lime,
peaches, and minerals, complemented by vanilla, butterscotch, and toasted oak. It's nicely balanced, with a
long finish.
Kitchen Fridge Survivor™ Grade: B
Your notes:_____

_____

Jacob's Creek Chardonnay   PC   T   V
Australia $ 20   22

Both trade and consumers clearly rate this a taste and value star. I give it extra credit for consistency and for keeping such a bright, mouthwatering, light-handed style where so many budget Chardonnays go heavy and flabby. Pear, melon, citrus, peach, yum.

Kitchen Fridge Survivor™ Grade: Avg.

Your notes:_____

_____

Jordan Chardonnay   PC   T   V
California $$$ 22   18

Jordan's Chardonnay has come a long way since the early vintages, which were criticized by pros as "over-rated," riding the coattails of the Cabernet's reputation. The new fruit sources have contributed a crisp vibrancy and length that the wine heretofore lacked. The creamy citrus flavors and gentle toastiness are subtle, classy, and built for food.

Kitchen Fridge Survivor™ Grade: B

Your notes:_____

_____

Joseph Drouhin Pouilly-Fuissé   PC   T   V
(*poo-YEE fwee-SAY*), **France** $$ 21   19

While it lacks the intricate flavors of P-F from a boutique Burgundy house, it doesn't have a boutiquey price either. It does offer classic, understated Pouilly-Fuissé character, with creamy apple and fresh almond scents, plus steely dryness and a long finish.

Kitchen Fridge Survivor™ Grade: A

Your notes:_____

_____

Kendall-Jackson Grand Reserve   PC   T   V
Chardonnay, California $$$ 22   19

K-J's trade-up Chardonnay is fuller-bodied and more intense than the Vintner's Reserve, with more

Price Ranges: **$** = $12 or less; **$$** = 12.01–20; **$$$** = 20.01–35; **$$$$** = > $35

Kitchen Countertop Survivor™ Grades: **Avg.** = a "one-day wine," tastes noticeably less fresh the next day; **B** = holds its freshness for 2–3 days after opening; **B+** = holds *and gets better* over 2–3 days after opening; **A** = a 3- to 4-day "freshness window"; **A+** = holds *and gets better* over 3–4 days

prominent oak and lots of tropical fruit flavor. Some trade buyers say it should be "a measuring stick for others" in the luxury Chardonnay category, due to the high quality for the price.

Kitchen Fridge Survivor™ Grade: Avg

Your notes:_____

_____

Kendall-Jackson Great Estates	PC	T	V
Monterey Chardonnay, California	$$$$	X	X

♥ According to the sales statistics, everyone is drinking and loving K-J's Vintner's Reserve Chardonnay. This is a completely different ball game. Great Estates refers to K-J's selection of outstanding lots from its top estate (meaning winery-owned) vineyards, coddled in the winery, then bottled separately to showcase the pedigree of the source vineyards (in this case in Monterey). It captures Monterey Chardonnay character well, with abundantly layered passion fruit, kiwi, peach, pineapple, and ginger flavors. The lavish oak leaves a touch of cinnamon in the scent. As with many exceptional wines, this one evolves beautifully in the glass, such that with each sip there's something new for the senses to take in. Very exciting!

Kitchen Fridge Survivor™ Grade: B

Your notes:_____

_____

Kendall-Jackson Vintner's Reserve	PC	T	V
Chardonnay, California	$$	20	19

This wine seems to trap snobby sommeliers in a catch-22—torn by the truth that the definition of "good wine" is whatever you like and the fact that the wine-loving public makes its preference crystal clear with this bottling, which is numero uno in the market. But what they complain about—a signature style based on a whisper of sweetness to kick up the juicy fruit—is widely imitated. And why not? Sweetness doesn't always taste sugary. Like oak, fruit, and other "rich" traits of wine, it often just tastes yummy. So if you count yourself among the legions of fans of this wine, enjoy it, but also know this: there are many other similarly styled, excellent Chardonnays out there at or below this price level. So you may want to experiment (and a good sommelier or shop will be happy to help you do just that).

Kitchen Fridge Survivor™ Grade: A

Your notes:_____

_____

| **Kenwood Chardonnay** | PC | T | V |
| California | $$ | 21 | 20 |

Although perhaps less well known than Kenwood's Sauvignon Blanc and reds, this Chardonnay gets good taste reactions, thanks to the clean, refreshing citrus and apple fruit, the bright acidity, and the fact that it's not overly oaky.

Kitchen Fridge Survivor™ Grade: Avg

Your notes:_____

_____

| **La Crema Chardonnay** | PC | T | V |
| California | $$ | 23 | 21 |

"Balanced and yummy" is one consumer's tasting note for this wine, whose value rating shows that many tasters appreciate that style for the price. I'd describe it as classically California—vividly ripe peach and tropical fruit, plus refreshing acidity, framed with toasty-sweet oak.

Kitchen Fridge Survivor™ Grade: Avg

Your notes:_____

_____

Labouré-Roi Puligny-Montrachet	PC	T	V
(*lah-boo-ray WAH poo-leen-YEE*	$$$$	21	19
mohn-rah-SHAY), France			

The steep prices of French Burgundy reflect tiny supply and high demand—especially for a classy white wine village like Puligny-Montrachet. The subtle apple and mineral complexity of this wine garners good marks for taste, but the value assessment shows that at that price most buyers want more. That said, buyers should remember that Burgundy is pretty

Price Ranges: **$** = $12 or less; **$$** = 12.01–20; **$$$** = 20.01–35; **$$$$** = > $35

Kitchen Countertop Survivor™ Grades: ***Avg.*** = a "one-day wine," tastes noticeably less fresh the next day; ***B*** = holds its freshness for 2–3 days after opening; ***B+*** = holds *and gets better* over 2–3 days after opening; ***A*** = a 3- to 4-day "freshness window"; ***A+*** = holds *and gets better* over 3–4 days

vintage-sensitive. Look for years with good harvest season weather to get this wine at its best.

Kitchen Fridge Survivor™ Grade: B

Your notes:_____

Leflaive (*luh-FLEV*) (Domaine)   PC   T   V
Puligny-Montrachet $$$$ 26   21
France

✔ Fans of Domaine Leflaive white Burgundies (and there are many) love their ability to make "delicious," "finessed" Chardonnays that sing with style, complexity, and concentrated layers of baked apple and peach fruit—even in difficult vintages. Although such quality comes at "a substantial price," its consistency, along with the wine's remarkable ability to get better with age, earns it points for value for the money.

Kitchen Fridge Survivor™ Grade: B+

Your notes:_____

Leflaive (Olivier) (*luh-FLEV*   PC   T   V
***oh-LIV-ee-ay*) Puligny-Montrachet** $$$$ 24   21
France

Because Olivier Leflaive blends wines from many growers, availability of this brand and sometimes prices can be better than the wines of Domaine Leflaive (the families are related). Tasters appreciate that, though not quite on a par with the Domaine's, Olivier's Puligny is a worthy example. The refined citrus and pear fruit, and hints of mineral and toasty oak on the scent, gain complexity with a few years' bottle age. Tasters consider it a good value in the context of Burgundy, because the wine's quality maintains good year-to-year consistency and in great vintages can really shine.

Kitchen Fridge Survivor™ Grade: B

Your notes:_____

Lindemans Bin 65 Chardonnay   PC   T   V
Australia $ 20   23

I wasn't at all surprised that this Chardonnay, a perennial player on every wine critic's best-buy list, was among the top Chardonnay values with my tasters, too. Even though it leans to the richer style—fragrant vanilla scent and tropical fruit, it maintains a lovely brightness from acidity, which gives it nice balance for food. The consistency of quality and style from year to year is impressive.

Kitchen Fridge Survivor™ Grade: B+

Your notes:_____

_____

Livingston Cellars Chardonnay	PC	T	V
California	$	16	14

Any Chardonnay at this price that actually tastes like Chardonnay deserves kudos. This is lemon-appley, soft, and perfectly pleasant.

Kitchen Fridge Survivor™ Grade: Avg

Your notes:_____

_____

Louis Jadot Mâcon-Villages	PC	T	V
(*LOO-ee jhah-DOUGH mah-COHN*	$	19	20
vill-AHJH) Chardonnay, France			

This French Chardonnay is popular for a reason. The clean, refreshing green apple and citrus fruit, punctuated with vivid acidity and unencumbered by oak heaviness, is wonderful by itself and with food. It also holds nicely for a few days in the fridge, so you can enjoy it with Tuesday's takeout sushi *and* Thursday's tortellini.

Kitchen Fridge Survivor™ Grade: B+

Your notes:_____

_____

Louis Jadot Pouilly-Fuissé	PC	T	V
(*poo-YEE fwee-SAY*) France	$$$	21	20

It seems the entire world of wine drinkers has tried this wine, which makes the consensus on taste quite impressive. For me, it's easy to see why. First, it's got classic Pouilly-Fuissé elegance with fresh, unoaked Chardonnay fruit flavor, a touch of mineral, and good length. Second, it's consistent from year to year, so no

Price Ranges: **$** = $12 or less; **$$** = 12.01–20; **$$$** = 20.01–35; **$$$$** = > $35

Kitchen Countertop Survivor™ Grades: *Avg.* = a "one-day wine," tastes noticeably less fresh the next day; *B* = holds its freshness for 2–3 days after opening; *B+* = holds *and gets better* over 2–3 days after opening; *A* = a 3- to 4-day "freshness window"; *A+* = holds *and gets better* over 3–4 days

vintage stress. Finally, it's available and reasonable. As this book went to press, you could find it at the two-dollar-sign level in some markets, thanks to favorable exchange rates at the time of importation.

Kitchen Fridge Survivor™ Grade: A

Your notes:_____

_____

	PC	T	V
Luna di Luna Chardonnay/ Pinot Grigio, Italy	$	15	16

I respect savvy marketing, and I also love a good package as much as the next person. But I have tasted this wine repeatedly and cannot recommend it, in light of the many other worthy wines in this price point.

Kitchen Fridge Survivor™ Grade: Avg.

Your notes:_____

_____

	PC	T	V
Mâcon-Lugny Les Charmes France	$	19	21

Here's a wine that, despite the fickleness of the marketplace, just powers on, giving the big-brand Cali and Aussie Chardonnay competitors at the same price point a flavor and value fight, at least with my tasters. Its amazing quality consistency throughout my career has also been impressive. And it's true to the Macon style—soft and elegant, with a little snap of green apple acidity and good fridge staying power. Even more interesting, it's quite possible many fans didn't even think of it as Chardonnay. They just recognized it as good, cheap wine.

Kitchen Fridge Survivor™ Grade: B

Your notes:_____

_____

	PC	T	V
Meridian Chardonnay California	$	19	20

"Best Carmen Miranda [tropical] Chardonnay for the money" aptly sums up the consensus here. Meridian is consistently ripe with pineapple fruit, lush in texture, and inexpensive for the flavor and quality. Thanks to its acidity, it's also one of the few ripe-style Chardonnays that are versatile with food.

Kitchen Fridge Survivor™ Grade: B

Your notes:_____

_____

Michel Laroche Chablis St. Martin,	PC	T	V
Burgundy, France	$$$	X	X

♥ Since every Chardonnay in the world is modeled after French white Burgundy, you may wonder why there are so few among the top sellers. The answer is simple: limited supply, and the resultant high prices, keep them out of bounds for most wine drinkers. But you must try true Chablis, whose classic style is so elegant, with piercingly pure apple and citrus fruit, a scent tinged with chamomile and a bit of earthiness (like the smell of wet rocks), and an amazing ability to age. That is all here, at a price that's cheaper than most and definitely fair for the high quality. A reminder for buyers: generic jug-type "chablis" bears no resemblance.

Kitchen Fridge Survivor™ Grade: A

Your notes:_____

_____

Nathanson Creek Chardonnay	PC	T	V
California	$	15	15

I find that this wine's value-for-money ratio has declined since it first hit the market in the early nineties. There are better choices for the money.

Kitchen Fridge Survivor™ Grade: Avg

Your notes:_____

_____

Penfolds Koonunga Hill	PC	T	V
Chardonnay, Australia	$	21	21

Sommeliers say, and it is quite true, that this Chard from one of Australia's leading winemakers practically sells itself. No wonder: buyers looking for a generous boatload of tropical fruit and creamy butterscotch character will get satisfaction—and a good bang for the buck.

Kitchen Countertop Survivor™ Grade: Avg

Your notes:_____

_____

Price Ranges: **$** = $12 or less; **$$** = 12.01–20; **$$$** = 20.01–35; **$$$$** = > $35

Kitchen Countertop Survivor™ Grades: *Avg.* = a "one-day wine," tastes noticeably less fresh the next day; *B* = holds its freshness for 2–3 days after opening; *B+* = holds *and gets better* over 2–3 days after opening; *A* = a 3- to 4-day "freshness window"; *A+* = holds *and gets better* over 3–4 days

R.H. Phillips Dunnigan Hills	PC	T	V
Chardonnay, California	$	19	20

Quite a few tasters, myself among them, consider this one "better than the more expensive Toasted Head Chard," referring to its more expensive sibling below. I wasn't surprised, given the consistent quality and value I've found in this wine over many years. It's got vivid citrus and nectarine fruit, with a nice kiss of oak that's not too heavy.

Kitchen Fridge Survivor™ Grade: A

Your notes:_____

R.H. Phillips Toasted Head	PC	T	V
Chardonnay, California	$$	20	21

Although I prefer the balance of the preceding wine, the consensus rules in favor of this pricier bottling for both taste and value. "Toasted Head" refers to more oakiness—they toast not only the inside of the barrel staves for flavor but the "head" (end piece) of the barrel, too. The result is very oaky, toasty, rich, butterscotch-scented Chardonnay. And the cool fire-breathing-bear label has earned practically cult status.

Kitchen Fridge Survivor™ Grade: Avg

Your notes:_____

Raymond Estates Napa Chardonnay	PC	T	V
California	$$	21	20

I'm a bigger fan of Raymond's red wines, but my tasters find this Napa Chard to be faithful, dependable, and consistent—delivering the requisite apple and pear flavors and toasty oak finish.

Kitchen Fridge Survivor™ Grade: Avg

Your notes:_____

Robert Mondavi Coastal	PC	T	V
Chardonnay, California	$	17	18

For this price and from this name, I'd like more harmony and complexity to the citrus and oak flavors.

Kitchen Fridge Survivor™ Grade: Avg

Your notes:_____

Robert Mondavi Napa Chardonnay PC T V
California $$$ 21 19

It seems true that "you pay for the name," as tasters
noted. Specifically, the baked apple and toasty-spice
flavor of Napa Chardonnay is there, but drinkers—
myself included—expect a bit more for the price.
Kitchen Fridge Survivor™ Grade: Avg

Your notes:_____

_____

Rodney Strong Chardonnay PC T V
California $$ 20 20

I'm always struck by the very oaky style of this wine,
but it definitely pleases my tasters. A coconut-sweet
scent and apple fruit are prominent characteristics of
this very popular wine.
Kitchen Fridge Survivor™ Grade: Avg

Your notes:_____

_____

Rosemount Diamond Label PC T V
Chardonnay, Australia $ 21 22

"Tastes expensive even though it's not," noted one
buyer, and as with nearly every Rosemount wine, it's
definitely great for the money. It's got a remarkably
fresh aroma of melons, peaches, and citrus fruits, a
little bit of oak richness, and a clean finish—all of
which make it delicious but also flexible with food.
Kitchen Fridge Survivor™ Grade: B+

Your notes:_____

_____

Sonoma Creek Chardonnay PC T V
California $ 19 18

One of my buyer friends calls it a "K-J look-alike" at
a cheaper price, which in her restaurants translates
to boatloads sold by the glass. That's due to the rich

Price Ranges: **$** = $12 or less; **$$** = 12.01–20; **$$$** = 20.01–35;
$$$$ = > $35
Kitchen Countertop Survivor™ Grades: *Avg.* = a "one-day wine,"
tastes noticeably less fresh the next day; *B* = holds its freshness for
2–3 days after opening; *B+* = holds *and gets better* over 2–3 days
after opening; *A* = a 3- to 4-day "freshness window"; *A+* = holds *and
gets better* over 3–4 days

flavors that fans liken to "a fresh fruit salad," with creamy vanilla oakiness and a smooth finish.

Kitchen Fridge Survivor™ Grade: B

Your notes:_____

_____

Sonoma-Cutrer Russian River Ranches Chardonnay, California	PC $$	T 23	V 20

This bottling has been a wine list stalwart as the "quintessential California Chardonnay" for years—interesting in light of the style. As pros rightly point out, it is "not of the monster Chardonnay genre"—rather, it holds out for elegance, complexity, and crispness of style. I have to caution that I have experienced some bottle-to-bottle inconsistency of late, so stay tuned.

Kitchen Fridge Survivor™ Grade: Avg.

Your notes:_____

_____

St. Francis Sonoma Chardonnay California	PC $	T 21	V 21

"Saints be praised" is my corny but sincere sentiment. This wine—along with Château St. Jean Chardonnay—seems to be among the few remaining Sonoma Chardonnays with real Sonoma character for an affordable price. That means ripe pear and tropical fruit, soft vanilla oak, and full but not flabby body, thanks to the nice acid balance. This one's a major fridge survivor, too.

Kitchen Fridge Survivor™ Grade: A+

Your notes:_____

_____

Sterling Vineyards North Coast Chardonnay, California	PC $$	T 21	V 20

This wine has made a jump in price but a quantum leap in quality in the last few vintages. It's actually quite subtly exotic, with a vanilla, brown sugar, and nutmeg scent reminiscent of crème brûlée but then lots of lovely and vibrant peach fruit on the palate.

Kitchen Fridge Survivor™ Grade: A

Your notes:_____

_____

Sutter Home Chardonnay   PC   T   V
California $ 15   17

Pretty controversial among my tasters, but I side with the fans who find it "pretty good for the price." It's got clean tangerine fruit flavor that's food-versatile and pleasant.

Kitchen Fridge Survivor™ Grade: Avg

Your notes:_____

Talbott (Robert) Sleepy Hollow   PC   T   V
Vineyard Chardonnay, California $$$$ 25   20

Buyers adore the exotic marzipan, toasted nut, and tart pear flavors of this wine, as has every guest to whom I've ever served it. As the price has risen, its perceived value has suffered. However, among California's big-ticket, trophy Chardonnays of comparable quality, it remains among the most reasonable for what you get.

Kitchen Fridge Survivor™ Grade: B

Your notes:_____

Talus Chardonnay   PC   T   V
California $ 14   14

Major marketing has gotten this wine in front of many tasters, but reactions are lackluster. The advertising-driven brand awareness ensures it sells well, but there are many better choices for the money.

Kitchen Fridge Survivor™ Grade: Avg

Your notes:_____

Turning Leaf Chardonnay   PC   T   V
California $ 12   14

Although my tasters gave higher marks to the Cabernet Sauvignon, I have always found Chardonnay to be the Turning Leaf brand's best foot forward—soft,

---

Price Ranges: **$** = $12 or less; **$$** = 12.01–20; **$$$** = 20.01–35; **$$$$** = > $35

Kitchen Countertop Survivor™ Grades: **Avg.** = a "one-day wine," tastes noticeably less fresh the next day; **B** = holds its freshness for 2–3 days after opening; **B+** = holds *and gets better* over 2–3 days after opening; **A** = a 3- to 4-day "freshness window"; **A+** = holds *and gets better* over 3–4 days

clean, and citrusy, not heavy and very food-versatile. You'll have to decide for yourself!

Kitchen Fridge Survivor™ Grade: Avg

Your notes:_____

_____

| Viña Santa Carolina Chardonnay/ | PC | T | V |
| Sauvignon Blanc, Chile | $ | 14 | 16 |

This untraditional combination of grapes seems to throw tasters for a loop. Tropical-style Chardonnay with herbal Sauvignon Blanc caused palates accustomed to either/or a bit of shock. I think the wine is sound and drinkable, and a fun match with spicy food, but the atypical flavor profile might catch you off guard.

Kitchen Fridge Survivor™ Grade: Avg

Your notes:_____

_____

| Woodbridge (Robert Mondavi) | PC | T | V |
| Chardonnay, California | $ | 15 | 17 |

Several tasters described this as "sweet and oaky," which may explain its popularity by the glass in many parts of the country. Given the pedigree, I wish it were a value leader for the category as it once was. The name recognition keeps it wildly popular.

Kitchen Fridge Survivor™ Grade: Avg

Your notes:_____

_____

Other Whites

Category Profile: A label of "other" for wines that don't fit neatly into a major category means some do not get the respect they deserve. The group does include a wildly diverse collection of wine types, from generic wines to uncommon grapes and regions to unique blends and proprietary branded wines—all of them commercially valid. Here is some background on each:

Generics—The major bag-in-box and jug wines made this survey because, although the category is losing ground to premium wines in a big way, the top brands still enjoy major popularity. They are typically commercial blends of unspecified grapes. What riles wine pros and purists is the generic naming, which uses classic regional names like Chablis, Burgundy, and Rhine, even though the wines aren't from the named region and bear no resemblance to their quality level.

Uncommon Grapes and Regions—This category includes the grapes Albariño (from Spain), Pinot Blanc, and Gewürztraminer, all meriting high marks from tasters and definitely worth your attention. The other–than–Pinot Grigio Italian whites are also here. (See the Wine List Decoder for more on these.)

Unique Blends—Although untraditional, blends of the white grapes Semillon and Chardonnay are proving successful, mainly in Australia and Washington state.

Proprietary Brands—These used to dominate the wine market in the seventies, and a few like Blue Nun have retained significant market presence.

Serve: Well chilled.

When: The uncommon grapes (like Gewürztraminer) and unique blends are wonderful when you want to surprise guests with a different flavor experience; see the notes that follow for ideas with the generic wines, but most tasters think of them when cost is a major consideration because ounce for ounce they're the least expensive wines in this book.

With: In my opinion, Gewürztraminer, Albariño, and the Semillon-Chardonnay blends are some of the most exciting food partners out there. My Best Bets indexes are full of specific food recommendations.

In: An all-purpose wineglass.

Price Ranges: **$** = $12 or less; **$$** = 12.01–20; **$$$** = 20.01–35; **$$$$** = > $35
Kitchen Countertop Survivor™ Grades: *Avg.* = a "one-day wine," tastes noticeably less fresh the next day; *B* = holds its freshness for 2–3 days after opening; *B+* = holds *and gets better* over 2–3 days after opening; *A* = a 3- to 4-day "freshness window"; *A+* = holds *and gets better* over 3–4 days

Almaden Mountain Chablis | PC | T | V
USA | $ | 7 | 10

Proof that bag-in-box wines are here to stay, this perennially popular "oldie but goodie" has been abandoned by the average buyer in favor of cork-finished varietal wines. It is still perfectly OK but decidedly after its time in many markets.

Kitchen Fridge Survivor™ *Grade: NA*

Your notes:_____

_____

Blue Nun Liebfraumilch | PC | T | V
(*LEEB-frow-milk*), Germany | $ | 11 | 13

"This one's proof of our sweet-tooth past," said one sommelier, referring to America's love of off-off-dry wines back in the 1970s. Honestly, I don't think our taste has changed much, just the number and quality of new alternatives. If you liked this then, you'll like it now. It's light, fresh, and soft like a fruit salad. Drink it with anything spicy to tone down the heat.

Kitchen Fridge Survivor™ *Grade: B*

Your notes:_____

_____

Bolla Soave (*BOWL-uh SWAH-vay*) | PC | T | V
Italy | $ | 14 | 15

Considering the brand muscle and huge distribution of this wine, it should have the spunk to inspire more enthusiasm among tasters. No one expects to be bowled over by complexity with Soave, but the responses on many competitor whites at this price point show a lot of the wine-buying public has moved on to more flavor.

Kitchen Fridge Survivor™ *Grade: Avg*

Your notes:_____

_____

Carlo Rossi Chablis | PC | T | V
USA | $ | 8 | 10

Many buyers disparage the use of the classic Burgundy name "Chablis" on a generic wine like this. But in the screw-top generic category of simple white wines, this is among the best.

Kitchen Fridge Survivor™ *Grade: Avg*

Your notes:_____

_____

Carlo Rossi Rhine	PC	T	V
USA	$	8	10

As another generic use of a classic wine region name, Rhine (as in Germany), this wine irritates pros. But it's soft and a little sweet, making it "OK for spritzers."

Kitchen Fridge Survivor™ Grade: Avg

Your notes:_____

Columbia Crest Semillon/	PC	T	V
(*sem-ee-YOHN*) Chardonnay	$	X	X
Washington			

♥ Blending Semillon (which is more commonly partnered with Sauvignon Blanc) into Chardonnay plays neat tricks with the flavor. It gives a tantalizing bite of acidity and earthiness to the ripe Chardonnay fruit and adds intriguing layers to the scent—honey, chamomile, and lime. This is a really great wine for Asian flavors like wasabi, ginger, and soy.

Kitchen Fridge Survivor™ Grade: B

Your notes:_____

Fetzer Echo Ridge Gewürztraminer	PC	T	V
(*guh-VERTZ-trah-mee-ner* or	$	18	19
simply *guh-VERTZ* as it's known			
in the trade), California			

Many buyers wonder how to pronounce this grape (see above). Plenty of tasters, however, knew how to praise its "beautiful" floral and apricot aromas and "luscious flavors." If you haven't tried Gewürz, you should, and this wine makes it affordable to do so. It's amazing with Thai and Chinese food.

Kitchen Fridge Survivor™ Grade: B

Your notes:_____

Price Ranges: **$** = $12 or less; **$$** = 12.01–20; **$$$** = 20.01–35; **$$$$** = > $35

Kitchen Countertop Survivor™ Grades: *Avg.* = a "one-day wine," tastes noticeably less fresh the next day; *B* = holds its freshness for 2–3 days after opening; *B+* = holds *and gets better* over 2–3 days after opening; *A* = a 3- to 4-day "freshness window"; *A+* = holds *and gets better* over 3–4 days

Franzia Chablis   PC   T   V
USA $ 8   9

	PC	T	V
Franzia Chablis			
USA	$	8	9

Another huge generic seller primarily for package and price. Aside from that, I know many buy it for the convenience—no corkscrew, no wasted leftovers.

Kitchen Fridge Survivor™ Grade: NA

Your notes:_____

	PC	T	V
Franzia Rhineflur			
USA	$	8	10

Another success story for Franzia's bag-in-box line of wines, delivering off-dry sweetness and a touch of the floweriness hinted at in the name. It's not the taste but the use of Rhine (a famous German region) in the name that riles pros.

Kitchen Fridge Survivor™ Grade: NA

Your notes:_____

	PC	T	V
Hugel (*hew-GELL*) Gewürztraminer			
France	$$	23	22

This wine was a runaway success with all my tasters, thanks to all that character-for-the-money. The beautiful floral and sweet spice scent—and lychee-nut/apricot flavor—deliver nearly cultlike seduction. "Drink more Gewürz!" entreats one taster, "especially with anything curry." I wholeheartedly agree!

Kitchen Fridge Survivor™ Grade: A

Your notes:_____

	PC	T	V
Hugel Pinot Blanc			
France	$	23	23

Pinot Blanc—the all-around best taste for the money in Alsace? It's certainly a contender, based on my tasters' responses. I, too, am continually taken by surprise by the concentrated apple-pear flavor, mineral complexity, and liveliness of this Pinot Blanc (and others). It is indeed "real wine" for the money.

Kitchen Fridge Survivor™ Grade: B

Your notes:_____

La Scolca Black Label Gavi   **PC**   **T**   **V**
Italy   **$$$$**   19   19

As with many Italian whites, it's a perfectly "nice, appley" food wine. But the prices these days for wines from the Gavi region are quite high, prompting one buyer to charge: "Cortese conspiracy." (Cortese is the grape used.) The forces of supply and demand are more likely at work, but there are plenty of places to look for more flavor for the money.

Kitchen Fridge Survivor™ *Grade: B*

Your notes:_____

_____

Livingston Cellars Chablis   **PC**   **T**   **V**
USA   **$**   10   11

A simple, fruity generic wine that's a huge seller and good in its category.

Kitchen Fridge Survivor™ *Grade: Avg*

Your notes:_____

_____

Marqués de Riscal Rueda (*mar-KESS***   PC**   **T**   **V**
deh ree-SCAHL roo-AY-duh), Spain**   **$**   19   21

Every time I come back to this wine I can't believe its value, and clearly I'm with the majority. It's a fresh, sleek, vibrant, and light white tasting of key lime and kiwi, completely free of oak flavor and delish with all manner of foods, from sandwiches to sushi.

Kitchen Fridge Survivor™ *Grade: B+*

Your notes:_____

_____

Martin Codax Albariño   **PC**   **T**   **V**
(*all-buh-REEN-yo***), Spain**   **$$**   23   24

✓ This wine evokes an instant "wow" from any taster—and that is the trick. The Albariño grape, a specialty of Galicia in the northwest corner of Spain, is still a fringe wine even among aficionados. But it's

Price Ranges: **$** = $12 or less; **$$** = 12.01–20; **$$$** = 20.01–35; **$$$$** = > $35
Kitchen Countertop Survivor™ Grades: *Avg.* = a "one-day wine," tastes noticeably less fresh the next day; *B* = holds its freshness for 2–3 days after opening; *B+* = holds *and gets better* over 2–3 days after opening; *A* = a 3- to 4-day "freshness window"; *A+* = holds *and gets better* over 3–4 days

gorgeous: floral and citrus scents, passion fruit and pear on the palate, all on an ultralight, oak-free frame. "Wow" is right.

Kitchen Fridge Survivor™ Grade: B+

Your notes:_____

_____

Miguel Torres Viña Sol	PC	T	V
Spain	$	20	21

I love this wine. Here's a fine bargain from one of Spain's preeminent winemaking families. It's dry and fresh, with crisp apple flavor and a tight, crisp finish. It's perfect with tapas.

Kitchen Fridge Survivor™ Grade: B+

Your notes:_____

_____

Penfolds Semillon/Chardonnay	PC	T	V
Australia	$	22	23

"Don't spoil our secret!" jokes one *Immer Guide* taster about this delicious "sleeper of a wine." But of course that is my job. Pros like it, too, for its provocative pear aromas and considerable citrus flavors, making for a mouthwatering wine that's great alone or with food.

Kitchen Fridge Survivor™ Grade: B+

Your notes:_____

_____

Pepperwood Grove Viognier	PC	T	V
(**vee-own-YAY**), California	$	X	X

♥ "Inexpensive Viognier" is practically an oxymoron. The grape is rare and tough to grow, so the few wineries that make it have to charge accordingly. I don't know how they do it, but this is an exception. It has real Viognier character—exotic honeysuckle, lavender, and ripe pineapple scents and flavors—at an affordable price. A tip to inspire you: sommeliers love to get wacky with Viognier and food matching, which explains why you see a lot of this varietal on the lists at exotic ethnic restaurants, including Indian, Asian, Japanese, pan-Latin, and southwestern.

Kitchen Fridge Survivor™ Grade: Avg

Your notes:_____

_____

Pierre Sparr Pinot Blanc   PC   T   V
France $ X   X

♥ For many Alsace wineries, Pinot Blanc is the budget bottling and tastes like it—light and simple. Pierre Sparr's is a notable exception. As is traditional in Alsace, there's no oak or high alcohol here to get your attention. This wine screams character through its lip-smacking pear and quince fruit, with a whisper of mineral scent, all on a sleek, light-bodied frame.
Kitchen Fridge Survivor™ Grade: B
Your notes:_____

_____

Rosemount Chardonnay/Semillon   PC   T   V
Australia $ 19   21

The "ultimate seafood wine," say fans of Rosemount's super citrus-styled blend, featuring gorgeous tangerine aromas, melon fruit, a creamy texture, and bright spiciness that makes it perfect with shellfish or just great on its own.
Kitchen Fridge Survivor™ Grade: A
Your notes:_____

_____

Ruffino Orvieto   PC   T   V
Italy $ 19   21

This wine is a favorite of tasters who love its crisp, refreshing acidity; pros like its fresh, clean melon and nutty qualities. I think it's what everyday Italian white wine should be, in both style and price: a light-bodied wine that makes a perfect *aperitivo*.
Kitchen Fridge Survivor™ Grade: B
Your notes:_____

_____

Price Ranges: **$** = $12 or less; **$$** = 12.01–20; **$$$** = 20.01–35; **$$$$** = > $35
Kitchen Countertop Survivor™ Grades: *Avg.* = a "one-day wine," tastes noticeably less fresh the next day; *B* = holds its freshness for 2–3 days after opening; *B+* = holds *and gets better* over 2–3 days after opening; *A* = a 3- to 4-day "freshness window"; *A+* = holds *and gets better* over 3–4 days

Schmitt Söhne (*SHMITT ZOHN-uh, Söhne is German for "sons"*)
Liebfraumilch, Germany

	PC	T	V
	$	14	14

"Definitely on the sweet side," says a pro of this off-off-dry wine that's still popular with Americans who like a little spritz in their wine.

Kitchen Fridge Survivor™ Grade: Avg

Your notes:_____

_____

Sokol Blosser Evolution
Oregon

	PC	T	V
	$	X	X

♥ The way-cool label will impress your friends, and the taste will delight them. It is a blend of a whole bunch of aromatic white grapes, and that's exactly what it tastes like. The scent and juicy flavor are like an aromatherapy treatment—honeysuckle, peach, apricot, pear, and more—but a lot cheaper!

Kitchen Fridge Survivor™ Grade: B

Your notes:_____

_____

Weingärtner Gruner Veltliner
(*WINE-gart-ner GROO-ner VELT-linn-er*) Federspiel, Austria

	PC	T	V
	$	X	X

♥ All right, this will take a bit of a search but is *so* worth the trouble. If you have not tried Austrian white wines, you are missing out. The easy price of this makes it a good rookie starting point to discover the amazing character of Austria's signature white grape, which the vintners call Gru-V (as in groovy) for short. And that it is—ginger, grapefruit, and cardamom scents; apple, peach, and lemon zest flavors, great acidity, great food compatibility. Go for it!

Kitchen Fridge Survivor™ Grade: A

Your notes:_____

_____

BLUSH/PINK/ROSÉ WINES

Category Profile: Although many buyers are snobby about the blush category, the truth is that for most of us white Zinfandel was probably the first wine we drank that had a cork. Clearly it's a juicy, uncomplicated style that makes a lot of buyers, and their wallets, very happy. Now for the gear switch—rosé. The only thing true rosés have in common with the blush category is appearance. Rosé wines are classic to many world-class European wine regions. They are absolutely dry, tangy, crisp, and amazingly interesting wines for the money. I often say that with their spice and complexity they have red wine flavor, but the lightness of body and chillability gives them white wine style. They are *great* food wines. Don't miss the chance to try my recommendations or those of your favorite shop or restaurant. You will love them.

Serve: The colder the better.

When: The refreshing touch of sweetness in blush styles makes them great as an aperitif. (Some wine drinkers are snobby about the slight sweetness in popular wines, but actually their style is right in sync with the other popular drinks out there—sodas and sweet cocktails like the cosmopolitan and the margarita.)

With: A touch of sweetness in wine can tone down heat, so spicy foods are an especially good partner for blush wine. Dry rosés go with everything.

In: An all-purpose wineglass.

Beringer White Zinfandel	PC	T	V
California	$	16	18

The standard-bearer in the WZ category, and for good reason. It's got lots of fresh strawberry, sweet raspberry, and lively citrus aromas and flavors and a juicy texture.
Kitchen Fridge Survivor™ Grade: B
Your notes:_____

_____

Price Ranges: **$** = $12 or less; **$$** = 12.01–20; **$$$** = 20.01–35; **$$$$** = > $35
Kitchen Countertop Survivor™ Grades: ***Avg.*** = a "one-day wine," tastes noticeably less fresh the next day; ***B*** = holds its freshness for 2–3 days after opening; ***B+*** = holds *and gets better* over 2–3 days after opening; ***A*** = a 3- to 4-day "freshness window"; ***A+*** = holds *and gets better* over 3–4 days

Bonny Doon Vin Gris de Cigare   PC   T   V
Pink Wine, California $ X   X

♥ "Quality is color-blind" is the wine message here.
Randall Grahm of Bonny Doon doesn't do anything
halfway, including a noncerebral quaffer like this
that's all about bone-dry, tangy, spicy refreshment.
Nor does he trifle with self-conscious window
dressing. This is *pink wine*—if there's an image
problem with that, it's in your head.
Kitchen Fridge Survivor™ Grade: B

Your notes:_____

_____

Buehler White Zinfandel   PC   T   V
California $ 18   20

A favorite of restaurant buyers because it's not as
sweet as its peers and has some nice berry flavors.
Kitchen Fridge Survivor™ Grade: B

Your notes:_____

_____

Ernest & Julio Gallo Twin Valley   PC   T   V
White Zinfandel, California $ 13   17

Quite light in the category. A summer staple for many,
thanks to the refreshing watermelon flavor.
Kitchen Fridge Survivor™ Grade: Avg

Your notes:_____

_____

Franzia Blush   PC   T   V
USA $ 8   12

A huge bag-in-box seller, among the most obviously
sweet of the bunch.
Kitchen Fridge Survivor™ Grade: NA

Your notes:_____

_____

Franzia White Zinfandel   PC   T   V
California $ 9   12

For white Zin drinkers, a mega-budget choice that's
decent.
Kitchen Fridge Survivor™ Grade: NA

Your notes:_____

_____

Inglenook White Zinfandel	PC	T	V
California	$	10	12

Experienced buyers note that as far as white Zins go, this one is nice for the price.

Kitchen Fridge Survivor™ Grade: Avg

Your notes:_____

Marqués de Cáceres Rioja Rosado	PC	T	V
Spain	$	X	X

♥ For goodness' sake, don't blame me if you're too wimpy to get your store to order this wine. Very few places stock it, but there's supply, so you have to ask. Why? Because it's rosé and we Americans all have this *thing* about rosés. (What it is, I can't understand.) Tangy strawberry-watermelon-spice . . . *yum.* You can invite *any* food to this party.

Kitchen Fridge Survivor™ Grade: Avg

Your notes:_____

McDowell Grenache Rosé	PC	T	V
California	$	X	X

♥ Lively strawberry and pomegranate flavor, tangy acidity and spice, clean as a whistle, great with food.

Kitchen Fridge Survivor™ Grade: B

Your notes:_____

Regaleali Rosato, Tasca D'Almerita	PC	T	V
Italy	$	X	X

♥ Proof that Italians put all their *passione* into reds (the hot-weather version of which are rosatos like this one). Why drink boring white when you can have this sort of snazzy, spicy, mouthwatering, and dry-style wine to cool you down and complement your summertime or seaside fare?

Kitchen Fridge Survivor™ Grade: B

Your notes:_____

Price Ranges: **$** = $12 or less; **$$** = 12.01–20; **$$$** = 20.01–35; **$$$$** = > $35

Kitchen Countertop Survivor™ Grades: *Avg.* = a "one-day wine," tastes noticeably less fresh the next day; *B* = holds its freshness for 2–3 days after opening; *B+* = holds *and gets better* over 2–3 days after opening; *A* = a 3- to 4-day "freshness window"; *A+* = holds *and gets better* over 3–4 days

René Barbier Mediterranean Rosado PC   T   V
Spain $ X   X

♥ This is the "umbrella drink" of wines—easy drinking and tons of fun. But since it's wine, it's got nice light cherry flavor and acidity, to actually *enhance* the poolside noshes. Even more fun is the cheap price.
Kitchen Fridge Survivor™ Grade: Avg
Your notes:_____

_____

Sutter Home White Zinfandel PC   T   V
California $ 14   17

Purportedly invented out of necessity (the winery had lots of red grapes planted, but taste trends shifted to favor white wines), Sutter Home's "incredibly successful" pink wine will probably go down as one of the most significant accidental innovations in the history of winemaking. It's juicy and pleasing, as it should be.
Kitchen Fridge Survivor™ Grade: B
Your notes:_____

_____

Vendange White Zinfandel PC   T   V
California $ 10   12

Great package, simple and fruity style, and widely available—but not a taste leader in the WZ category.
Kitchen Countertop Survivor™ Grade: Avg
Your notes:_____

_____

RED WINES

Beaujolais/Gamay

Category Profile: Beaujolais Nouveau (*bow-jhoe-LAY*), the new wine of the vintage that each year is shipped from France on the third Thursday in November (just in time for Thanksgiving), dominates sales in this category. (It also inspires scores of nouveau imitators riding its cash-cow coattails.) You can have fun with nouveau, but don't skip the real stuff—particularly Beaujolais-Villages (*vill-AHJH*) and Beaujolais Cru (named for the town where they're grown, e.g., Morgon, Brouilly, Moulin-à-Vent, etc.). These Beaujolais categories are a wine world rarity, in that they offer real character at a low price. The signature style of Beaujolais is a juicy, grapey fruit flavor and succulent texture with, in the crus, an added layer of earthy spiciness. All red Beaujolais is made from the Gamay grape.

Serve: Lightly chilled, to enhance the vibrant fruit.

When: Great as an aperitif and for alfresco occasions such as picnics and barbecues.

With: Many tasters said they swear by it for Thanksgiving. It's so soft, smooth, and juicy I think it goes with everything, from the simplest of sandwich meals to brunch, lunch, and beyond. It's often a great buy on restaurant wine lists and versatile for those really tough matching situations where you've ordered everything from oysters to osso bucco but you want one wine.

In: An all-purpose wineglass.

Barton & Guestier (B&G) Beaujolais	PC	T	V
France	$	17	18

Here's a good-value, food-friendly wine that's great for parties, because it won't break your bank. What more could you ask for?" (FYI: Insiders call it "B&G" for short.)
Kitchen Countertop Survivor™ Grade: Avg
Your notes:_____

_____

Duboeuf (*Duh-BUFF*) (Georges)	PC	T	V
Beaujolais Nouveau, France	$	17	19

Although nouveau remains a hugely popular seasonal French wine, I'm with those pros who've seen consumers—especially in restaurants—cool a bit to the hype. Duboeuf's nouveau is always a festive, juicy crowd-pleaser that consumers find "drinkable with or without food," great with Thanksgiving dinner, and bargain-priced.
Kitchen Countertop Survivor™ Grade: Avg
Your notes:_____

_____

Price Ranges: **$** = $12 or less; **$$** = 12.01–20; **$$$** = 20.01–35; **$$$$** = > $35
Kitchen Countertop Survivor™ Grades: *Avg.* = a "one-day wine," tastes noticeably less fresh the next day; *B* = holds its freshness for 2–3 days after opening; *B+* = holds *and gets better* over 2–3 days after opening; *A* = a 3- to 4-day "freshness window"; *A+* = holds *and gets better* over 3–4 days

Duboeuf (Georges) Beaujolais-Villages, France | PC | T | V
| | $ | 19 | 20

🔖 I agree with trade colleagues that it's "hard not to love" this widely available bottling from the King of Beaujolais. Its plump berry flavor is great with a wide variety of foods and a good wine to offer those who don't normally drink red.

Kitchen Countertop Survivor™ Grade: B

Your notes:_____

_____

Louis Jadot Beaujolais-Villages France | PC | T | V
| | $ | 21 | 21

I've tasted—and sold in restaurants—*every* vintage of this wine for the last ten years, and my reaction is as consistent as the wine: delish! Both pro and consumer tasters love its light body and raspberry and cherry fruit, which make it "the perfect sipping wine." Its food versatility impresses, too, with tasters recommending everything from "roasted chicken and salad" to "sushi if you want a red." I'd throw in Chinese food, too.

Kitchen Countertop Survivor™ Grade: B

Your notes:_____

_____

Pinot Noir

Category Profile: Pinot Noir is my favorite of the major classic red grape varieties, because I love its smoky-ripe scent, pure fruit flavor, and, most of all, silken texture. It also offers red wine intensity and complexity, without being heavy. Although Pinot Noir's home turf is the Burgundy region of France, few of those wines make the list of top sellers in the U.S., because production is tiny. The coolest parts of coastal California (especially the Russian River Valley, Carneros, Monterey, and Santa Barbara County) specialize in Pinot Noir, as does Oregon's Willamette (*will-AM-ett*) Valley. I believe New Zealand will also become an important Pinot source in the near future. Pinot Noir from all the major regions is typically oak aged, but as with other grapes the amount of oakiness is matched to the intensity of the fruit. Generally the budget bottlings are the least oaky.

Serve: *Cool* room temperature; don't hesitate to chill the bottle briefly if needed.

When: Although the silky texture makes Pinot Noir quite bewitching on its own, it is also the ultimate "food wine." It is my choice to take to dinner parties and to order in restaurants, because I know it will probably delight both white and red wine drinkers and will go with everything.

With: Pinot's versatility is legendary, but it is *the* wine for mushroom dishes, salmon, rare tuna, and any bird (especially duck).

In: An all-purpose wineglass. Or try a larger balloon stem; the extra air space enhances the wine's aroma.

Anapamu Pinot Noir	PC	T	V
California	$$	18	19

It is indeed "a very good wine if you can get past the name," which is tough to pronounce, as pros pointed out. Just say *ah-nuh-PAH-moo* and enjoy the classic Pinot Noir character that's often hard to find at this price point: "elegant and supple" texture, "juicy cherry" fruit.

Kitchen Countertop Survivor™ Grade: B

Your notes:_____

_____

Archery Summit Arcus Estate	PC	T	V
Pinot Noir, Oregon	$$$$	25	20

Pinot Noir in the "intense and opulent" style is an apt description here. Oakiness, black cherry fruit, and layers of flavor are part of the package, which quite a few tasters even compared to "top French Burgundy." Both trade and consumers call it "an Oregon Pinot best bet" that's "pricey but worth it."

Kitchen Countertop Survivor™ Grade: B

Your notes:_____

_____

Price Ranges: $ = $12 or less; **$$** = 12.01–20; **$$$** = 20.01–35; **$$$$** = > $35

Kitchen Countertop Survivor™ Grades: ***Avg.*** = a "one-day wine," tastes noticeably less fresh the next day; ***B*** = holds its freshness for 2–3 days after opening; ***B+*** = holds *and gets better* over 2–3 days after opening; ***A*** = a 3- to 4-day "freshness window"; ***A+*** = holds *and gets better* over 3–4 days

Au Bon Climat Pinot Noir Santa Barbara, California

PC	T	V
$$$	X	X

✗ *Oh-bohn-clee-MAHT* has a cult following and a nickname—"ABC"—among those of us who love its exciting Pinot Noirs. To me, here are the virtues that distinguish truly great Pinots: crystalline purity of fruit, structural components (the oak, body, and tannin) in perfect, subtle balance, and an aromatic "identity" connecting the wine to its vineyard or growing zone. Magically, ABC achieves all three, in this its basic bottling and the more limited releases from single vineyards. Try them to experience their luxurious but never heavy-handed fruit and a savory-sweet, slightly animal note in the scent that to me marks the ABC style. They age nicely, too.

Kitchen Countertop Survivor™ Grade: B+

Your notes:_____

_____

Beaulieu Vineyards (BV) Carneros Pinot Noir, California

PC	T	V
$$	21	21

Although Cabernet Sauvignon is BV's longtime signature wine, this Pinot Noir has been consistently a nice example of "classic Carneros Pinot"—silky cherry fruit, spicy, and soft. The reasonable price and blue chip name make it a great wine for business or casual entertaining—cachet, real Pinot character, great food compatibility.

Kitchen Countertop Survivor™ Grade: B

Your notes:_____

_____

Beringer Founders' Estate Pinot Noir California

PC	T	V
$	19	20

Here's an inexpensive Pinot Noir, which to wine purists might seem like an oxymoron, but this one's good and getting better every year since the Founders' Estate line was launched. Its soft berry flavors and silky texture, without heavy alcohol, are probably what people looking for the smoothness credited to Merlot actually want.

Kitchen Countertop Survivor™ Grade: B

Your notes:_____

_____

Buena Vista Carneros Pinot Noir	PC	T	V
California	$$	X	X

♥ Wow—real Pinot Noir character for well under $20. It's even got classic Carneros elegance, with aromas of potpourri and exotic tea leaves and flavors of dried fruit and spices. A triumph, especially for the money.

Kitchen Countertop Survivor™ Grade: B

Your notes:_____

Byron Santa Maria Valley Pinot Noir	PC	T	V
California	$$	24	21

A good choice if you like "earthier Pinots," say pros of this "classic style" wine that is medium-bodied, complex in character, and driven by pure fruit components: namely ripe dark cherries; the texture is silky and the finish is mild. I find Byron to be consistently good for the money—a tall order for Pinot Noir. Look also for its Estate bottling, a bit more expensive but delicious.

Kitchen Countertop Survivor™ Grade: B+

Your notes:_____

Calera Central Coast Pinot Noir	PC	T	V
California	$$	19	20

⚜ Calera Pinot Noirs deliver a rare and impressive combination among American wineries: a blue chip track record in hand-crafted but available quantities. It's impressive that, year in and year out, the "supple, earthy" style, redolent of "dried cherry fruit," comes through—because it's definitely a house style I've loved since at least the late eighties. If you like it, you can confidently trade up to the utterly original single-vineyard Calera Pinots. White wine drinkers shouldn't miss their Viognier and Chardonnay.

Kitchen Countertop Survivor™ Grade: B+

Your notes:_____

Price Ranges: **$** = $12 or less; **$$** = 12.01–20; **$$$** = 20.01–35; **$$$$** = > $35

Kitchen Countertop Survivor™ Grades: *Avg.* = a "one-day wine," tastes noticeably less fresh the next day; *B* = holds its freshness for 2–3 days after opening; *B+* = holds *and gets better* over 2–3 days after opening; *A* = a 3- to 4-day "freshness window"; *A+* = holds *and gets better* over 3–4 days

Cambria (*CAME-bree-uh*) Julia's PC T V
Vineyard Pinot Noir, California **$$** 24 21

This wine's signature style—savory earth and spice
character alongside chunky, concentrated plum flavor
and a tug of tannin in the mouth—have been consis-
tent since it was launched. Buyers are noticing: this
is a wine that's classic Santa Barbara but with its own
unique profile—no McWine here.
Kitchen Countertop Survivor™ Grade: B
Your notes:_____

_____

Clos du Bois Pinot Noir PC T V
California **$$** X X

♥ Smoke, raspberry preserves, sweet tobacco, and
leather in the scent and taste; plus succulent, almost
syrupy texture in the mouth. This is omigod gorgeous
Pinot Noir fruit, allowed to shine, unladen with too
much oak.
Kitchen Countertop Survivor™ Grade:
Your notes:_____

_____

Cristom Willamette Pinot Noir PC T V
Oregon **$$$** 23 22

A "Pinot to write home about," says a trade colleague,
"at great length, about great length." I couldn't agree
more. I have been bewitched by the smoky/cocoa
scent of this wine since its debut. "Exotic," "seductive,"
and "deeply perfumed" are all right-on descriptors,
too, and the satiny texture is amazing.
Kitchen Countertop Survivor™ Grade: B+
Your notes:_____

_____

David Bruce Central Coast Pinot PC T V
Noir, California **$$** X X

✗ Lots of MIA inquiries about this characterful
vibrant Pinot laced with savory spice, earth, and
raspberry fruit. Production limits keep it out of the
statistics, but the quality for the price keep it top-of-
mind for trade buyers and consumers alike.
Kitchen Countertop Survivor™ Grade: B
Your notes:_____

_____

Domaine Drouhin (*droo-AHN*)	PC	T	V
Willamette Valley Pinot Noir, Oregon	$$$$	25	20

This wine is "dripping" with "exuberant raspberry and cherry fruit," which appeals to many tasters. Be prepared, however, for heavy oak that to my taste overpowers the fruit a bit, giving the wine a candied character that can seem cloying.

Kitchen Countertop Survivor™ *Grade: Avg*

Your notes:_____

_____

Duck Pond Pinot Noir	PC	T	V
Oregon	$	19	19

Look for this "light on the wallet," supple, and fruity Pinot on wine lists when you want to impress, because it's true Pinot for a great price. It has really nice strawberry aromas, ripe raspberry flavors, and great food compatibility.

Kitchen Countertop Survivor™ *Grade: B*

Your notes:_____

_____

Elk Cove Pinot Noir	PC	T	V
Oregon	$$	23	21

This is a nice Oregon Pinot Noir in the lighter-bodied style, whose savory spice and dried cherry character make it really versatile with food.

Kitchen Countertop Survivor™ *Grade: Avg*

Your notes:_____

_____

Estancia Pinnacles Pinot Noir	PC	T	V
California	$$	20	20

You get impressive complexity at this price, with a distinct herbal, strawberry compote, and smoky character. I am also impressed with Estancia's consistent track record over the last five years: true Pinot Noir character and great flavor for the money.

Price Ranges: **$** = $12 or less; **$$** = 12.01–20; **$$$** = 20.01–35; **$$$$** = > $35

Kitchen Countertop Survivor™ Grades: **Avg.** = a "one-day wine," tastes noticeably less fresh the next day; **B** = holds its freshness for 2–3 days after opening; **B+** = holds *and gets better* over 2–3 days after opening; **A** = a 3- to 4-day "freshness window"; **A+** = holds *and gets better* over 3–4 days

Look also for the Reserve, which is incredible for the price.

Kitchen Countertop Survivor™ Grade: B+

Your notes:_____

Etude Pinot Noir
California

PC	T	V
$$$$	26	22

🍴 I have been serving this gorgeous Pinot Noir for my restaurant guests ever since winemaker Tony Soter first launched his own label in the 1980s. It is not only "one of the best from California," as my trade tasters concur but also "consistently well made" and in my view gets extra points for its distinctive style that resisted the trend to layer on too much oak. Rather, its hallmark is an elegant, sleek texture, lovely berry and spice scents and flavors, and artful balance. It develops additional complexity with a few years' bottle age. Bravo!

Kitchen Countertop Survivor™ Grade: B+

Your notes:_____

Firesteed Pinot Noir
Oregon

PC	T	V
$	21	20

The delicious cranberry and dried cherry fruit and nice kick of acid make this wine a great food partner—and consequently a favorite among restaurant buyers. We in the trade marvel when a winery can produce Pinot Noir that is this "true to the grape at such a great price."

Kitchen Countertop Survivor™ Grade: B

Your notes:_____

Gallo of Sonoma Pinot Noir
California

PC	T	V
$	20	21

Both trade and consumer tasters tagged this wine as probably the best-value Pinot Noir from California. Indeed it is quite a special wine, redolent of fresh, pure "raspberry and cherry" fruit, a soft vanilla-cream oakiness, and supple-but-lively texture—in other words, classic Pinot Noir.

Kitchen Countertop Survivor™ Grade: B+

Your notes:_____

Indigo Hills Pinot Noir | PC | T | V
California | **$$** | 18 | 18

Light-bodied and tangy, with sour cherry and savory spice notes. Another Gallo brand offering good Pinot Noir character at a value price.

Kitchen Countertop Survivor™ Grade: Avg

Your notes:_____

Joseph Drouhin Chorey Les Beaune | PC | T | V
***(shore-ay lay BONE)*, France** | **$$$$** | 23 | 20

"A lot of money" for "such fleeting fruit," say pros about this pretty, delicate Burgundy that's "got more aroma than flavor," citing scents of raspberries and red currant, but "not much more." Unfortunately, I think that's a common problem with red Burgundy in general.

Kitchen Countertop Survivor™ Grade: Avg

Your notes:_____

Kendall-Jackson Vintner's Reserve | PC | T | V
Pinot Noir, California | **$$** | 20 | 20

You can "always count on K-J" to deliver "big" "hearty flavor," say fans of this Pinot that "never disappoints." I agree, it's another great example of how the K-J Vintner's Reserve line makes wines true to the varietal. Another good introductory Pinot that shows you its classic character at an affordable price.

Kitchen Countertop Survivor™ Grade: A

Your notes:_____

King Estate Pinot Noir | PC | T | V
Oregon | **$$** | 21 | 20

This "lovely Pinot" is "always a good pouring wine" as my trade tasters point out. I say it's also one of the most consistent and widely available of the Oregon

---

Price Ranges: **$** = $12 or less; **$$** = 12.01–20; **$$$** = 20.01–35; **$$$$** = > $35

Kitchen Countertop Survivor™ Grades: ***Avg.*** = a "one-day wine," tastes noticeably less fresh the next day; ***B*** = holds its freshness for 2–3 days after opening; ***B+*** = holds *and gets better* over 2–3 days after opening; ***A*** = a 3- to 4-day "freshness window"; ***A+*** = holds *and gets better* over 3–4 days

Pinots, and it follows the Burgundy model: medium bodied and elegant.

Kitchen Countertop Survivor™ Grade: B

Your notes:_____

_____

La Crema Pinot Noir   PC   T   V
California $$ 23   22

Here's a controversial wine that's a "favorite Pinot" for some and disappointing to others, perhaps, who find the oak and tannin a bit heavy-handed for the delicate Pinot Noir grape. It does have deep cherry-cola flavor, and I think it needs food to tame its brawn.

Kitchen Countertop Survivor™ Grade: Avg

Your notes:_____

_____

Lindemans Bin 99 Pinot Noir   PC   T   V
Australia $ 19   20

Pros say you "can't beat the price" of this light, approachable wine, and I agree: soft and uncomplicated, it is a very pleasant Pinot for the price.

Kitchen Countertop Survivor™ Grade: Avg

Your notes:_____

_____

Louis Latour Côte de Beaune   PC   T   V
(*coat duh BONE*), France $$$ 21   20

Pro opinions are mixed about the consistency—or lack thereof—of this pretty but one-dimensional wine from a great producer. Again we face the "Burgundy challenge" with this wine: to find enough complexity and fruit for the "hefty price" typically charged.

Kitchen Countertop Survivor™ Grade: B+

Your notes:_____

_____

Louis Latour Nuits-St.-Georges   PC   T   V
(*nwee-saint-GEORGE*), France $$$$ 23   22

This wine is "not one to share with friends," "considering it costs a small fortune," say some. This French Pinot Noir has a beautifully perfumed berry nose punctuated with hints of violets and a supple tannic structure. For the price I'd like more fruit concentration.

Kitchen Countertop Survivor™ Grade: B

Your notes:_____

Meridian Pinot Noir   PC   T   V
California $ 19   18

This has always been one of my favorite value-priced Pinot Noirs, and I've obviously got company. So many tasters pointed out that this wine is perfect for every day, especially for the price. The mouthwatering flavor "tastes like biting into fresh cherries."

Kitchen Countertop Survivor™ Grade: B

Your notes:_____

Morgan Pinot Noir   PC   T   V
California $$ 24   22

Morgan has built up quite a track record for its Pinot Noirs, which are known for their ripe cherry fruit and exotic, smoky character. Their consistency and quality of style, year after year, are something very few Pinot Noir producers achieve. Bravo!

Kitchen Countertop Survivor™ Grade: B+

Your notes:_____

Robert Mondavi Coastal Pinot Noir   PC   T   V
California $$ 18   18

One of the best varietals in the Mondavi Coastal line, and true to the grape with its light berry fruit. It's not one of my favorite Pinots at this price point, however; given the pedigree and Mondavi's winemaking resources, this should lead the value Pinot pack for quality—though at present it does not.

Kitchen Countertop Survivor™ Grade: B

Your notes:_____

Price Ranges: **$** = $12 or less; **$$** = 12.01–20; **$$$** = 20.01–35; **$$$$** = > $35

Kitchen Countertop Survivor™ Grades: *Avg.* = a "one-day wine," tastes noticeably less fresh the next day; *B* = holds its freshness for 2–3 days after opening; *B+* = holds *and gets better* over 2–3 days after opening; *A* = a 3- to 4-day "freshness window"; *A+* = holds *and gets better* over 3–4 days

Robert Mondavi Napa Pinot Noir | PC | T | V
California | $$$ | 21 | 19

Although this wine could benefit from a bit of bottle age, as trade buyers pointed out, I have found that aeration—a few swirls in a large wine glass with plenty of air space—usually does the trick. The style is quite distinctive, with "gorgeous cherry fruit," plus a lot of smoky spice and complexity. I give it extra-high marks for being true to this style for over ten years.

Kitchen Countertop Survivor™ Grade: B

Your notes:_____

_____

Robert Sinskey Napa Pinot Noir | PC | T | V
California | $$$ | 24 | 21

This wine has developed a loyal following over the years for its chunky, oaky "big Pinot" style, as the taste scores make clear. My personal experience is that in some years the fruit intensity hasn't been sufficient to balance all the oak and tannin. As the price creeps up, I find myself looking toward other California Pinots.

Kitchen Countertop Survivor™ Grade: B

Your notes:_____

_____

Turning Leaf Pinot Noir | PC | T | V
California | $ | 14 | 15

"Plain" and "simple," say tasters of this Gallo Pinot, and I agree. Light and skimpy on fruit, it's a disappointment in comparison to the exemplary job Gallo does with its Chardonnay in the same price range.

Kitchen Countertop Survivor™ Grade: Avg

Your notes:_____

_____

Wild Horse Pinot Noir | PC | T | V
California | $$ | 23 | 20

Many of my trade tasters cited this as a "standard-bearer" in an increasingly prominent Pinot region, namely Santa Barbara. The cherry-cola aromas and plump berry fruit—hallmarks of this regional style—are in abundance here, and indeed it is not "over-oaked" as many relieved tasters noted. The price makes it an easy initiation for anyone new to Santa Barbara Pinot.

Kitchen Countertop Survivor™ Grade: B

Your notes:_____

Willakenzie Willamette Valley	PC	T	V
Pinot Noir, Oregon	**$$$**	**26**	**23**

✓ The Willakenzie name comes from the distinctive soil type in this growing area, which itself is named for the two rivers that converge there: the Willamette and the McKenzie. The wine is consistently tasty and elegant and a value for this quality. Indeed it delivers big-time character. From "luscious black cherry fruit" to "lovely cedar and herbal nuances," it's clearly a home run. They also make an outstanding Pinot Gris, and the winery is beautiful to visit if you find yourself in Oregon wine country.

Kitchen Countertop Survivor™ Grade: B

Your notes:_____

Willamette Valley Vineyards Pinot	PC	T	V
Noir, Oregon	**$$**	**22**	**20**

This winery delivers consistent quality every year in a cherry-and-spice-scented style that's subtle and doesn't hit you over the head with too much wood. Look also for the small-production reserve Pinot Noir.

Kitchen Countertop Survivor™ Grade: Avg

Your notes:_____

Chianti and Sangiovese

Category Profile: Remember the days when "Chianti" meant those kitschy straw-covered bottles? Tuscany's signature red has come a long way in quality

---

Price Ranges: **$** = $12 or less; **$$** = 12.01–20; **$$$** = 20.01–35; **$$$$** = > $35

Kitchen Countertop Survivor™ Grades: ***Avg.*** = a "one-day wine," tastes noticeably less fresh the next day; ***B*** = holds its freshness for 2–3 days after opening; ***B+*** = holds *and gets better* over 2–3 days after opening; ***A*** = a 3- to 4-day "freshness window"; ***A+*** = holds *and gets better* over 3–4 days

since then, pulling much of the Italian wine world with it. As one retailer in the trenches put it, wine lovers are "missing some great values" in this category, but I think that's due to some understandable confusion about the labels and styles. Specifically, as quality has improved, Chianti itself has "morphed" into three tiers of wine—varietal Sangiovese (*san-joe-VAY-zay*), labeled with the grape name; traditional Chianti in a range of styles; and the luxury tier, which includes top regional wines like Brunello, and the so-called "Super Tuscan" reds. Many of the major Tuscan wineries produce wines in all three categories. The basic Sangioveses largely populate the one-dollar-sign price tier, and many offer good value. Chianti itself now spans the entire price and quality spectrum from budget quaff to boutique collectible, with the top-quality *classico* and *riserva* versions worthy of aging in the cellar. Finally, the Super Tuscans emerged because wineries wanted creative license to use international grapes outside the traditional Chianti "recipe" (and, I guess, with fantasy names like Summus, Sassicaia, and Luce, poetic license, too!). What they all have in common is that Italian "zest"—savory spice in the scent, plus vibrant acidity and texture that seems "alive" in the mouth. It's a flavor profile that truly sings with food, and, coming from the joyously food-frenzied Italians, would you expect anything less?

Serve: Room temperature (the varietal Sangioveses are also nice with a light chill); the "bigger" wines—classicos, riservas, and Super Tuscans—benefit from aeration (pour into the glass and swirl, or decant into a pitcher or carafe with plenty of air space).

When: Any food occasion, from snack to supper to celebration.

With: Especially great wherever tomato sauce, cheese, olive oil, or savory herbs (rosemary, basil, oregano) are present.

In: An all-purpose wineglass or larger-bowled red wine stem.

Antinori (Marchese) (*ahn-tee-*	PC	T	V
NORE-ee mar-KAY-zee)	$$$	24	22

Antinori (Marchese) (*ahn-tee-NORE-ee mar-KAY-zee*) Chianti Classico Riserva, Italy

✓ From the "King of Chianti" comes this well-made wine, whose flavor concentration and balance some pros caution can be vintage sensitive. With a string of recent good vintages in Tuscany, look for the classic strawberry fruit, tannic grip, and peppery spice of traditional Chianti Classico Riserva to shine though.
Kitchen Countertop Survivor™ Grade: B+
Your notes:_____

_____

Banfi Brunello di Montalcino	PC	T	V
Italy	$$$$	23	20

This "big," "almost chocolaty" Brunello is a rare combination for wine lovers: easy to find, consistently classy, and true to the Brunello character. That means palate-coating tannin but with dense fig and mocha flavors. The whole package comes across as big but balanced, and as such I highly recommend decanting or aerating in the glass to soften it up.
Kitchen Countertop Survivor™ Grade: A
Your notes:_____

_____

Castello di Gabbiano Chianti	PC	T	V
Italy	$	17	19

A soft, simple Chianti, with red cherry flavors and spicy nuances. It's a versatile food partner and, as my tasters point out, can't be beat for the price.
Kitchen Countertop Survivor™ Grade: B
Your notes:_____

_____

Castello di Gabbiano Chianti	PC	T	V
Classico Riserva, Italy	$$	21	21

I agree with tasters who label this "mouthwatering" wine as a perfect example of Chianti Classico Riserva.

Price Ranges: **$** = $12 or less; **$$** = 12.01–20; **$$$** = 20.01–35; **$$$$** = > $35
Kitchen Countertop Survivor™ Grades: *Avg.* = a "one-day wine," tastes noticeably less fresh the next day; *B* = holds its freshness for 2–3 days after opening; *B+* = holds *and gets better* over 2–3 days after opening; *A* = a 3- to 4-day "freshness window"; *A+* = holds *and gets better* over 3–4 days

It delivers a cornucopia of red fruit, lively acidity, and a nice tug of tannin. Great food partner.

Kitchen Countertop Survivor™ Grade: B

Your notes:_____

_____

	PC	T	V
Cecchi (*CHECK-ee*) Chianti Classico Italy	$	21	21

This is the fun version of Chianti Classico, soft and easy drinking, plus easy on the wallet. The soft berry fruit character, tinged with a bit of spice, makes it *perfetto* with pasta or pizza.

Kitchen Countertop Survivor™ Grade: Avg

Your notes:_____

_____

	PC	T	V
Felsina (*FELL-si-nuh*) Chianti Classico, Italy	$$	23	21

Yes, it's terrific and hard to find, as my tasters pointed out. Restaurants buy up most of it, so this is one to seek out on wine lists. Subtle, strawberry-raspberry fruit balanced with savory-earthy notes means it goes with everything on the table from antipasti to osso bucco. It is a wonderful food wine.

Kitchen Countertop Survivor™ Grade: B+

Your notes:_____

_____

	PC	T	V
Frescobaldi Chianti Rufina (*ROO-fin-uh*) Riserva, Italy	$$$	22	21

Frescobaldi, one of the oldest winemaking families in Tuscany, is always dependable, from its budget-priced Chianti to this luxurious Riserva from Rufina, the Chianti subdistrict where its estate is located. Though fans say it's hard to find, you'll be rewarded with plenty of ripe cherry fruit and peppery nuances. It's a bit on the pricey side but still worth it.

Kitchen Countertop Survivor™ Grade: B+

Your notes:_____

_____

	PC	T	V
Querciabella (*Kwair-chuh-BELL-uh*) Chianti Classico Riserva, Italy	$$$	24	22

I used to serve this wine by the glass at Windows on the World as a textbook example of top Chianti

Classico Riserva. It delivers ample berry fruit flavors, nuances of wood and earth, and a firm backbone of tannin and acidity. Fans say it is "hard to drink in small quantities" and "what *all* Chianti should taste like."

Kitchen Countertop Survivor™ Grade: A
Your notes:_____

_____

Ruffino Chianti Classico Riserva Ducale (*ri-ZUR-vuh doo-CALL-eh*) Gold Label, Italy

	PC	T	V
	$$$$	23	21

As one taster put it, it's, "as good as gold but costs almost as much." Although I wish the price had not risen so steeply of late, I have to agree that it is a benchmark of quality and authenticity of Chianti Classico Riserva. The A+ survivor grade is well deserved: the open bottle of this wine actually gets better and increasingly complex over many days. Ruffino's other bottlings, the tan label Riserva Ducale and Aziano, are less expensive and true to the red fruit, spicy Chianti profile.

Kitchen Countertop Survivor™ Grade: A+
Your notes:_____

_____

Santa Cristina Sangiovese, Antinori Italy

	PC	T	V
	$	22	23

I couldn't put it better than the consumer who wrote "a trip to Italy in a glass," but not the big city—rather, a trattoria in the countryside. Its easy-to-drink, fresh cranberry fruit makes it very food friendly, and the price is "unbeatable."

Kitchen Countertop Survivor™ Grade: Avg
Your notes:_____

_____

Price Ranges: **$** = $12 or less; **$$** = 12.01–20; **$$$** = 20.01–35; **$$$$** = > $35
Kitchen Countertop Survivor™ Grades: **Avg.** = a "one-day wine," tastes noticeably less fresh the next day; **B** = holds its freshness for 2–3 days after opening; **B+** = holds *and gets better* over 2–3 days after opening; **A** = a 3- to 4-day "freshness window"; **A+** = holds *and gets better* over 3–4 days

Selvapiana (*SELL-vuh-pee-AH-nuh*)   PC   T   V
Chianti Rufina, Italy $$ 23   23

This was the first Chianti estate I ever visited, and it remains my sentimental favorite, for it was here I discovered what it's like to be "adopted" as family in that inimitable Italian way. I also discovered, via a wine opened from my birth year, the incredible quality and longevity these wines can achieve. The earthy mushroom and spice scents, bright cherry fruit, and velvety texture of this wine comprise a love letter to food.

Kitchen Countertop Survivor™ Grade: A

Your notes:_____

_____

Straccali Chianti   PC   T   V
Italy $ X   X

✗ Here's an uncomplicated, soft, juicy Chianti that's totally drinkable and always a basic Chianti bargain.

Kitchen Countertop Survivor™ Grade: Avg

Your notes:_____

_____

Merlot

Grape Profile: When early nineties news reports linked heart health and moderate red wine drinking, Merlot was there with some very user-friendly virtues: the two-syllable name made it easy to pronounce, the smooth style made it easy to drink. And the rest, as we say in the trade, was history. Sales skyrocketed, and Merlot joined the ranks of go-to wine names that inspire instant customer recognition and confidence—a great thing indeed! As with other market-leading varietals like Chardonnay and Cabernet Sauvignon, Merlot can range both in price, from budget to boutique, and in complexity, from soft and simple to "serious." Across the spectrum, Merlot is modeled on the wines from its home region of Bordeaux, France. At the basic level, that means medium body and soft texture, with nice plum and berry fruit flavor. The more ambitious versions have more body, tannin, and fruit concentration and usually a good bit of oakiness in the scent and taste. Washington state,

SPECIAL NOTE to Merlot devotees: If you are looking for something new but similar, at a great price, check out these two South American specialties. First, Argentinean Malbec (*MAHL-beck*), a red grape originally from Bordeaux, has emerged as a major wine specialty from tango country. It's similar in body and smoothness to Merlot, with lots of aromatic complexity. Some wineries to look for: Trapiche, Navarro Correas, Catena, and Chandon Terrazas. Second, from Chile, try Carmenere (*car-muh-NAIR-eh*), also a Bordeaux import that was originally misidentified as Merlot in many Chilean vineyards. Its smooth texture and plum fruit are complemented by an exotically spicy scent. Look for Carmeneres from Concha y Toro's Terrunyo label, Veramonte Primus, and Arboleda (check out the Top 50 Wines You're Not Drinking section for more on these).

California's Sonoma and Napa regions, and Chile are my favorite growing regions for varietal Merlot. Most Merlot producers follow the Bordeaux practice of blending in some Cabernet Sauvignon (or another of the classic Bordeaux red grapes) to complement and enhance the wines' taste and complexity.

Serve: *Cool* room temperature.

When: With meals, of course; and the basic bottlings are soft enough to enjoy on their own as a cocktail alternative.

With: Anything with which you enjoy red wine, especially cheeses, roasts, and grilled foods.

In: An all-purpose wineglass or larger-bowled red wine stem.

Price Ranges: **$** = $12 or less; **$$** = 12.01–20; **$$$** = 20.01–35; **$$$$** = > $35

Kitchen Countertop Survivor™ Grades: *Avg.* = a "one-day wine," tastes noticeably less fresh the next day; *B* = holds its freshness for 2–3 days after opening; *B+* = holds *and gets better* over 2–3 days after opening; *A* = a 3- to 4-day "freshness window"; *A+* = holds *and gets better* over 3–4 days

Barton & Guestier (B&G) Merlot | PC | T | V
France | $ | 15 | 17

Although France is the traditional HQ for Merlot, New World regions like Washington state and Chile beat it on the value-for-money front more often than not. This wine is light and simple, and I think Merlot drinkers will want more than that.

Kitchen Countertop Survivor™ *Grade: Avg*

Your notes:_____

_____

Beaulieu Vineyard (BV) Coastal | PC | T | V
Merlot, California | $ | 18 | 18

"Very consistent quality and a good value," say my pro tasters, and I think this is among the best "coastal" Merlots on the market, with all the plump berry fruit and smooth, juicy texture that you look for in an everyday Merlot

Kitchen Countertop Survivor™ *Grade: Avg*

Your notes:_____

_____

Beringer Founders' Estate Merlot | PC | T | V
California | $ | 19 | 20

As Beringer's Founders' Estate line gets better and better every year, its legions of loyal trade and consumer fans who "buy it again and again" grow. Nothing cerebral here, just a tasty, mouth-filling glass of plum and berry flavor. And it's got better kitchen countertop staying power than a lot of Merlots, giving extra value to the bargain price.

Kitchen Countertop Survivor™ *Grade: B*

Your notes:_____

_____

Blackstone Merlot | PC | T | V
California | $$ | 20 | 21

A lot of buyers find both the "smooth and flavorful" taste of this wine—*and* its name—easy to remember. I think it's soft and well balanced but hope the price, which has crept up over the last few years, will level off.

Kitchen Countertop Survivor™ *Grade: Avg*

Your notes:_____

_____

Bogle Merlot	PC	T	V
California	$$	20	20

While it's not the bargain price it used to be, many pros say this Bogle Merlot is "still a great value." I think its character, however, is not as complex as it should be for the money.

Kitchen Countertop Survivor™ Grade: Avg

Your notes:_____

_____

Bolla Merlot	PC	T	V
Italy	$	13	14

The Bolla name and Merlot grape keep this wine selling, but even at this price its very light style and thinness of fruit flavor fall short of what Merlot devotees would expect.

Kitchen Countertop Survivor™ Grade: Avg

Your notes:_____

_____

CK Mondavi Merlot	PC	T	V
California	$$	17	16

This is a light and fruity crowd-pleaser Merlot, with berry flavors and a smooth finish. Good for the price; good for parties.

Kitchen Countertop Survivor™ Grade: Avg

Your notes:_____

_____

Carmenet Dynamite Merlot	PC	T	V
California	$$$	22	20

A full-bodied, mouthwatering Merlot, redolent with black cherry flavor. Fans of the oaky style will be happy with the vanilla and sweet spice character, which is intense but balanced.

Kitchen Countertop Survivor™ Grade: B+

Your notes:_____

_____

Price Ranges: **$** = $12 or less; **$$** = 12.01–20; **$$$** = 20.01–35; **$$$$** = > $35

Kitchen Countertop Survivor™ Grades: *Avg.* = a "one-day wine," tastes noticeably less fresh the next day; *B* = holds its freshness for 2–3 days after opening; *B+* = holds *and gets better* over 2–3 days after opening; *A* = a 3- to 4-day "freshness window"; *A+* = holds *and gets better* over 3–4 days

Casa Lapostolle Classic Merlot   PC   T   V
California $ 22   22

⚓ I have to agree with the consumer who declared this "the best find of the last five years." To my taste, that could be said of all the varietals in Casa Lapostolle's under-$10 "classic" line. Plum and cherry flavors, a gentle tug of tannin, nice staying power after the bottle's opened—I don't think there is better Merlot for the money.

Kitchen Countertop Survivor™ Grade: B

Your notes:_____

Casa Lapostolle Cuvée Alexandre   PC   T   V
Merlot, Chile $$$ X   X

✗ Both trade and consumers rave "superb stuff at really fair prices" about Casa Lapostolle in general and this wine specifically. With its sweet vanilla and coffee scents, extremely ripe and concentrated plum fruit, velvety tannins, and very long finish, it really does drink "like top Bordeaux at triple the price." That amount of flavor and quality for the money place it among the truly great values on the market, though increasingly difficult to find outside restaurants and fine wine boutiques. Definitely worth the search. Look for the Cuvée Alexandre Cabernet and Chardonnay, too.

Kitchen Countertop Survivor™ Grade: B

Your notes:_____

Château Ste. Michelle Columbia   PC   T   V
Valley Merlot, Washington $$ 22   22

Year in and year out, this is one of the nicest Merlots coming out of Washington, whose aromas of "mocha" and "ripe raspberries"—plus a juicy and soft texture— make it a great bottle for the price. With a string of nice vintages coming recently out of Washington, it's set to shine even brighter.

Kitchen Countertop Survivor™ Grade: B

Your notes:_____

Château Simard Bordeaux   PC   T   V
France $$$ 20   19

The entire world models its Merlots on the château wines from Bordeaux's so-called "right bank" villages—namely, Pomerol and St. Emilion, which are the source of this wine. Both trade and consumers say it's "wonderful stuff" that "beats other Bordeaux at twice the cost." The subtle but powerful profile, with scents of earth, cedar, and coffee cloaking the plum fruit and soft-but-structured tannins, is a great entree to the St. Emilion style. This wine also presents the opportunity to sample a red with some bottle age, with some older vintages currently available in the marketplace.

Kitchen Countertop Survivor™ Grade: B+

Your notes:_____

_____

Christian Moueix (*MWEXX*) Merlot	**PC**	**T**	**V**
France	**$**	**20**	**20**

Coming from the maker of Bordeaux's famous Château Petrus—arguably the world's most coveted Merlot—this wine should deliver more fruit and flavor than it does. Even at this price, I prefer other Merlots.

Kitchen Countertop Survivor™ Grade: Avg

Your notes:_____

_____

Clos du Bois Sonoma Merlot	**PC**	**T**	**V**
California	**$$$**	**21**	**21**

Maybe if you looked up "mixed feelings" in the dictionary, you'd see this wine. Trade buyers call it "a must on wine lists," because the name recognition makes it a sure seller, but this wine earned its consumer reputation for "yummy" fruit at around the $12 price point. Now it costs nearly twice that, and I'm with trade buyers who feel that if you have to pay more, you should get more flavor.

Kitchen Countertop Survivor™ Grade: Avg

Your notes:_____

_____

Price Ranges: **$** = $12 or less; **$$** = 12.01–20; **$$$** = 20.01–35; **$$$$** = > $35

Kitchen Countertop Survivor™ Grades: *Avg.* = a "one-day wine," tastes noticeably less fresh the next day; *B* = holds its freshness for 2–3 days after opening; *B+* = holds *and gets better* over 2–3 days after opening; *A* = a 3- to 4-day "freshness window"; *A+* = holds *and gets better* over 3–4 days

Columbia Crest Merlot   PC   T   V
Washington $ 21   22

"Great for the money," say both trade and consumer tasters of what I call a textbook Merlot: velvety texture, medium body, and subtle plum-berry fruit, layered with a bit of earth, all in balance. Yum!
Kitchen Countertop Survivor™ Grade: B
Your notes:_____

_____

Concha y Toro Frontera Merlot   PC   T   V
Chile $ 18   21

A no-nonsense, easy-drinking glass of red, with berry fruit flavors and "a price that's easy to swallow."
Kitchen Countertop Survivor™ Grade: Avg
Your notes:_____

_____

Corbett Canyon Merlot   PC   T   V
California $ 13   15

This is a soft, pleasant wine, with nice berry flavors, that is "great for sipping with friends, either over a light meal or just by itself."
Kitchen Countertop Survivor™ Grade: Avg
Your notes:_____

_____

Duckhorn Napa Merlot   PC   T   V
California $$$$ 26   21

I've been selling this "wine list must-have" since the early days of my restaurant career. Its full-throttle, lush fig and blackberry fruit, toasty oak, and ample tannins pretty much defined the category of serious California Merlot, and it remains a benchmark against which the others are judged. Along with its impressive consistency, collectors discovered that it ages nicely, launching demand for the wine, and thus its price leaped into the stratosphere.
Kitchen Countertop Survivor™ Grade: B+
Your notes:_____

_____

Ecco Domani Merlot   PC   T   V
Italy $ 15   16

Like other budget-priced Italian Merlots, this one has light, clean fruit flavor that's meant to complement and not overpower a wide range of foods. It does that nicely.

Kitchen Countertop Survivor™ Grade: Avg

Your notes:_____

Ernest & Julio Gallo Twin Valley | **PC** | **T** | **V**
Merlot, California | **$** | **16** | **17**

At this price, I don't expect the wine to scream Merlot character, but it delivers what I *do* expect: a simple, soft quaffing red wine.

Kitchen Countertop Survivor™ Grade: Avg

Your notes:_____

Fetzer Eagle Peak Merlot | **PC** | **T** | **V**
California | **$** | **18** | **19**

For the money this "well-known and well-made" Merlot is among the best basic California Merlots on the market. The soft texture, cherry berry flavors, and impressive survivor grade make it "a sure winner" offered by the glass or as your everyday "house" Merlot.

Kitchen Countertop Survivor™ Grade: B

Your notes:_____

Forest Glen Merlot | **PC** | **T** | **V**
California | **$$** | **17** | **18**

"Always a very safe bet," say fans of this soft, ripe, plummy Merlot that's become very popular. Sometimes so much name recognition leads to higher prices for less quality, but Forest Glen's have both held pretty steady.

Kitchen Countertop Survivor™ Grade: Avg

Your notes:_____

Price Ranges: **$** = $12 or less; **$$** = 12.01–20; **$$$** = 20.01–35; **$$$$** = > $35

Kitchen Countertop Survivor™ Grades: *Avg.* = a "one-day wine," tastes noticeably less fresh the next day; *B* = holds its freshness for 2–3 days after opening; *B+* = holds *and gets better* over 2–3 days after opening; *A* = a 3- to 4-day "freshness window"; *A+* = holds *and gets better* over 3–4 days

Franciscan Oakville Estate Merlot | PC | T | V
California | $$$ | 22 | 20

This winery consistently offers "great bang for your buck" in all its wines, and this one's no exception. You get quintessential Napa Merlot character here— lush cherry fruit, plush tannins, and just enough light, toasty oak to make it "formidable, without being too heavy." Look also for Franciscan's Chardonnays and excellent red Bordeaux-style blend, called Magnificat.

Kitchen Countertop Survivor™ Grade: B

Your notes:_____

Franzia Merlot | PC | T | V
California | $ | 12 | 13

"What you see is what you get": a simple, off-dry bag-in-a-box red, whose fruity style would be good in sangria.

Kitchen Countertop Survivor™ Grade: NA

Your notes:_____

Frei Brothers Reserve Merlot | PC | T | V
California | $$ | X | X

♥ Really top-rank Merlot character and complexity for under $20? I thought that was a relic of the past until I tried this wine. The plum-berry fruit is concentrated but subtle, the oak and tannins are beautifully integrated and plush, and the finish is long. Classy wine, real-world price.

Kitchen Countertop Survivor™ Grade: B

Your notes:_____

Frog's Leap Merlot | PC | T | V
California | $$$ | 23 | 21

Though it's expensive, devotees find the big, beautiful flavor of this Merlot "worth every penny." I give it extra points for balance—though the fruit is intense, the oak and alcohol are not.

Kitchen Countertop Survivor™ Grade: A

Your notes:_____

Gallo of Sonoma Merlot   PC   T   V
California $ 20   21

No, it's not a technical term, but "Wow!" is how pro buyers laud the "amazing quality-to-price ratio" of this wine. The succulent ripe plum fruit flavor and satiny-smooth texture are exemplary. To my taste, it is the best Merlot on the market at this price point, and exceeds the quality and pleasure quotient of many higher-priced Merlots.

Kitchen Countertop Survivor™ Grade: A

Your notes:_____

_____

Glen Ellen Proprietor's Reserve   PC   T   V
Merlot, California $ 14   14

The use of the word *reserve* in the name is misleading, because it suggests a special quality status for the wine. In reality, the "nice fruit" makes this a "decent everyday red."

Kitchen Countertop Survivor™ Grade: B

Your notes:_____

_____

Gossamer Bay Merlot   PC   T   V
California $ 11   12

Like so many California Merlots at this price point, it's soft, simple, and fruity.

Kitchen Countertop Survivor™ Grade: Avg

Your notes:_____

_____

Kendall-Jackson Vintner's Reserve   PC   T   V
Merlot, California $$ 20   19

Pros and consumers alike say this Merlot is a "great wine for the price." I feel that's true for all the varietals in K-J's Vintner's Reserve line. Their secret? Great vineyard sources that yield extremely high-quality

Price Ranges: **$** = $12 or less; **$$** = 12.01–20; **$$$** = 20.01–35; **$$$$** = > $35

Kitchen Countertop Survivor™ Grades: ***Avg.*** = a "one-day wine," tastes noticeably less fresh the next day; ***B*** = holds its freshness for 2–3 days after opening; ***B+*** = holds *and gets better* over 2–3 days after opening; ***A*** = a 3- to 4-day "freshness window"; ***A+*** = holds *and gets better* over 3–4 days

grapes, whose flavor intensity makes it into the bottle. This is Merlot in the luscious style—redolent with black cherry flavor.

Kitchen Countertop Survivor™ Grade: B+

Your notes:_____

_____

Lindemans Bin 40 Merlot	PC	T	V
Australia	$	20	21

Pros laud the "great quality and "tremendous value" of this wine as "a good by-the-case buy." Indeed the plump plum and berry fruit flavor *really* dusts many of the California Merlots at the same price.

Kitchen Countertop Survivor™ Grade: Avg

Your notes:_____

_____

Markham Merlot	PC	T	V
California	$$$	X	X

✗ This wine-list stalwart was a Merlot category leader well before the category took off. Demand has pushed the price up a little, but the quality remains so consistent and high that it's still a value compared to other California Merlots. The rich plum fruit and silky texture say "serious Merlot," something for which you usually expect to pay a lot more.

Kitchen Countertop Survivor™ Grade: B+

Your notes:_____

_____

Meridian Merlot	PC	T	V
California	$	18	19

Consumers credit Meridian with "some of the best-value," "most reliable" wines on the market, and its Merlot is no exception. The plump flavor reminds me of black cherry Jell-O, balanced with a nice tang of vibrant acidity.

Kitchen Countertop Survivor™ Grade: B+

Your notes:_____

_____

Montes Merlot	PC	T	V
Chile	$	20	22

Montes remains a standard-bearer among Chilean Merlots: concentrated dark-berry flavors and cedar

and earth scents—all on an elegant frame. For this price the complexity and quality are a triumph.
Kitchen Countertop Survivor™ Grade: B
Your notes:_____

Mouton-Cadet Bordeaux	PC	T	V
France	$	17	16

Reviews are mixed on this "light," basic Bordeaux that pros say can be "soft and elegant when it's on, but thin tasting and one-dimensional when it's off." I suspect, however, that there may be some label snobbery at work here, as we used to serve it with the label hidden to our Windows on the World wine students—to generally positive responses. Look also for the Mouton-Cadet Reserve, which has a lot more flavor and complexity for just a little more money.
Kitchen Countertop Survivor™ Grade: Avg
Your notes:_____

Nathanson Creek Merlot	PC	T	V
California	$	14	14

While it used to be one of the best California value brands, Nathanson Creek has slipped a bit in my opinion. Still, this Merlot is a "no bells and whistles" kind of wine, with some "redeeming red-berry fruit."
Kitchen Countertop Survivor™ Grade: Avg
Your notes:_____

Pine Ridge Crimson Creek Merlot	PC	T	V
California	$$$$	23	19

Here's a "fuller-bodied Merlot for the Cabernet lover," says a savvy retailer, and I agree it's intense and concentrated. But it's also beautifully balanced, having resisted the trend toward too much oak and alcohol that plagues many California Merlots. The deep blackberry fruit, subtle earthiness, and long

Price Ranges: **$** = $12 or less; **$$** = 12.01–20; **$$$** = 20.01–35; **$$$$** = > $35
Kitchen Countertop Survivor™ Grades: ***Avg.*** = a "one-day wine," tastes noticeably less fresh the next day; ***B*** = holds its freshness for 2–3 days after opening; ***B+*** = holds *and gets better* over 2–3 days after opening; ***A*** = a 3- to 4-day "freshness window"; ***A+*** = holds *and gets better* over 3–4 days

finish combine in a really classy package. Look for Pine Ridge's delicious white wines, too—Chardonnay and Chenin Blanc.

Kitchen Countertop Survivor™ Grade: B+

Your notes:_____

Ravenswood Vintners Blend Merlot | **PC** | **T** | **V**
California	**$$**	**21**	**21**

As my pro tasters put it very plainly, "Ravenswood never disappoints." For that reason it's been a mainstay brand on every wine list I have ever written. This Merlot, layered with plum and cherry fruit and "a touch of vanilla-scented oak," is "a fabulous wine" at a great price.

Kitchen Countertop Survivor™ Grade: B+

Your notes:_____

Robert Mondavi Coastal Merlot | **PC** | **T** | **V**
California	**$$**	**18**	**18**

Although Merlot is one of the strongest varietals in the Robert Mondavi Coastal line, I have found some bottle-to-bottle quality variation, which is disturbing, since so many restaurants offer this wine by the glass. When it's "on form," there's nice plum fruit and silky tannin.

Kitchen Countertop Survivor™ Grade: Avg

Your notes:_____

Rodney Strong Merlot | **PC** | **T** | **V**
California	**$$**	**22**	**21**

This is Merlot in the intense style, with strong alcohol and very prominent scents of coconut and butter coming from aging in American oak. To my taste the oak overshadows the fruit a bit. Then again, a big steak might tame it nicely.

Kitchen Countertop Survivor™ Grade: Avg

Your notes:_____

Shafer Merlot | **PC** | **T** | **V**
California	**$$$$**	**26**	**21**

✓ I remember longingly the days when I served this wine as a superpremium by-the-glass offering ($18 per glass—in case you were wondering!) at Windows on the World. Now tight supplies and higher prices mean this Merlot is rarely encountered outside the finest restaurants. If the occasion dictates a splurge, you will love this rich, classy wine that compares in quality and style to top French Bordeaux, but in the lush, powerful California style.

Kitchen Countertop Survivor™ Grade: B+

Your notes:_____

| St. Francis Sonoma Merlot | PC | T | V |
| California | $$$ | 23 | 23 |

When Merlot boomed in the 1990s, quite a few wineries raised prices drastically, and/or compromised on quality, in the rush to cash in on the new demand. Not St. Francis. Yes, the price has gone up some, but this wine remains a relative value in the category of ultrapremium Merlot. And the style is distinctly St. Francis—velvety texture, berry compote and fig flavors, clove, coconut, and eucalyptus scents, and a long finish.

Kitchen Countertop Survivor™ Grade: B

Your notes:_____

| Stag's Leap Wine Cellars Napa | PC | T | V |
| Merlot, California | $$$$ | 25 | 21 |

The classic Napa style, "great structure" and "depth" make this one of the best-selling California Merlots on restaurant lists. To me the hallmark of this wine is complexity—earth, mocha, and mint in the scent; cassis and licorice flavors, and great balance. It has also proven to be age-worthy.

Kitchen Countertop Survivor™ Grade: B

Your notes:_____

Price Ranges: **$** = $12 or less; **$$** = 12.01–20; **$$$** = 20.01–35; **$$$$** => $35

Kitchen Countertop Survivor™ Grades: *Avg.* = a "one-day wine," tastes noticeably less fresh the next day; *B* = holds its freshness for 2–3 days after opening; *B+* = holds *and gets better* over 2–3 days after opening; *A* = a 3- to 4-day "freshness window"; *A+* = holds *and gets better* over 3–4 days

Sterling Vineyards Napa Merlot	PC	T	V
California	$$$	23	21

As the first California winery to release a vintage-dated Merlot, Sterling was ahead of its time in launching the category. After a lull in quality, Sterling is back with Merlot to match the pedigree of this venerable Napa Valley name—medium-bodied, with jammy berry fruit and good balance.

Kitchen Countertop Survivor™ Grade: B

Your notes:_____

_____

Sutter Home Merlot	PC	T	V
California	$	15	16

In the "friendly crowd-pleaser" category, the Sutter Home wines always impress me because they're well made. The soft, clean fruit flavor makes this a good everyday Merlot for the money.

Kitchen Countertop Survivor™ Grade: Avg

Your notes:_____

_____

Talus Merlot	PC	T	V
California	$$	15	16

Mixed reviews here, with some tasters calling it "great for the price" but others quite underwhelmed by the taste. In my opinion it's not a standout in this crowded price category.

Kitchen Countertop Survivor™ Grade: Avg

Your notes:_____

_____

Turning Leaf Merlot	PC	T	V
California	$	13	15

Pros want more from this Merlot "made under the Gallo umbrella," given their reputation as leaders in the value-for-money category. But consumers do credit the "drinkability at a great price" offered by this wine, which is soft and smooth. The Coastal Reserve bottling, for not much more money, has a lot more flavor.

Kitchen Countertop Survivor™ Grade: Avg

Your notes:_____

_____

| **Vendange Merlot** | PC | T | V |
| California | $ | 10 | 11 |

Consumers say this Merlot is a "crowd pleaser for big parties." Although I used to count Vendange as a core value brand for large-scale by-the-glass programs on my wine lists, I think other brands now top it in flavor per dollar.

Kitchen Countertop Survivor™ Grade: Avg

Your notes:_____

_____

| **Walnut Crest Merlot** | PC | T | V |
| Chile | $ | 17 | 20 |

After launching as an amazing winner for the price (under $5 at the time!), this Merlot stumbled on the quality front. Now it's back on my value-for-the-money radar screen, with "easy-drinking, supple" plum fruit and a hint of the savory spice and tobacco in the scent that I consider to be a hallmark of Chilean reds.

Kitchen Countertop Survivor™ Grade: Avg

Your notes:_____

_____

| **Woodbridge (Robert Mondavi)** | PC | T | V |
| Merlot, California | $ | 15 | 16 |

Trade buyers call this Merlot "flavor-shy," saying it "has basic berry fruit" but "doesn't make a memorable impression." Still, the Mondavi name and the price "make guests happy."

Kitchen Countertop Survivor™ Grade: Avg

Your notes:_____

_____

Price Ranges: **$** = $12 or less; **$$** = 12.01–20; **$$$** = 20.01–35; **$$$$** = > $35

Kitchen Countertop Survivor™ Grades: **Avg.** = a "one-day wine," tastes noticeably less fresh the next day; **B** = holds its freshness for 2–3 days after opening; **B+** = holds *and gets better* over 2–3 days after opening; **A** = a 3- to 4-day "freshness window"; **A+** = holds *and gets better* over 3–4 days

Cabernet Sauvignon and Blends

Grape Profile: Merlot may have been the *mucho*-trendy red of the late 1990s, but Cabernet Sauvignon remains by far the top-selling red varietal wine, I think for good reason. Specifically, Cabernet (for short) grows well virtually all over the wine world and gives excellent quality and flavor at every price level, from steal to splurge. Its flavor intensity and body can vary, based on the wine's quality level—from uncomplicated everyday styles to the superintense boutique and collector bottlings. Nearly every major wine-growing country produces Cabernets across that spectrum, but the most famous and plentiful sources are Bordeaux in France, California (especially Sonoma and Napa), Washington state, and Italy on the high end with its Super Tuscan versions. I think Chile rules the value category, with a high proportion of its budget bottlings still offering true Cabernet character. Classically, that means a scent and taste of dark berries (blueberry, blackberry), plus notes of spice, earth, cocoa, cedar, and even mint that can be very layered and complex in the best wines. It also means medium to very full body and often more tannin—that bit of a tongue-gripping sensation that one of my waiters once described, perfectly I think, as "a slip-cover for the tongue, ranging from terry cloth to suede to velvet," depending on the wine in question. Oakiness, either a little or a lot, depending on the growing region and price, is also a common Cabernet feature. Combined, these can make for a primo mouthful of a wine, which surely explains why Cabernet rules the red wine world.

A note about "blends": As described previously for Merlot, Cabernet Sauvignon wines follow the Bordeaux blending model, with one or more of the traditional Bordeaux red grapes—Merlot, Cabernet Franc, Petit Verdot, and Malbec—blended in for balance and complexity. Australia pioneered blending Cabernet Sauvignon with Shiraz—a delicious combination that the wine buying market has embraced. Those blends are listed either here or in the Shiraz section, according to which of the two grapes is dominant in the blend (it will be listed first on the label, too).

Serve: Cool room temperature; the fuller-bodied styles benefit from aeration—pour into the glass a bit ahead of time or decant into a carafe (but if you forget, don't sweat it; if you care to, swirling the glass does help).

When: With your favorite red wine meals, but the everyday bottlings are soft enough for cocktail-hour sipping.

With: Anything you'd serve alongside a red; especially complements beef, lamb, goat cheese, and hard cheeses, pesto sauce, and dishes scented with basil, rosemary, sage, or oregano.

In: An all-purpose wineglass or larger-bowled red wine stem.

	PC	T	V
Barton & Guestier (B&G) Cabernet Sauvignon, France	$	16	17

This surprisingly nice French Cabernet has decent backbone and nice cherry and spice aromas; it "tastes peppery" and has a "pretty nice" finish. It's also a survivor that you can enjoy the next day with cheese or a BLT . . . or whatever's handy.
Kitchen Countertop Survivor™ Grade: Avg
Your notes:_____

	PC	T	V
Beaulieu Vineyard (BV) Coastal Cabernet Sauvignon, California	$	18	20

Retail buyers especially cite this wine as a "terrific value and huge seller." I am always impressed when the varietal character comes through—even at these bargain prices—as it does here with ripe blackberry fruit, a "lovely anise scent," and nice structure—but not too much tannin.
Kitchen Countertop Survivor™ Grade: B+
Your notes:_____

Price Ranges: **$** = $12 or less; **$$** = 12.01–20; **$$$** = 20.01–35; **$$$$** = > $35
Kitchen Countertop Survivor™ Grades: ***Avg.*** = a "one-day wine," tastes noticeably less fresh the next day; ***B*** = holds its freshness for 2–3 days after opening; ***B+*** = holds *and gets better* over 2–3 days after opening; ***A*** = a 3- to 4-day "freshness window"; ***A+*** = holds *and gets better* over 3–4 days

Beaulieu Vineyard (BV) Rutherford	PC	T	V
Cabernet Sauvignon, California	$$$	22	22

In the early days of my wine career, this was my go-to bottle for guests who wanted to see what classic California Cabernet (then just emerging) was about—without spending a fortune. Prices across the category have risen precipitously since then, but this wine still offers ripe, jammy Cabernet at a relative value. A great vine grower in California once described to me the character of "Rutherford dust" (Rutherford is a tiny Napa Valley town cloaked in Cabernet vineyards), which supposedly comes through in the scent of her Cabernets, saying: "jammy cherry, mint, cedar, and wet dirt." This wine definitely earns the name.

Kitchen Countertop Survivor™ Grade: A

Your notes:_____

Beringer Founders' Estate	PC	T	V
Cabernet Sauvignon, California	$	21	21

The first vintages of this wine disappointed me, but no more. Now it's among the top players in the value game, with real Cabernet character—blackberry fruit, cedar scent—acknowledged by a most intriguing array of tasters, from trade to consumer novice to collector. Everyone respects a value.

Kitchen Countertop Survivor™ Grade: A

Your notes:_____

Beringer Knights Valley Cabernet	PC	T	V
Sauvignon, California	$$$	24	22

Although the price of this California classic has risen with the rest of the market, pros note that you're paying for "consistent quality," "year after year," that's relatively reasonable when compared to the cult Cabernets with monster alcohol and oak and little if any track record. In this wine the cedar and mint scent with dense, chewy cassis fruit cloaks an elegant but powerful frame, with vanilla-scented oak and alcohol in balance.

Kitchen Countertop Survivor™ Grade: B+

Your notes:_____

Black Opal Cabernet Sauvignon	PC	T	V
Australia	$	19	19

It's "not rocket science" to see "why people like this wine," say pros who describe it as a "straightforward" Cabernet with "nice, juicy fruit flavor" and "a great price tag." As the survivor grade indicates, it holds up, making it a good "house" wine for every day.

Kitchen Countertop Survivor™ Grade: B

Your notes:_____

_____

Black Opal Cabernet/Merlot	PC	T	V
Australia	$	20	21

We give California, Chile, and Washington credit for the best values in these varietals, but the blends from Australia such as this "best buy" can match them all. The "bold fruit" that "goes with anything," according to both trade and consumers, make it the perfect everyday wine. The "pretty berry" flavors and staying power of the leftovers do, too.

Kitchen Countertop Survivor™ Grade: B

Your notes:_____

_____

Cain Cuvée Bordeaux Style Red	PC	T	V
California	$$$	24	21

Easier to find and much easier on the wallet than the luxury Bordeaux-style Cain Five red. I agree with pro and consumer buyers who noted that this wine is "so much better" than many other, "higher-priced California blends" featuring the Bordeaux red grapes. Expect beautiful cassis fruit and cedar-oak aromas and flavors and a long, complex finish.

Kitchen Countertop Survivor™ Grade: A

Your notes:_____

_____

Price Ranges: **$** = $12 or less; **$$** = 12.01–20; **$$$** = 20.01–35; **$$$$** = > $35

Kitchen Countertop Survivor™ Grades: ***Avg.*** = a "one-day wine," tastes noticeably less fresh the next day; ***B*** = holds its freshness for 2–3 days after opening; ***B+*** = holds *and gets better* over 2–3 days after opening; ***A*** = a 3- to 4-day "freshness window"; ***A+*** = holds *and gets better* over 3–4 days

Cakebread Napa Cabernet	PC	T	V
Sauvignon, California	$$$$	25	20

All the superpremium California wines in this book drew complaints about their high prices, and this excellent Cabernet is no exception. It's definitely joined the pricey ranks that most buyers, regardless of income, term "special-occasion wine." With its gorgeous and classic blackberry fruit, soft, spicy-vanilla oak, long finish, and aging power, the wine certainly delivers on that term. I just wish normal people could experience "special" in a wine context more often. The Reserve Cab is great, too.

Kitchen Countertop Survivor™ Grade: A+

Your notes:_____

_____

Caliterra Cabernet Sauvignon	PC	T	V
Chile	$	18	20

Thank God for Chile! Here's a Cabernet with character that's "good and cheap," as my tasters commented. I agree it doesn't get much better than this at this price, with its ripe berry fruit flavors and pleasant tannins. It's a great "party wine."

Kitchen Countertop Survivor™ Grade: B+

Your notes:_____

_____

Canyon Road Cabernet Sauvignon	PC	T	V
California	$	X	X

✗ This is the second label for Geyser Peak, whose wines also rate high with buyers. They lauded the "real Cabernet character"—blackberry fruit and cedar-chocolate scent—"for a great price." It was those virtues that first prompted me to use this wine for the lists at luxury hotels I bought for. Although it is not at all heavy, it has a plush richness that immediately conveys "this is the good stuff," even though it's not the expensive stuff.

Kitchen Countertop Survivor™ Grade: B

Your notes:_____

_____

Carmenet Dynamite Cabernet	PC	T	V
Sauvignon, California	$$$	23	22

Both trade and consumers love this "consistently great" Cab. I agree: the classic California Cabernet

character—cassis fruit, cedar, spice and vanilla scents—make it one of the best in its price range.
Kitchen Countertop Survivor™ Grade: A+
Your notes:_____

_____

Casa Lapostolle Classic Cabernet	PC	T	V
Sauvignon, Chile	$	20	22

Pros say Casa Lapostolle "makes an extraordinary wine," some finding it "the best wine in their line." In fact, all the varietals got great feedback from my tasters. As Chilean Cabernets go, this one stands out for its ripe red fruit, rich texture, and overall elegance.
Kitchen Countertop Survivor™ Grade: B
Your notes:_____

_____

Casa Lapostolle Cuvée Alexandre	PC	T	V
Cabernet Sauvignon, Chile	$$	X	X

♥ It's not that no one drinks this wine, but I think not enough buyers are aware this is a world-class wine with decent availability at a fair price (which actually makes it a rarity!). Insiders know it's one of the few Cabernets on the market that has classic structure and flavors, modeled very much on French red Bordeaux, juxtaposed with Southern Hemisphere fruit vibrancy. The cedar, vanilla, cinnamon, dark, dusky fruit, and earth scents all seem Old World. But on the palate, the richness and immediacy of the fruit are very modern. Together, they are stunning.
Kitchen Countertop Survivor™ Grade: A
Your notes:_____

_____

Château Gloria Bordeaux	PC	T	V
France	$$$$	23	22

This is a Bordeaux classic, blending Cabernet and Merlot primarily into a smooth, subtle expression of

Price Ranges: **$** = $12 or less; **$$** = 12.01–20; **$$$** = 20.01–35; **$$$$** = > $35
Kitchen Countertop Survivor™ Grades: *Avg.* = a "one-day wine," tastes noticeably less fresh the next day; *B* = holds its freshness for 2–3 days after opening; *B+* = holds *and gets better* over 2–3 days after opening; *A* = a 3- to 4-day "freshness window"; *A+* = holds *and gets better* over 3–4 days

what Bordeaux does best—black currant fruit, touched with cedar, coffee, and mocha scents. It benefits a lot from aeration, so plan to decant.

Kitchen Countertop Survivor™ Grade: B+

Your notes:_____

_____

Château Greysac Bordeaux	PC	T	V
France	$$	22	22

Even serious collectors and elite sommeliers rate this a terrific value that gives people a chance to experience Bordeaux without having to go broke. In my experience the classic cedar spice scent and powerful but elegant plum fruit have fooled many an expert in blind tastings into thinking it was one of the top châteaus.

Kitchen Countertop Survivor™ Grade: B

Your notes:_____

_____

Château Gruaud-Larose (*GROO-oh*	PC	T	V
***lah-ROSE*) Bordeaux, France**	$$$$	25	22

Many tasters—me among them—"remember it when it was cheap." Still, it's more affordable than many Bordeaux of comparable quality, as it's both classy and classic: deeply concentrated and powerful, with palate-coating tannins. The dark fruit, cedar, and toasty coffee scents and long finish, are the style model for Cabernet-based wine worldwide.

Kitchen Countertop Survivor™ Grade: A

Your notes:_____

_____

Château Larose-Trintaudon	PC	T	V
(*la-ROSE TRENT-oh-DOAN*)	$$	22	23
Bordeaux, France			

This wine combines classic Bordeaux characteristics and real-world virtues. The rich, round tannins and mouthwatering fruit are true to the region, but the drink-it-young suppleness and affordable price keep it accessible.

Kitchen Countertop Survivor™ Grade: A+

Your notes:_____

_____

Chât. Ste. Michelle Columbia Valley   **PC**   **T**   **V**
Cabernet Sauvignon, Washington   **$$**   **22**   **22**

I think this Cabernet is one of the best coming from Washington—especially for the price—with intense black cherry aromas, concentrated blackberry flavors, and a toasty-oak finish. It's big but not heavy-handed.

Kitchen Countertop Survivor™ Grade: A

Your notes:_____

Clos du Bois Sonoma Cabernet   **PC**   **T**   **V**
Sauvignon, California   **$$**   **22**   **21**

With this wine (and the Chardonnay and Pinot Noir in this book), Clos du Bois proves it's one of California's blue chip wineries. Having survived the 1990s boutique—and "badge"—wine movement, it has emerged as an overall quality-for-the-price leader. This soft but solid Cabernet is textbook "Sonoma," with that distinctive wild berry, anise, and eucalyptus character. With the price having risen slightly in the last few years, trade buyers recommend, "buy on sale." But even at the regular price, I think it delivers.

Kitchen Countertop Survivor™ Grade: B+

Your notes:_____

Columbia Crest Cabernet Sauvignon   **PC**   **T**   **V**
Washington   **$**   **20**   **21**

This terrific wine is "just consistently good," say pros, who recommend Columbia Crest as "a go-to winery in general" for solid quality; fans say it's fruity and complex; and "the price can't be beat." I like it because with one taste you know where you are, Washington state, where Cabernets are always concentrated yet still elegant.

Kitchen Countertop Survivor™ Grade: B+

Your notes:_____

Price Ranges: **$** = $12 or less; **$$** = 12.01–20; **$$$** = 20.01–35; **$$$$** = > $35

Kitchen Countertop Survivor™ Grades: *Avg.* = a "one-day wine," tastes noticeably less fresh the next day; *B* = holds its freshness for 2–3 days after opening; *B+* = holds *and gets better* over 2–3 days after opening; *A* = a 3- to 4-day "freshness window"; *A+* = holds *and gets better* over 3–4 days

Concha y Toro Sunrise Cabernet	PC	T	V
Sauvignon/Merlot, Chile	$	18	20

For "the budget-minded host," this wine will do you proud. It's light-bodied and soft, but still tastes like the grapes used to make it—plummy and succulent. It even has that tinge of earthiness in the scent that says "Chile" to me.

Kitchen Countertop Survivor™ Grade: Avg

Your notes:_____

_____

Corbett Canyon Cabernet	PC	T	V
Sauvignon, California	$	11	12

Corbett Canyon's Sauvignon Blanc fared better with my tasters than this Cabernet, which they found to be "lightweight" and "simple." Not a top performer in the price range.

Kitchen Countertop Survivor™ Grade: Avg

Your notes:_____

_____

Ernest & Julio Gallo Twin Valley	PC	T	V
Cabernet Sauvignon, California	$	15	16

This simple, one-dimensional, fruity Cabernet is "priced right for experimentation," according to tasters, but since there are better Cabernets at the same price point, why not experiment with one of those?

Kitchen Countertop Survivor™ Grade: Avg

Your notes:_____

_____

Escudo Rojo Cabernet Blend,	PC	T	V
Baron Philippe de Rothschild, Chile	$$	X	X

♥ "Wow. What *is* that?" Everyone to whom I've ever introduced this as "a new wine from Chile" has responded in like fashion. Undoubtedly they weren't expecting such detailed complexity from a Chilean wine. Especially at this price, it would surprise any- one—meaty-smokiness, dried spices, leather, coffee, figs, mint . . . But all this exoticism is borne on an elegant, balanced frame, making it a completely intriguing and delicious match for food, especially rustic cheeses.

Kitchen Countertop Survivor™ Grade: A

Your notes:_____

_____

Estancia Cabernet Sauvignon | PC | T | V
California | **$$** | 21 | 22

Make this wine your "house wine" (and we'll all be right over), implore my tasters, saying it has "great taste" and a "good price." Pros agree, saying it's "a good 'any night' Cabernet" that's "chewy and chocolaty." I concur: it certainly delivers at its price point.

Kitchen Countertop Survivor™ Grade: B+

Your notes:_____

_____

Far Niente Cabernet Sauvignon | PC | T | V
California | **$$$$** | X | X

✗ As the write-in voters pointed out, Far Niente "isn't produced in enough quantity to be included" among the nation's top-selling Cabernets. But it does have a great track record for quality and ageability and an amazing following on top restaurant wine lists. For California Cabernet lovers who like the classic, classy Napa style—big fruit and body without the overwhelming oak and alcohol that became trendy in the 1990s, this is a home-run choice. Look for their excellent Chardonnay as well.

Kitchen Countertop Survivor™ Grade: A

Your notes:_____

_____

Fetzer Valley Oaks Cabernet | PC | T | V
Sauvignon, California | **$** | 17 | 20

Pros think that Fetzer offers exactly what a "bargain"-priced Cab should: "generous fruit" and "mild, food-friendly tannins."

Kitchen Countertop Survivor™ Grade: B

Your notes:_____

_____

Price Ranges: **$** = $12 or less; **$$** = 12.01–20; **$$$** = 20.01–35; **$$$$** => $35
Kitchen Countertop Survivor™ Grades: *Avg.* = a "one-day wine," tastes noticeably less fresh the next day; *B* = holds its freshness for 2–3 days after opening; *B+* = holds *and gets better* over 2–3 days after opening; *A* = a 3- to 4-day "freshness window"; *A+* = holds *and gets better* over 3–4 days

Forest Glen Barrel Select Cabernet	PC	T	V
Sauvignon, California	$	17	18

Trade are mixed on this one. Some say it's a "no brainer" that "hits all the buttons." Others say the fruit and flavors are "just OK," even at this price. I say it's not bad, but you can do better for the same money.
Kitchen Countertop Survivor™ Grade: Avg.

Your notes:_____

_____

Franciscan Napa Cabernet	PC	T	V
Sauvignon, California	$$	23	22

Trade buyers point out that this wine "tastes like real Napa Cabernet at a great price," and I agree. It's got a whiff of mintiness, dark cassis fruit, a balanced oak profile of sweet vanilla and spice and velvety tannins— all classic hallmarks of the Napa Cabernet style. Its year-in and year-out consistency is impressive, too.
Kitchen Countertop Survivor™ Grade: B

Your notes:_____

_____

Gallo of Sonoma Cabernet	PC	T	V
Sauvignon, California	$	21	22

No wine in the book inspired more trade comments than this one. And I quote: ". . . a beauty, I drink it often," ". . . most underrated wine on the list," and ". . . you have to wonder if Gallo has a committee that decides what the American public wants, then produces it flawlessly and at a great price too." Yet pros say it's a "tough sell" because of the Gallo name. Clearly, based on this wine and the others in the line, all of which rank high with tasters, the public needs to get over it. I hope you enjoy drinking better and spending less.
Kitchen Countertop Survivor™ Grade: B+

Your notes:_____

_____

Glen Ellen Proprietor's Reserve	PC	T	V
Cabernet Sauvignon, California	$	14	14

A good wine for new red wine drinkers, because its fruity, almost-sweet, entry-level taste won't offend. And neither will the price.
Kitchen Countertop Survivor™ Grade: Avg

Your notes:_____

_____

Gossamer Bay Cabernet Sauvignon | **PC** | **T** | **V**
California | **$** | **12** | **13**

With little varietal character, this wine is over-shadowed by others in this price range for both taste and value.

Kitchen Countertop Survivor™ Grade: Avg

Your notes:_____

_____

Greg Norman Cabernet/Merlot | **PC** | **T** | **V**
Australia | **$$** | **X** | **X**

♥ No, Greg hasn't traded in his clubs for wine-glasses, but he is the man, along with one of Australia's most prestigious wineries, behind this brand. This Cabernet/Merlot blend is plump, concentrated, and silky, with mint, dark berry, and chocolate notes. The entire line of wines, including Shiraz and Chardonnay, is good stuff.

Kitchen Countertop Survivor™ Grade: Avg

Your notes:_____

_____

Groth Napa Cabernet Sauvignon | **PC** | **T** | **V**
California | **$$$$** | **24** | **21**

Although some call it pricey, I think this wine remains fairly reasonable within the category of luxury Cabernets. And with its plush tannins and deep cassis fruit, elegantly framed with vanilla oak, it's a benchmark Napa Valley Cabernet. Although this wine definitely will improve with age, it's also nicely drinkable in youth.

Kitchen Countertop Survivor™ Grade: B+

Your notes:_____

_____

Price Ranges: **$** = $12 or less; **$$** = 12.01–20; **$$$** = 20.01–35; **$$$$** = > $35

Kitchen Countertop Survivor™ Grades: *Avg.* = a "one-day wine," tastes noticeably less fresh the next day; *B* = holds its freshness for 2–3 days after opening; *B+* = holds *and gets better* over 2–3 days after opening; *A* = a 3- to 4-day "freshness window"; *A+* = holds *and gets better* over 3–4 days

Guenoc Cabernet Sauvignon   PC   T   V
California $$ 22   21

This is real California Cabernet flavor, yet silky
smooth in texture—a rare breed, indeed. The high
quality for the money is also a rarity, making this easy
to enjoy with any food or no food—and often.
Kitchen Countertop Survivor™ Grade: B
Your notes:_____

_____

Heitz Napa Cabernet Sauvignon   PC   T   V
California $$$$ 24   19

Both pros and consumers alike give Heitz top marks.
Even this Napa bottling has some of the "fabulous
earthy-minty qualities" for which its famous Martha's
Vineyard is widely coveted by collectors. The firm-
but-integrated tannins and powerful elegance of the
dark fruit are, to most tasters, worth every juicy cent.
Kitchen Countertop Survivor™ Grade: B+
Your notes:_____

_____

Heritage Cabernet Sauvignon   PC   T   V
California $ 14   15

The simple red wine flavor "could really be anything,"
say pros. Not a bad wine, but there are better Caber-
nets at this price.
Kitchen Countertop Survivor™ Grade: Avg.
Your notes:_____

_____

Hess Select Cabernet Sauvignon   PC   T   V
California $$ 23   21

Although the good-quality competition at this price
point is growing, most tasters still rate this an all-
around good drinking Cabernet. To me the plum
and blackberry flavors and touch of earthy spiciness
definitely make it a leader among its peers.
Kitchen Countertop Survivor™ Grade: B
Your notes:_____

_____

Inglenook Cabernet Sauvignon   PC   T   V
California $ 15   15

Inglenook is a jug producer that joined the varietal
market to keep up with consumers' increasing wine

sophistication. Unfortunately this light Cabernet is not sufficiently better than its generic jug wine.

Kitchen Countertop Survivor™ Grade: Avg

Your notes:_____

_____

J. Lohr 7 Oaks Cabernet Sauvignon	**PC**	**T**	**V**
California	**$$**	**22**	**22**

This is one of my favorite California Cabernets at any price, so its affordability is, to me, a major bonus. The style—powerful, exotic berry fruit and luxurious coconut cream scent from American oak—is incredibly consistent from year to year.

Kitchen Countertop Survivor™ Grade: B+

Your notes:_____

_____

Jacob's Creek Cabernet Sauvignon	**PC**	**T**	**V**
Australia	**$**	**21**	**22**

Nice minty-berry varietal character, soft tannin, great price. Hard to go wrong with this one.

Kitchen Countertop Survivor™ Grade: B

Your notes:_____

_____

Jordan Cabernet Sauvignon	**PC**	**T**	**V**
California	**$$$$**	**24**	**20**

This wine sparked great debate among pro respondents, with some calling it "elegant," "very reliable," and "worth the money." Others are decidedly underwhelmed. I think this: the elegant, cedar-scented, silky style is out of fashion, as tastes have turned to huge "fruit and oak bomb" styles. Still, Jordan is delicious to drink and ages quite well, too, so it's really a matter of what style you prefer. Personally, I love it.

Kitchen Countertop Survivor™ Grade: B+

Your notes:_____

_____

Price Ranges: **$** = $12 or less; **$$** = 12.01–20; **$$$** = 20.01–35; **$$$$** = > $35

Kitchen Countertop Survivor™ Grades: *Avg.* = a "one-day wine," tastes noticeably less fresh the next day; *B* = holds its freshness for 2–3 days after opening; *B+* = holds *and gets better* over 2–3 days after opening; *A* = a 3- to 4-day "freshness window"; *A+* = holds *and gets better* over 3–4 days

Joseph Phelps Napa Cabernet   PC   T   V
Sauvignon, California   **$$$$**   **25**   **22**

✓ I agree with pros who enthuse, "It tastes like real Napa Cabernet." Although not cheap, the price is doable and fair for what you get: great structure, mint, cedar, coffee-spice scents, and classic Cabernet fruit flavors.

Kitchen Countertop Survivor™ Grade: B

Your notes:_____

_____

Kendall-Jackson Vintner's Reserve   PC   T   V
Cabernet Sauvignon, California   **$$**   **21**   **19**

As one pro aptly put it, "The trend is to turn your nose up at Kendall-Jackson, but I like this Cabernet." So do I. It's hard to find real varietal character—blackberry flavor, a touch of earth, and a tug of tannin—for this price. I use it to introduce novice tasters to what Cabernet is like.

Kitchen Countertop Survivor™ Grade: B

Your notes:_____

_____

Kenwood Cabernet Sauvignon   PC   T   V
California   **$$**   **22**   **21**

After a few years of finding that the fruit tasted a bit dried out, I think Kenwood is back to solid form. It's a good example of the Sonoma Cabernet style, which emphasizes wild berry fruit with a touch of Asian spice and smooth tannin.

Kitchen Countertop Survivor™ Grade: Avg.

Your notes:_____

_____

Los Vascos Cabernet Sauvignon   PC   T   V
Chile   **$**   **19**   **21**

Definitely a great value every year and one of Chile's most elegant, classically styled Cabernets. It's got dark cherry fruit and a cedary scent, with smooth but structured tannins.

Kitchen Countertop Survivor™ Grade: B

Your notes:_____

_____

Meridian Cabernet Sauvignon	PC	T	V
California	$	19	19

This juicy wine is "consistent" and "always a great value," say my tasters. I say the in-your-face style has appealing aromas of black cherry and fruitcake and a soft texture.

Kitchen Countertop Survivor™ Grade: B

Your notes:_____

_____

Mt. Veeder Napa Cabernet	PC	T	V
Sauvignon, California	$$$	25	19

The Mt. Veeder district (a sub-appellation of Napa Valley) is known for a very distinctive style: big, mouth-filling structure, with gripping tannins and dense figlike fruit. The winemaking for Mt. Veeder seems to get better every year, and the wine offers great ageability. If you plan to drink it young, decant and invite a big steak or a fine cheese to the table.

Kitchen Countertop Survivor™ Grade: A

Your notes:_____

_____

Mystic Cliffs Cabernet Sauvignon	PC	T	V
California	$	10	11

There is no reason that a California Cabernet should be this shy on fruit. You can find Cabernet flavor at this price, so there's no need to sacrifice.

Kitchen Countertop Survivor™ Grade: Avg

Your notes:_____

_____

Napa Ridge Coastal Cabernet	PC	T	V
Sauvignon, California	$	17	19

My fears this brand would decline after Beringer sold it appear to have been unfounded. It earns solid taste and value marks from tasters of every stripe, including me. With plum-blackberry fruit and a soft

Price Ranges: **$** = $12 or less; **$$** = 12.01–20; **$$$** = 20.01–35; **$$$$** = > $35

Kitchen Countertop Survivor™ Grades: *Avg.* = a "one-day wine," tastes noticeably less fresh the next day; *B* = holds its freshness for 2–3 days after opening; *B+* = holds *and gets better* over 2–3 days after opening; *A* = a 3- to 4-day "freshness window"; *A+* = holds *and gets better* over 3–4 days

spiciness, it's got nice Cabernet varietal character for the price.

Kitchen Countertop Survivor™ Grade: Avg

Your notes:_____

_____

Nathanson Creek Cabernet   PC   T   V
Sauvignon, California $ 15   15

This used to be a value home run, but the taste, having faded from pleasant to generic, left the field open, and other players fill the void.

Kitchen Countertop Survivor™ Grade: Avg

Your notes:_____

_____

Penfolds Bin 389 Cabernet   PC   T   V
Sauvignon/Shiraz, Australia $$$ 23   22

"What's not to like?" ask pros about this excellent, "absolutely great restaurant wine" that delivers on all counts: complexity, density of flavor, the "yum" factor, and value. It happens to be one of my favorite all-time wines in any color or style. The vivid raspberry fruit and pepper/cedar/spice/coconut scent are delicious young, but the wine also develops breathtaking complexity with age.

Kitchen Countertop Survivor™ Grade: A+

Your notes:_____

_____

Raymond Napa Cabernet Sauvignon PC   T   V
California $$ 23   21

Retail pros note that although "this wine sells well," it should sell even better, "considering the great bang for the buck." The Raymond family are longtime farmers of premium Napa vineyards, so they can put quality in the bottle for a good price. The style, balanced and not heavy, makes it a very food-versatile Cabernet.

Kitchen Countertop Survivor™ Grade: B

Your notes:_____

_____

Robert Mondavi Coastal Cabernet   PC   T   V
Sauvignon, California $$ 18   19

I'd have expected Mondavi, longtime leader in California's signature red grape, to be easily the coastal category's best. It is not. Though the wine is not unpleasant, many others, including cheaper ones, beat it for flavor and quality.

Kitchen Countertop Survivor™ Grade: Avg

Your notes:_____

_____

Robert Mondavi Napa Cabernet	PC	T	V
Sauvignon, California	$$$	22	20

I agree this is a "consistently great Cab," which, compared to others of its quality, remains "good value for the money." The deeply concentrated cassis and licorice flavor and cedary, spicy, minty scent are consistent style signatures and a benchmark for the category.

Kitchen Countertop Survivor™ Grade: B

Your notes:_____

_____

Rodney Strong Cabernet Sauvignon	PC	T	V
California	$$	21	21

To my taste the quality has not kept up with the name recognition, which is very strong. Although quite a few pros say it's "good Cab for the money," I've felt the oak overpowers the fruit for several years running.

Kitchen Countertop Survivor™ Grade: Avg

Your notes:_____

_____

Rosemount Diamond Label	PC	T	V
Cabernet Sauvignon, Australia	$	21	22

Pros rave that this "big," "jammy," "very-well-made" Aussie Cab is "simply one of the best buys in wine." I agree and love the minty, cedary varietal character, too. And of course anyone could love the price.

Kitchen Countertop Survivor™ Grade: B

Your notes:_____

_____

Price Ranges: **$** = $12 or less; **$$** = 12.01–20; **$$$** = 20.01–35; **$$$$** = > $35

Kitchen Countertop Survivor™ Grades: *Avg.* = a "one-day wine," tastes noticeably less fresh the next day; *B* = holds its freshness for 2–3 days after opening; *B+* = holds *and gets better* over 2–3 days after opening; *A* = a 3- to 4-day "freshness window"; *A+* = holds *and gets better* over 3–4 days

Rosemount Diamond Label	PC	T	V
Cabernet Sauvignon/Merlot	$	21	22
Australia			

An absolutely "fantastic value" that I'd recommend by the glass and for everyday drinking on the home front for those who love juicy, dark, plummy fruit.

Kitchen Countertop Survivor™ Grade: B

Your notes:_____

_____

Santa Rita 120 Cabernet Sauvignon	PC	T	V
Chile	$	19	20

It is indeed "a price that's hard to believe" for the quality and flavor punch it delivers. The nice tannic grip and meaty-spicy scent and flavor show the rustic Chilean Cabernet character that I love.

Kitchen Countertop Survivor™ Grade: B

Your notes:_____

_____

Seven Peaks Cabernet Sauvignon	PC	T	V
California	$	X	X

♥ If you want to know what tasters mean by "velvety" wine, try this. I can't think of another Cabernet at this price level with this much true-to-the-grape character. It has scents of coconut (from the wood), licorice, cedar, and blackberries, flavors to match, and a long finish. Rather than ask "How do they do it for this price?" I'll just say *"Please keep it up!"*

Kitchen Countertop Survivor™ Grade: B

Your notes:_____

_____

Silver Oak Alexander Valley	PC	T	V
Cabernet Sauvignon, California	$$$$	25	19

Whether in auction rooms, on wine lists, or in those few fine wine shops that score a few bottles, this wine counts a sea of die-hard devotees who find its consistency and quality "worth the price." But more than just "yummy" to drink, it is utterly original, known for really intense wild berry fruit, velvety-thick tannins, a coconut-dill scent coming from American oak barrels, and an overall density in the mouth that, like it or not, seizes your senses unforgettably.

Kitchen Countertop Survivor™ Grade: B

Your notes:_____

_____

Silverado Napa Cabernet Sauvignon, California	PC $$$$	T X	V X

✗ This wine is "the reason I love Cabernet, the perfect balance of soft and tough, sorta like your favorite leather jacket," writes one aficionado. Silverado's elegant but firm style is classy, with cassis flavor scented with sweet oak and a wet-clay earthiness—original and special.

Kitchen Countertop Survivor™ Grade: A

Your notes:_____

_____

Simi Sonoma Cabernet Sauvignon California	PC $$	T 22	V 20

This terrific wine is, as one pro aptly put it, "a sleeper hiding in plain sight." Simi's blue chip reputation, today more than ever, offers excellent value for the money and classy, true California Cabernet flavors: blackberry, earth, and spice.

Kitchen Countertop Survivor™ Grade: B+

Your notes:_____

_____

Stag's Leap Wine Cellars Napa Cabernet Sauvignon, California	PC $$$$	T 25	V 20

Pros overwhelmingly laud this wine's "incredible flavors" of dark spices, mint, and berry; smooth character; and "year after year" consistency in quality and style. Restaurateurs note that "it's quite pricey, but people don't mind because the stuffing's there." Major Cabernet fans should note that many sommeliers say Stag's Leap's more limited SLV bottling "more than rewards the extra cost."

Kitchen Countertop Survivor™ Grade: B

Your notes:_____

_____

Price Ranges: **$** = $12 or less; **$$** = 12.01–20; **$$$** = 20.01–35; **$$$$** = > $35

Kitchen Countertop Survivor™ Grades: *Avg.* = a "one-day wine," tastes noticeably less fresh the next day; *B* = holds its freshness for 2–3 days after opening; *B+* = holds *and gets better* over 2–3 days after opening; *A* = a 3- to 4-day "freshness window"; *A+* = holds *and gets better* over 3–4 days

Sterling Vineyards Napa Cabernet PC T V
Sauvignon, California $$$$ 23 20

Devotees of this classic name in Cabernet praise its "concentrated," "jammy fruits." I think it is good but outperformed of late by many old Napa neighbors, as well as new names from Sonoma, Paso Robles, and beyond.

Kitchen Countertop Survivor™ Grade: Avg
Your notes:_____

_____

Stonestreet Alexander Valley PC T V
Cabernet Sauvignon, California $$$ X X

♥ This is very classy California Cabernet, unencumbered by excessive oak and alcohol, but with plenty of power and concentration. The scents of vanilla, damp earth, crushed mint, and blackberry are classic Alexander Valley. The big but balanced flavor wears the same attributes on an elegant structure. Proof that power and subtlety can cohabit in a wine with beautiful results.

Kitchen Countertop Survivor™ Grade: Avg
Your notes:_____

_____

Sutter Home Cabernet Sauvignon PC T V
California $ 15 16

Though not particularly expressive of Cabernet character, as a simple red it's "perfectly light and easy" and a "crowd pleaser."

Kitchen Countertop Survivor™ Grade: Avg
Your notes:_____

_____

Talus Cabernet Sauvignon PC T V
California $ 15 16

Though it's not a star in this Cabernet price range, this is the best varietal in the Talus line, with some good fruit flavor and a soft texture.

Kitchen Countertop Survivor™ Grade: Avg
Your notes:_____

_____

Turning Leaf Cabernet Sauvignon	PC	T	V
California	$	14	16

The Chardonnay under this label is a much stronger performer. Although it's not unpleasant, the fruit of this wine seems a little tired and dull compared to others in the price category.

Kitchen Countertop Survivor™ Grade: B

Your notes:_____

Vendange Cabernet Sauvignon	PC	T	V
California	$	13	16

I side with those tasters who find this wine a little "one-dimensional." Still, others find it's "a good value" but acknowledge that "you sacrifice some taste for money."

Kitchen Countertop Survivor™ Grade: Avg

Your notes:_____

Veramonte Cabernet Sauvignon	PC	T	V
Chile	$	17	19

Retail buyers tag this a "real value find for consumers," and I agree. It's got great color, good concentration, and some substance—licorice-berry fruit, some chewy tannin, and a savory spice note.

Kitchen Countertop Survivor™ Grade: Avg

Your notes:_____

Viña Carmen Cabernet Sauvignon	PC	T	V
Chile	$	17	19

So cheap and so drinkable, with "nice berry aromas" and a tug of tannin. What's not to love?

Kitchen Countertop Survivor™ Grade: B

Your notes:_____

Price Ranges: **$** = $12 or less; **$$** = 12.01–20; **$$$** = 20.01–35; **$$$$** = > $35

Kitchen Countertop Survivor™ Grades: *Avg.* = a "one-day wine," tastes noticeably less fresh the next day; *B* = holds its freshness for 2–3 days after opening; *B+* = holds *and gets better* over 2–3 days after opening; *A* = a 3- to 4-day "freshness window"; *A+* = holds *and gets better* over 3–4 days

Walnut Crest Cabernet Sauvignon	PC	T	V
Chile	$	17	18

"Tastes more expensive than it is," say tasters, who rank it accordingly for both taste and value. The peppery, fruity, and crowd-pleasing style is at once smooth and savory. Chalk up another one for Chile, and for the wine-buying public.

Kitchen Countertop Survivor™ Grade: Avg

Your notes:_____

_____

Woodbridge (Robert Mondavi)	PC	T	V
Cabernet Sauvignon, California	$	15	17

Both pros and consumers rate Woodbridge as "sturdy," reliable for everyday drinking and affordable wine by the glass. Still, it's not a leader in either taste or value for its increasingly competitive price category, despite the Mondavi pedigree.

Kitchen Countertop Survivor™ Grade: Avg

Your notes:_____

_____

Rioja, Ribera del Duero, and Other Spanish Reds

Category Profile: Haven't tried one? Busted! You see, if I were chief of the "wine police," I'd put all wine drinkers on probation until they'd tried at least one Spanish red. My hope, for every buyer's taste and budget's sake, is that in a few years Spanish reds will be like Caesar salad—they'll be consumed everywhere, often, and we'll hardly remember the time when they were a "fringe" item. If, like so many Americans, your kitchen table is presently a "crime scene" (as described here), you can quickly destroy the evidence by trying any one of these wines or another that your favorite store or restaurant recommends. There aren't many familiar grapes on the label, so you'll just have to go with them as classical, wholesome, centuries-old products of nature. (Can you say that about the other things you ingest regularly?) Now, for the background: Red Rioja (*ree-OH-huh*) and Ribera del Duero (*ree-BEAR-uh dell DWAIR-oh*) are Spain's two most famous wines and regions—like other classic Euro wines, it's the place rather than the grape on the label. Both are made mainly from the local Tempranillo (*temp-rah-NEE-oh*) grape. Depending on quality level, Rioja ranges from everyday easy-drinking/spicy to seriously rich, leathery/toffee in character—never ho-hum. The other Spanish reds here show emerging regions—Priorat (*pre-oh-RAHT*) for strong, inky-dark cellar candidates (some made from Cabernet and/or Grenache), and Navarra (*nuh-VAHR-uh*), perhaps better known to Americans for the running of the bulls in Pamplona, but a good source of value wines in all colors. Though not represented in the top red wine sellers, Penedes (*pen-eh-DESS*), which is better known for cava sparkling wines, is also an outstanding source of values in every style and color.

Serve: Cool room temperature; as a rule Spanish reds are exemplary food wines, but basic reds from Navarra, Penedes, and Rioja (with the word Crianza on the label) are good "anytime" wines and tasty on their own.

When: Rioja Crianza is my personal "house" red wine. Also, if you dine out often in wine-focused restaurants, Spanish reds are *the* red wine category for world-class drinking that's also affordable.

With: Your next pig roast (!) . . . Seriously, the classic matches are pork and lamb, either roasted or grilled; also amazing with slow-roasted chicken or turkey and hams, sausages, and other cured meats. Finally, if you enjoy a cheese course in lieu of dessert, or are interested in trying one of the world's great pairings that's also easy to pull off, try a Spanish Ribera del Duero, Priorat, or Rioja Reserva or Gran Reserva with good-quality cheese. (Spanish Manchego is wonderful and available in supermarkets.)

In: An all-purpose wineglass or larger-bowled red wine stem.

Price Ranges: **$** = $12 or less; **$$** = 12.01–20; **$$$** = 20.01–35; **$$$$** = > $35

Kitchen Countertop Survivor™ Grades: *Avg.* = a "one-day wine," tastes noticeably less fresh the next day; *B* = holds its freshness for 2–3 days after opening; *B+* = holds *and gets better* over 2–3 days after opening; *A* = a 3- to 4-day "freshness window"; *A+* = holds *and gets better* over 3–4 days

Alvaro Palacios Les Terrasses | PC | T | V
(all-VAHR-oh puh-LAH-see-os lay | $$$ | 25 | 23
tear-AHSS) Priorat, Spain

For sheer drama it's hard to top this dark, brooding beauty from Priorat, the tiny Spanish wine region that has sommeliers and fine wine buyers buzzing. This one from Alvaro Palacios, a premier producer, is lush, intense, and inky, with beautiful black cherry flavors, toasty oak, and a finish that seems hours long.
Kitchen Countertop Survivor™ Grade: B
Your notes:_____

_____

Arzuaga *(ahr-ZWAH-guh)* **Crianza** | PC | T | V
Ribera del Duero, Spain | $$$ | 23 | 22

My tasters, both trade and consumers, gave this high taste and value marks for its power, concentration, ripeness, and complexity. Though it's "expensive," most tasters felt the gorgeous, rich flavor and length do deliver the goods. The price, though, does make it "tough to get people to try it."
Kitchen Countertop Survivor™ Grade: Avg
Your notes:_____

_____

Faustino *(fau-STEEN-oh)* **Rioja** | PC | T | V
Crianza, Spain | $ | 20 | 20

This is Rioja in the rustic, earthy, Old World style, possessing chewy cherry-berry flavor and full-on tannins that are surprisingly complex for a wine of this price. This is one to buy by the case, say pro tasters, who recommend to lovers of assertive red, "Make it your house wine."
Kitchen Countertop Survivor™ Grade: A
Your notes:_____

_____

Marqués de Cáceres *(mahr-KESS* | PC | T | V
deh CAH-sair-ess) **Rioja Crianza** | $$ | 22 | 23
Spain

With "lots of cherry fruit" and "typical toffee-spice," this Rioja is true to type—delicious, drinkable, and food friendly. It is among my very favorite widely avail-able, basic Riojas. In light of that success, one might fear the wine would become "commercial"—meaning no character. Happily, I'm still pleasantly surprised.

Kitchen Countertop Survivor™ *Grade: A*

Your notes:_____

| **Marqués de Riscal** (*mahr-KESS deh ree-SKALL*) **Rioja Crianza, Spain** | PC $ | T 22 | V 22 |

"What Wine Lovers Want!" It seems you could begin the dossier for such a wine file with this wine, based on the extremely high number of good to very good to outstanding scores for this wine, from the entire base of seriously committed wine buyers, pro and consumer, responding to this survey. In other words, they were all the Master Sommeliers, top buyers, and serious wine consumers (the collectors and wine aficionados who interact with the aforementioned pros). I know that their praise is based on these simple features—lovely spice in the nose, silken texture but with a tactile grip, and savory-strawberry flavor. This isn't the exclusive definition of "What Wine Lovers Want," but any version that's this cheap warrants special mention.

Kitchen Countertop Survivor™ *Grade: B+*

Your notes:_____

| **Montecillo** (*mohn-teh-SEE-yoh*) **Rioja Crianza, Spain** | PC $ | T 21 | V 22 |

Another wine well known to—and well regarded by the professional and "wine aficionado" inner circle, who say they are impressed with this "lean but solid" Rioja. It's got savory spiciness that's round and thick on the palate and long and full in the finish, combining Old World depth with New World technique. Very nice indeed.

Kitchen Countertop Survivor™ *Grade: Avg*

Your notes:_____

Price Ranges: **$** = $12 or less; **$$** = 12.01–20; **$$$** = 20.01–35; **$$$$** = > $35

Kitchen Countertop Survivor™ Grades: *Avg.* = a "one-day wine," tastes noticeably less fresh the next day; *B* = holds its freshness for 2–3 days after opening; *B+* = holds *and gets better* over 2–3 days after opening; *A* = a 3- to 4-day "freshness window"; *A+* = holds *and gets better* over 3–4 days

Muga (*MOO-guh*) Rioja Reserva Spain

PC	T	V
$$$	25	24

✓ "With wine like this, who needs Antonio Banderas?" quipped a fellow wine woman, prompting me to subordinate my own quote of "Omigod . . . geez!" Now, regaining my composure: this classic, sturdy Rioja is a great wine and a good value in the serious wine category. The stunningly generous fig, prune, and dried cherry fruit and dense but suede-smooth tannins make it "a brooding red" that's fabulous with cheese, lamb, and game.

Kitchen Countertop Survivor™ Grade: A+

Your notes:_____

_____

Pesquera (*pess-CARE-uh*) Ribera del Duero, Spain

PC	T	V
$$$	25	22

For years Pesquera's style consistency—gorgeous cherry fruit and firm tannins—a style that "provides an easy alternative to Bordeaux," has been legendary. This wine, on the edge of taste and value greatness, had for some respondents fallen off and slid far down the quality slope. While the consensus among tasters was quite high, the intense frustration voiced by some, that the wine has declined—becoming "devoid of fruit flavor"—had to be mentioned.

Kitchen Countertop Survivor™ Grade: B

Your notes:_____

_____

Vega Sindoa (*VAY-guh sin-DOUGH-uh*) Tempranillo/Merlot Navarra Tinto, Spain

PC	T	V
$	22	23

There are multiple *tinto* (meaning "red") choices from this brand made by Bodegas Nekeas. Tempranillo-Merlot, the least expensive of the three, is to me the most "Spanish," with a rustic, spicy note and soft fruit that buyers consistently rate a "great crowd pleaser," especially for the money. Look also for the Merlot and Cabernet-Tempranillo, both one-dollar-sign wines, with impressive flavor for the money.

Kitchen Countertop Survivor™ Grade: B

Your notes:_____

_____

Other Reds

Category Profile: As with the whites, this isn't a cohesive category but rather a spot to put big-selling reds that don't neatly fit a grape or region category—namely, generic wines, proprietary blends, and uncommon varietals.

Generics—Recapping the definition in the white wine section, this category uses classic regional names Chianti and Burgundy for basic bulk wines.

Proprietary blends—There is just one such wine here, Francis Coppola Presents Rosso. It is excellent and well loved by consumers for its high quality for the money. Based on its success, perhaps we can hope for more such tasty, inexpensive blends to hit the market.

Uncommon varietals—These are quite exciting. I introduced Malbec and Carmenere in the Merlot section, because I think they are distinctive and delicious alternatives for Merlot lovers. Although the names and even the style (bold and a little peppery) are similar, Petite Sirah and Syrah (Shiraz) are not the same grape.

Serve: Cool, even slightly chilled.

When: Anytime you need an uncomplicated, value-priced red. Many tasters recommended them for big parties, picnics (even with ice cubes), and other casual occasions. Quite a few pros also said they are a good-tasting and low-cost base for sangria and other wine-based punches.

With: Snacks and everyday meals.

In: An all-purpose wineglass.

Price Ranges: **$** = $12 or less; **$$** = 12.01–20; **$$$** = 20.01–35; **$$$$** = > $35
Kitchen Countertop Survivor™ Grades: ***Avg.*** = a "one-day wine," tastes noticeably less fresh the next day; ***B*** = holds its freshness for 2–3 days after opening; ***B+*** = holds *and gets better* over 2–3 days after opening; ***A*** = a 3- to 4-day "freshness window"; ***A+*** = holds *and gets better* over 3–4 days

Carlo Rossi Burgundy   PC   T   V
USA $ 9   12

The assessments here clearly reflect the fact that
Americans have traded up to varietal wines. "Great for
cooking," quips a sommelier, and it is indeed widely
used in restaurant kitchens in New York for just that.
While the taste is indeed as "simple as the twist-off
cap it comes with," it is sound and competently made.
Kitchen Countertop Survivor™ *Grade: B*
Your notes:_____

Concha y Toro Terrunyo Carmenere   PC   T   V
Chile $$ X   X

♥ You'll have to search a bit for this, but it's worth the
trouble. The flavor is like the concentrated essence
of wild berries (huckleberries, raspberries), with a
velvety-plush texture and seductive sweet spice-cola
scents.
Kitchen Countertop Survivor™ *Grade: B*
Your notes:_____

Concannon Petite Sirah   PC   T   V
California $ X   X

♥ Take a black pepper and berry scent, add explode-
in-your-mouth fruit-pie flavor, chewy tannins, and a
long licorice finish, and you've got this unique, fun,
and utterly delicious wine. It's got all the virtues of
California Syrah, Zinfandel, and Cabernet wrapped
into one and is bargain priced.
Kitchen Countertop Survivor™ *Grade: B+*
Your notes:_____

Coppola (Francis) Presents Rosso   PC   T   V
California $ 19   20

"Bring on the spaghetti," and "serve it cool," recom-
mended tasters of this juicy, fruity, and simple
Coppola wine (yes, *that* Coppola). A delicious,
fun-for-everyday red.
Kitchen Countertop Survivor™ *Grade: B+*
Your notes:_____

Franzia Red   PC   T   V
USA $ 8   9

"Perfect for sangria," suggested one sommelier, but the consensus was that most tasters wouldn't "go there" even for wine punch. There is surely no more convenient package for wine than bag-in-a-box: no corkscrew needed, and no wasted leftovers lost to oxidation. Wouldn't it make sense to put some more impressive everyday wine inside?

Kitchen Countertop Survivor™ Grade: NA

Your notes:_____

_____

Livingston Cellars Burgundy   PC   T   V
California $ 12   12

Yet another famous wine name used generically (which drives the pros insane), this light, simple red is neither Burgundy from France nor Pinot Noir, the grape used to make Burgundy. It is a basic blended red wine—not bad, but not real Burgundy.

Kitchen Countertop Survivor™ Grade: Avg

Your notes:_____

_____

Navarro Correas Malbec   PC   T   V
Argentina $ X   X

♥ Another example of amazing character for the price from the Southern Hemisphere. This is rustic but really inviting, with earthy, leathery, savory spice and dried fruits on the scent. The grip of tannin is followed by silky, subtle plum fruit and a smoky, earthy finish.

Kitchen Countertop Survivor™ Grade: B+

Your notes:_____

_____

Price Ranges: **$** = $12 or less; **$$** = 12.01–20; **$$$** = 20.01–35; **$$$$** = > $35

Kitchen Countertop Survivor™ Grades: **Avg.** = a "one-day wine," tastes noticeably less fresh the next day; **B** = holds its freshness for 2–3 days after opening; **B+** = holds *and gets better* over 2–3 days after opening; **A** = a 3- to 4-day "freshness window"; **A+** = holds *and gets better* over 3–4 days

Veramonte Primus	PC	T	V
Chile	$$	X	X

♥ This was one of the first Chilean wines from the Carmenere grape on these shores. It was given Primus as a proprietary name, because the grape wasn't yet recognized by our government label-regulations. It's still one of the best, with a lot of exotic berry fruit and both savory and sweet spices and flavors that almost mimic Asian flavors like hoisin or teriyaki. Yum!

Kitchen Countertop Survivor™ Grade: B

Your notes:_____

Italian Regional Reds

Category Profile: This group includes small Italian regions like Valpolicella and Lambrusco, whose market presence is dominated by a few big-selling, well-known brands.

Serve: Cool room temperature or slightly chilled.

When: As the Italians would, for everyday drinking.

With: Snacks and everyday meals.

In: An all-purpose wineglass.

Allegrini Valpolicella (*al-uh-GREE-*	PC	T	V
nee val-pole-uh-CHELL-uh), Italy	$$	21	21

Pros rave that this wine represents great winemaking from the "Master of Valpolicella," saying Allegrini is "as good as it gets on a viable, commercial level," with pure fruit, balance, and velvety tannins.

Kitchen Countertop Survivor™ Grade: B

Your notes:_____

Bolla Valpolicella	PC	T	V
Italy	$	16	18

This Valpolicella is fruity, soft, and a little spicy and definitely "made to drink young." Pros point out that, in true Italian wine fashion, it "doesn't compete with food."

Kitchen Countertop Survivor™ Grade: Avg

Your notes:_____

Citra Montepulciano d'Abruzzo	PC	T	V
(*CHEE-truh mon-teh-pool-CHAH-no*	$	16	18
dah-BROOT-so), Italy			

This is just a yummy little wine for the money and has been for years. When I see the magnums on back bars being poured as the house "rosso," I know the restaurant cares about its customers and food. Its light and fruity nature makes it an easy everyday quaff, while the touch of earthy spiciness makes almost any dish taste better. And, of course, the "price can't be beat."

Kitchen Countertop Survivor™ Grade: B

Your notes:_____

_____

Falesco Vitiano (*fuh-LESS-co*	PC	T	V
vee-tee-AH-no), Italy	$	X	X

♥ This wine gives you major yum for a song, something no one does better than the Italians. It's a spicy, plummy, lip-smacking blend of Merlot, Cabernet Sauvignon, and Sangiovese, from the Umbria region of Italy.

Kitchen Countertop Survivor™ Grade: B

Your notes:_____

_____

Riunite Lambrusco (*ree-you-NEE-tee*	PC	T	V
lam-BROO-scoe), Italy	$	11	13

For many *Immer Guide* respondents, this was their "first wine," the one that got them "hooked"—despite the fact that "it still drinks like soda" (as in Riunite on ice). But I'm with the trade buyer who notes, "Hey, if Riunite starts people on the road to wine, then so be it: this one is as good as any."

Kitchen Countertop Survivor™ Grade: Avg

Your notes:_____

_____

Price Ranges: **$** = $12 or less; **$$** = 12.01–20; **$$$** = 20.01–35; **$$$$** = > $35

Kitchen Countertop Survivor™ Grades: ***Avg.*** = a "one-day wine," tastes noticeably less fresh the next day; ***B*** = holds its freshness for 2–3 days after opening; ***B+*** = holds *and gets better* over 2–3 days after opening; ***A*** = a 3- to 4-day "freshness window"; ***A+*** = holds *and gets better* over 3–4 days

Syrah/Shiraz and
Other Rhône-Style Reds

Category Profile: This category of reds has stirred up great and growing excitement in the market and among my tasters. For example, some pros share my belief that Shiraz, Australia's signature red, is so hot it may be poised to unseat Merlot as consumers' go-to grape, due to its high quality for the money. It is true that even at the one-dollar-sign level you get a scent of sweet spice and jammy, succulent fruit flavor that, in my opinion, dusts many of the popular reds out there based on Merlot and Cabernet Sauvignon. The same grape, under the French spelling *Syrah,* also forms the backbone for France's revered Rhône Valley reds with centuries-old reputations. These include Côtes-du-Rhône (*coat-duh-ROAN*), Côte-Rôtie (*ro-TEE*), Hermitage (*uhr-muh-TAHJ*), and Châteauneuf-du-Pape (*shah-toe-NUFF-duh-POP*). Like Shiraz, Côtes-du-Rhône, with its lovely spicy fruit character, is a one-dollar-sign wonder. The latter three are true French classics and in my view currently lead that elite group in quality for the money. They are full-bodied, powerful, peppery, earthy, concentrated, and oak-aged. Finally, most major American wineries, and many smaller players, are bottling California or Washington state versions, often labeled with the Aussie spelling *Shiraz* rather than the French *Syrah.*

Serve: Room temperature; aeration enhances the aroma and flavor.

When: Basic Shiraz and Côtes-du-Rhône are great everyday drinking wines; in restaurants, these are great go-to categories for relative value.

With: Grilled, barbecued, or roasted anything (including fish and vegetables); outstanding with steaks, fine cheeses, and other dishes that call for a full red wine; I also love these styles with traditional Thanksgiving fare.

In: An all-purpose wineglass or a larger-bowled red wine stem.

Arboleda Estate Syrah	PC	T	V
Chile	$$	X	X

♥ Chile is an unexpected source for Syrah, but if this is a sample of its quality and excitement potential, we have every reason to hope for more. This estate is owned jointly by Errazuriz and Robert Mondavi, and the wines (like the luxury Seña Cabernet blend from Chile) are a joint venture. This wine achieves what I think a lot of California Syrahs are going for—wild raspberry fruit, with seductive and tough-to-label aromas that smell like everything from flowers to licorice to ink to smoked meat. It's full and gripping, but balanced.

Kitchen Countertop Survivor™ Grade: B

Your notes:_____

_____

Black Opal Shiraz	PC	T	V
Australia	$	19	20

Consensus is that you couldn't ask for much more from a wine at this price. It's light, friendly and perfectly juicy, which makes it great to serve to a big group, and with all sorts of foods.

Kitchen Countertop Survivor™ Grade: Avg.

Your notes:_____

_____

Château de Beaucastel	PC	T	V
Châteauneuf du Pape, France	$$$$	26	22

✓ Although some tasters pointed out that this Chateauneuf is "expensive" and "hard to get," that depends on what you're comparing to. Among the peer group of truly collectible, ageable, world-class wines, Beaucastel is a relative value. One taster's suggestion to "wait a year" is a good one, and it will age far longer. Still, it offers up the beauty of its Asian spice scent and incredibly deep, powerful fig and dark berry fruit fairly young, which I'm sure contributes to

Price Ranges: **$** = $12 or less; **$$** = 12.01–20; **$$$** = 20.01–35; **$$$$** = > $35

Kitchen Countertop Survivor™ Grades: *Avg.* = a "one-day wine," tastes noticeably less fresh the next day; *B* = holds its freshness for 2–3 days after opening; *B+* = holds *and gets better* over 2–3 days after opening; *A* = a 3- to 4-day "freshness window"; *A+* = holds *and gets better* over 3–4 days

the long list of fans for this "real special experience" of a wine.

Kitchen Countertop Survivor™ *Grade:* A+

Your notes:_____

Château La Nerthe (*shah-TOE lah*   PC   T   V
***NAIRT*) Châteauneuf-du-Pape,** $$$ 24   21
France

While trade buyers and serious wine devotees rave about this "lovely," "smooth" wine, some also rightly point out that all the really good Rhône juice around is giving it stiff competition, often at lower prices. The pepper/spicy/leathery scents, gripping tannins, and dried cranberry-anise flavors are textbook Château-neuf, built for rich meats and stews.

Kitchen Countertop Survivor™ *Grade:* A

Your notes:_____

Duboeuf (Georges) Côtes-du-Rhône   PC   T   V
(*du-BUFF coat-duh-ROAN*), France $ 19   19

Although Duboeuf is virtually synonymous with Beaujolais, look for his other French regional wines that, like this Côtes-du-Rhône, are consistently well made and often at best-deal prices. This wine shows perfectly how Côtes-du-Rhône delivers character for cheap. It is juicy and fresh tasting, with red cherry and a spicy pomegranate note. Yum!

Kitchen Countertop Survivor™ *Grade:* B

Your notes:_____

E & M Guigal (*ghee-GALL*)   PC   T   V
Côtes-du-Rhône, France $ 22   22

So many tasters, obviously enticed by the famous Guigal name, have discovered and enjoyed the cherry fruit and pepper-spice notes of this classic Côtes-du-Rhône. For consistency and flavor for the money, it has for years been on my short list of go-to wines for everyday drinking. It is true, as one taster noted, "There are a lot of terrific Côtes-du-Rhône for the same money or less," meaning this is a great introduction to a category that's definitely worth more exploration.

Kitchen Countertop Survivor™ *Grade:* A

Your notes:_____

| **Hill of Content Grenache/Shiraz** | **PC** | **T** | **V** |
| **Australia** | **$** | **X** | **X** |

♥ The smell of this wine, with raspberry-syrup fruit and an animal meatiness, always strikes me as somehow faintly naughty. In the taste it's got ripe, jammy Aussie-bold berry fruit and succulent texture.
Kitchen Countertop Survivor™ Grade: A
Your notes:_____

| **Jaboulet (*jhah-boo-LAY*)** | **PC** | **T** | **V** |
| **Côtes-du-Rhône, France** | **$** | **22** | **23** |

Jaboulet perfectly fits my definition of a true blue chip winery: one whose quality rings through across the price spectrum. While it stakes its reputation on its luxurious and collectible Hermitage, this bottling is an equally impressive calling card in the budget price category with succulent red-berry fruit and smoky black pepper scents.
Kitchen Countertop Survivor™ Grade: B
Your notes:_____

| **Jacob's Creek Shiraz/Cabernet** | **PC** | **T** | **V** |
| **Sauvignon, Australia** | **$** | **21** | **22** |

"This wine is tough to beat in the 'great taste and great value' category," said one of my tasters, and I have to agree. The exotic raspberry and eucalyptus notes and plump texture make it easy to see why Australia has been so successful at blending its signature Shiraz grape with Cabernet.
Kitchen Countertop Survivor™ Grade: B+
Your notes:_____

La Vieille Ferme (*lah vee-yay*	**PC**	**T**	**V**
***FAIRM; means "the old farm"*)**	**$**	**20**	**22**
Côtes-du-Ventoux, France			

A vacation tip from one taster who recommends the "great biking on Ventoux" and this tasty wine for day's

Price Ranges: **$** = $12 or less; **$$** = 12.01–20; **$$$** = 20.01–35; **$$$$** = > $35
Kitchen Countertop Survivor™ Grades: *Avg.* = a "one-day wine," tastes noticeably less fresh the next day; *B* = holds its freshness for 2–3 days after opening; *B+* = holds *and gets better* over 2–3 days after opening; *A* = a 3- to 4-day "freshness window"; *A+* = holds *and gets better* over 3–4 days

end. I wasn't the slightest bit surprised by tasters'
comments that this raspberry-ripe, lively red is a
favorite, with "great character" and "wonderful for
the price." It has been that way for years. Look for
its sister white from the Côtes du Luberon (loo-
bear-OHN).
Kitchen Countertop Survivor™ Grade: B+
Your notes:_____

| **Lindemans Bin 59 Shiraz** | PC | T | V |
| **Australia** | $ | 21 | 21 |

I agree with pros who say that this Shiraz—"like all
Lindemans products—sings!" It's got "pushy varietal
character"—meaning ripe raspberry fruit and a top
note of black pepper scent, plus a plump and round
mouthfeel. An all-around great drink and great buy.
Kitchen Countertop Survivor™ Grade: B+
Your notes:_____

| **Lindemans Shiraz/Cabernet** | PC | T | V |
| **Sauvignon, Cawarra, Australia** | $ | 21 | 21 |

Proof that an inexpensive wine can be quite distinctive. It's got ripe raspberry fruit, peppery spiciness,
and even a little mint scent. And the soft plump
texture makes it easy drinking.
Kitchen Countertop Survivor™ Grade: B
Your notes:_____

| **Rosemount Diamond Label Shiraz** | PC | T | V |
| **Australia** | $ | 23 | 24 |

This wine is just one big annual encore of delicious
raspberry-vanilla fruit and a lively but succulent
mouthfeel that seizes your senses without ever being
overwhelming to the palate or the food. It manages to
book a perennial return engagement on every critic's
"best buy" list, and counts legions of devotees among
both consumer and trade buyers, whose "guests love
it." It creates converts, too, as one taster's story attests:
"It converted my wife from drinking light white wines
to buying this one by the case—honest!"
Kitchen Countertop Survivor™ Grade: A+
Your notes:_____

Rosemount Diamond Label Shiraz/	PC	T	V
Cabernet Sauvignon, Australia	$	23	24

It's true, there's "no need to spend more," because this wine delivers the complete package for an unbelievable price. As its sister bottlings in this book attest, that's true for virtually the entire Diamond Label line. This bottling really shows the virtues of blending the Cabernet and Shiraz grapes, with juicy, mouthwatering berry fruit, a touch of mint in the scent, and a gentle tug of tannin.

Kitchen Countertop Survivor™ Grade: A+

Your notes:_____

_____

Rosemount GSM (Grenache-Shiraz-	PC	T	V
Mourvedre), Australia	$$	X	X

✗ A major presence on write-in lists, with one devotee noting, "Everyone I have introduced it to has thanked me to excess!" Of course, you'll want to see for yourself. It shows all the hallmarks of blends from these three Rhône red grapes—both savory and sweet spices, polished tannins, an irresistible smoky/meaty character in the scent, and rich, jammy black cherry and blueberry flavors.

Kitchen Countertop Survivor™ Grade: A

Your notes:_____

_____

Red Zinfandel

Category Profile: I'd say *groupie* is the apt moniker for devotees of this lovely red grape, a California specialty that ranges in style from medium-bodied, with bright and juicy raspberry flavors, to lush and full-bodied, with intense blueberry, licorice, and even chocolate scents and flavors. Many of the best vineyards are pre-Prohibition plantings, whose gnarled

Price Ranges: **$** = $12 or less; **$$** = 12.01–20; **$$$** = 20.01–35; **$$$$** = > $35

Kitchen Countertop Survivor™ Grades: *Avg.* = a "one-day wine," tastes noticeably less fresh the next day; *B* = holds its freshness for 2–3 days after opening; *B+* = holds *and gets better* over 2–3 days after opening; *A* = a 3- to 4-day "freshness window"; *A+* = holds *and gets better* over 3–4 days

old vines, often interplanted with other grapes (formerly a common European practice, brought to California by Italian immigrants), produce some amazingly intense, complex wines. In addition to big, bold red wine fruit and body, the wines usually are oaky—a little or a lot depending on the intensity of the grapes used. The grape intensity is a function of the vineyard—its age and its location. California's most famous red Zinfandel areas are Sonoma (especially the Dry Creek Valley subdistrict), Napa, Amador, and the Sierra foothills, whose most ambitious bottlings can be worthy of aging in the cellar. Lodi, in California's Central Valley, is also a good source. The value bottlings are usually regionally labeled as California or North Coast.

Serve: Room temperature; aeration enhances the aroma and flavor.

When: Value Zinfandels are excellent for everyday drinking; good restaurant lists (not necessarily the "big" ones) usually have a selection worth exploring across the price spectrum.

With: Burgers, pizza, lamb (especially with Indian or Moroccan spices), and quality cheeses are favorite matches. I have even enjoyed very rich, juicy Zinfandels with dark chocolate!

In: An all-purpose wineglass or a larger-bowled red wine stem.

Beaulieu Vineyard (BV) Coastal Zinfandel, California	PC	T	V
	$	19	19

This is a soft, pleasant, cherry-flavored Zinfandel in the lighter style. While there are others at this easy-does-it price point with more assertive "Zin" character (namely, spice and wild-berry fruit), it's a nice drink. If you like soft reds with up-front fruit, skip the budget Merlots you'd normally turn to. This is the flavor you *really* want.

Kitchen Countertop Survivor™ *Grade:* A

Your notes:_____

_____

Beringer North Coast Zinfandel	PC	T	V
California	$$	20	19

This fruity, uncomplicated Zin, with cherry-berry flavors and soft tannins, is medium-bodied, so it won't overpower food. I personally prefer more assertively Zinful character, but it's a well-made wine.

Kitchen Countertop Survivor™ Grade: A

Your notes:_____

_____

Cline Zinfandel	PC	T	V
California	$	23	22

It is rare that you get "wow" wine for this price, but it is here. Once you try what I'd agree is the "best value Zin in California," you'll want to try other offerings from Cline, one of California's great producers that keeps a lower profile in Contra Costa County, outside the spotlight of Napa and Sonoma. *Lots* of spice and fruit prompted tasters to describe it as at once "sexy and urgent" and "the perfect house wine." Who knew it could be so easy and cheap to spice up your everyday dinner?

Kitchen Countertop Survivor™ Grade: A+

Your notes:_____

_____

Clos du Bois Sonoma Zinfandel	PC	T	V
California	$$	21	20

Although this isn't the star of the Clos du Bois stable, it's certainly in keeping with its reliable quality standard. This is Zin in the medium style, with sweet oak in the scent, raspberry fruit, and soft tannins.

Kitchen Countertop Survivor™ Grade: B

Your notes:_____

_____

Price Ranges: **$** = $12 or less; **$$** = 12.01–20; **$$$** = 20.01–35; **$$$$** = > $35

Kitchen Countertop Survivor™ Grades: *Avg.* = a "one-day wine," tastes noticeably less fresh the next day; *B* = holds its freshness for 2–3 days after opening; *B+* = holds *and gets better* over 2–3 days after opening; *A* = a 3- to 4-day "freshness window"; *A+* = holds *and gets better* over 3–4 days

Dry Creek Vineyard Reserve   PC   T   V
Zinfandel, California $$$ X   X

♥ Old-vines Zinfandel, made from some of the earliest northern California plantings, is the signature wine of Sonoma's Dry Creek Valley. It's a style that wine insiders, and especially Californiaphiles, cherish. This wine is a perfect introduction—"blueberries and chocolate," as one of my sommelier colleagues describes the flavor, with thick and velvety tannins. Yes, it drips flavor, but without the oak and alcohol burn of some of the trendy heavy-handed Zins. It's a mouthful that deserves a mouthful—some great cheese or a top-shelf prime steak.

Kitchen Countertop Survivor™ Grade: A

Your notes:_____

_____

Fetzer Valley Oaks Zinfandel   PC   T   V
California $ 17   18

This light-bodied and uncomplicated Zinfandel has nice cherry flavors and the consistency you can count on from Fetzer's Valley Oaks line (though I prefer the Cabernet).

Kitchen Countertop Survivor™ Grade: B

Your notes:_____

_____

Gallo of Sonoma Dry Creek Valley   PC   T   V
Zinfandel, California $$ 21   22

An outstanding example of the Dry Creek Valley Zin style, whose hallmarks are complex wild-raspberry-spice character and exuberant, packed-in flavor. As tasters point out, it's quite impressive for the money. This is one to try with dark chocolate.

Kitchen Countertop Survivor™ Grade: B+

Your notes:_____

_____

Grgich Hills Sonoma Zinfandel   PC   T   V
California $$$ 24   20

In keeping with the Grgich style, this wine's complexity, firm structure, and restraint deliver the power of Zinfandel, with a subtler expression of scent and flavor. The cherry fruit and very delicate spice are framed firmly in oak and tannin. Improves with bottle age, if you can wait. Definitely a food wine—preferably dinner for two!

Kitchen Countertop Survivor™ Grade: A

Your notes:_____

_____

•

Kendall-Jackson Vintner's Reserve   PC   T   V
Zinfandel, California $$ 20   19

This is a rich, ripe "fruit bomb of a Zin," with ample cherry-cola flavors. It drinks nicely by itself and with bold food, especially anything from the grill.

Kitchen Countertop Survivor™ Grade: B

Your notes:_____

_____

Monteviña Amador Zinfandel   PC   T   V
California $ 20   21

This wine will give you—at a bargain price—a taste of the Amador Zin style, which is quite distinctive. Specifically, you'll notice a more earthy, savory-spice scent (think cumin and cardamom), prune and licorice flavors, and a firm tannic grip. It's a nice combination with Moroccan- or Indian-spiced dishes, as well as Mediterranean flavors—oregano, thyme, garlic, olive.

Kitchen Countertop Survivor™ Grade: B+

Your notes:_____

_____

Rabbit Ridge Zinfandel   PC   T   V
California $ 21   20

Rabbit Ridge staked its reputation on this balanced, fruit-forward Zinfandel, which gets good marks from tasters for taste and value. The brand appears to be in a state of flux, though, as growing production may force it to move from its Sonoma base. Stay tuned.

Kitchen Countertop Survivor™ Grade: B

Your notes:_____

_____

Price Ranges: **$** = $12 or less; **$$** = 12.01–20; **$$$** = 20.01–35; **$$$$** = > $35

Kitchen Countertop Survivor™ Grades: ***Avg.*** = a "one-day wine," tastes noticeably less fresh the next day; ***B*** = holds its freshness for 2–3 days after opening; ***B+*** = holds *and gets better* over 2–3 days after opening; ***A*** = a 3- to 4-day "freshness window"; ***A+*** = holds *and gets better* over 3–4 days

Rancho Zabaco Heritage Vines   PC   T   V
Zinfandel, California $$ X   X

✗ This is Zin with medium body but concentrated, rustic flavor that's thick with dried-cherry fruit and tobacco spice scents.

Kitchen Countertop Survivor™ Grade: B

Your notes:_____

_____

Ravenswood Vintners Blend   PC   T   V
Zinfandel, California $$ 22   22

Whither this "always reliable" fruity Zinfandel? That seems to be the question among legions of trade and consumer buyers who, like me, have counted Ravenswood as a Zin pioneer and leader for years. It gets high marks for taste and value, but the winery's recent purchase by a large conglomerate, and production and price increases, have caught buyers' notice. Hopefully, it'll maintain the Zin taste excitement for which Ravenswood was an industry benchmark—so far, so good. If you want to trade up, try the single-vineyard and "county" (Sonoma, Amador, etc.) Zins, too.

Kitchen Countertop Survivor™ Grade: A

Your notes:_____

_____

Ridge Geyserville (Zinfandel)   PC   T   V
California $$$ 26   23

✓ This "touchstone" for Zins happens to be one of my favorite wines, period. Clearly, I am not alone, as this wine garnered many superlatives from buyers of every stripe for its elegant, powerful style and quality that's simply great, every year. It is true that the price is climbing with its success; however, I think the price is a relative value for this sort of world-class, memorable drinking experience. The scent is complex cedar, savory-sweet spice, and dark fruit that's very intense. The texture feels like the finest chamois upholstery for your mouth, and "mind bending" is not an exaggeration for the finish. It also cellars beautifully.

Kitchen Countertop Survivor™ Grade: A+

Your notes:_____

_____

Robert Mondavi Coastal Zinfandel | PC | T | V
California | $ | 18 | 19

The Zinfandel is a standout in the Robert Mondavi Coastal line, for both taste and value. It's plump with cherry fruit and balanced with a lively acid/tannin structure that makes it versatile with food.

Kitchen Countertop Survivor™ Grade: Avg

Your notes:_____

_____

Seghesio Sonoma Zinfandel | PC | T | V
California | $$ | 22 | 22

This has long been on my list of favorite Zins, because it offers real Sonoma character—wild-berry fruit, dried spices—at a good price. However, my tasters rightly point out that the growing list of "better Zins for less" should keep them watching their Ps and Qs, when compared to the rest of the marketplace.

Kitchen Countertop Survivor™ Grade: Avg

Your notes:_____

_____

St. Francis Sonoma Zinfandel | PC | T | V
California | $$ | 23 | 23

This classic Sonoma Zin is both consistent and very popular. The dark blackberry and fig fruit are framed by lots of American oak—to some tastes "a bit heavy on the coconut sweetness," a reference to the signature scent that American oak barrel aging often contributes to wine. But others, I think in this case the majority, absolutely love that sort of intensity.

Kitchen Countertop Survivor™ Grade: B+

Your notes:_____

_____

Price Ranges: **$** = $12 or less; **$$** = 12.01–20; **$$$** = 20.01–35; **$$$$** = > $35

Kitchen Countertop Survivor™ Grades: *Avg.* = a "one-day wine," tastes noticeably less fresh the next day; *B* = holds its freshness for 2–3 days after opening; *B+* = holds *and gets better* over 2–3 days after opening; *A* = a 3- to 4-day "freshness window"; *A+* = holds *and gets better* over 3–4 days

Sutter Home Zinfandel	PC	T	V
California	$	14	17

Although Sutter Home was historically a Zin leader,
tasters were underwhelmed, as they see better Zin for
the money elsewhere—even right in the same family
under the Montevina brand. The wine is light and
quaffable but not particularly Zin-like.

Kitchen Countertop Survivor™ Grade: Avg

Your notes:_____

_____

Turning Leaf Zinfandel	PC	T	V
California	$	13	14

This Zinfandel lags the category in both price and
value, which is a shame considering the Gallo winemaking resources (which yield good Zin under other
brands) behind it. As a supersoft red for use in
punches and sangria, it would be fine. But for Zin
character, there are better choices (like its sister
brand, Rancho Zabaco, which was a write-in).

Kitchen Countertop Survivor™ Grade: Avg

Your notes:_____

_____

Vendange Zinfandel	PC	T	V
California	$	11	13

Both trade and consumer tasters say this light, fruity
wine is "just OK." I agree; it really doesn't taste much
like Zinfandel but rather like a pleasant jug wine.

Kitchen Countertop Survivor™ Grade: Avg

Your notes:_____

_____

Woodbridge (Robert Mondavi)	PC	T	V
Zinfandel, California	$	15	15

I agree with Chairman Michael Mondavi, who calls
this his favorite wine for everyday drinking ("with
pizza," he suggests). I also think this is the best
varietal in the Woodbridge line, with nice ripe plump
fruit, nice food versatility, and a very nice price.

Kitchen Countertop Survivor™ Grade: Avg

Your notes:_____

_____

DESSERT WINES

Category Profile: No, none of these have major market presence. The "dessert" wines (or at least those sweet enough to qualify) that are statistically the biggest sellers are unfortunately weak commercial products that fulfill purposes other than a fine ending to a meal. There are plenty of great and available dessert wines to choose from, many of them affordable enough to enjoy often, with or instead of dessert (they're fat free!). These are the dessert selections from my Top 50 Wines You're Not Drinking list. I hope you'll try them, because they will really jazz up your wine and food life.

Serve: Serving temperature depends on the wine, so see the individual entries.

When: With dessert, or as dessert; the lighter ones also make nice aperitifs. If you like to entertain, they're great. Add fruit, cheese, or some cookies, and you have a very classy end to a meal with very low hassle.

With: Blue cheese, chocolate, or simple cookies (like biscotti or shortbread) are classic. I've given specific matches in the individual entries.

In: An all-purpose wineglass or a smaller wineglass (the standard serving is 3 ounces rather than the traditional 6 for most wines.

Baron Philippe de Rothschild	**PC**	**T**	**V**
Sauternes, France	**$$$**	**X**	**X**

♥ You have to taste it to believe that real Sauternes character is available at this price. (Most are collectors' items, priced accordingly.) It has the classic and beautiful honeyed, crème brûlée and peach scent and flavors of Sauternes. The French serve it as an aperitif, or with foie gras, or at meal's end with Roquefort cheese—a combo that has to be tasted to be

---

Price Ranges: **$** = $12 or less; **$$** = 12.01–20; **$$$** = 20.01–35; **$$$$** = > $35
Kitchen Countertop Survivor™ Grades: **Avg.** = a "one-day wine," tastes noticeably less fresh the next day; **B** = holds its freshness for 2–3 days after opening; **B+** = holds *and gets better* over 2–3 days after opening; **A** = a 3- to 4-day "freshness window"; **A+** = holds *and gets better* over 3–4 days

believed. It is also lovely with crème brûlée and even
cheesecake. Serve slightly chilled.
Kitchen Countertop Survivor™ *Grade: A*
Your notes:_____

_____

Blandy's 10-Year-Old Malmsey   PC   T   V
Madeira, Portugal $$$ X   X
♥ Oh, how I love this wine—its flavor is so tantaliz-
ingly "out there." There's caramel, burnt sugar, toffee,
burnt orange, toasted nuts, spice, and a cut of tangy
acidity that keeps your palate on edge—all of that
from grapes! It would go well with any nut or caramel
dessert or just vanilla ice cream. The most amazing
dessert combination I have *ever* tasted, though, was
this wine with warm flourless chocolate cake. Omigod.
Serve at room temp. The open bottle will not go bad.
Kitchen Countertop Survivor™ *Grade: A+*
Your notes:_____

_____

Ferreira Doña Antonia Port NV   PC   T   V
Portugal $$$ X   X
♥ This is a tawny-style Port—all amber-gold color,
toasted nut, cinnamon sugar, cappuccino, and maple
scents and flavors. I love it with bread pudding, any
banana dessert, spice cake, carrot cake, pumpkin pie,
and just by itself. Serve at room temp. The open
bottle will not go bad.
Kitchen Countertop Survivor™ *Grade: A+*
Your notes:_____

_____

Ficklin Tinta "Port" NV   PC   T   V
California $$$ X   X
♥ "Port" is in quotes, because the real thing is from
Portugal. But this is a very worthy version of the style.
Chocolate, nuts, dried figs, and sweet spices
permeate both the scent and the taste. It would be
great with Stilton cheese (an English blue), dark
chocolate desserts, or nut cookies (pecan sandies, pis-
tachio biscotti, etc.). Serve at room temp.
Kitchen Countertop Survivor™ *Grade: A+*
Your notes:_____

_____

Michele Chiarlo Nivole ("Clouds")	PC	T	V
Moscato d'Asti, Italy	$$$	X	X

♥ This delicately sparkling, honeysuckle-scented wine from the Piedmont region of Italy should completely replace the brunch mimosa. It's got the bubbles, is low in alcohol, high in fruit (apricot and tangerine) and refreshment, and so much better tasting. For dessert it is lovely with fruit—fresh or in crêpes Suzette, strawberry shortcake, pavlova, and so on. It's also a beautiful, delicate aperitif. Serve chilled.

Kitchen Countertop Survivor™ *Grade: B*

Your notes:_____

_____

Price Ranges: **$** = $12 or less; **$$** = 12.01–20; **$$$** = 20.01–35; **$$$$** = > $35

Kitchen Countertop Survivor™ Grades: *Avg.* = a "one-day wine," tastes noticeably less fresh the next day; *B* = holds its freshness for 2–3 days after opening; *B+* = holds *and gets better* over 2–3 days after opening; *A* = a 3- to 4-day "freshness window"; *A+* = holds *and gets better* over 3–4 days

THE GREAT WINE MADE SIMPLE MINI-COURSE: A WINE CLASS IN A GLASS

How do you go about choosing wine? Many buyers assume the quick answer is to "trade up"—if you spend more, the wine will be better, right? Not necessarily, because price and quality are rarely proportional, meaning you cannot assume that a twenty-dollar bottle is twice as good as a ten-dollar one. And more important, preferences are individual. So the best way to ensure you'll be happy with your wine choices is to learn your taste.

Here are two quick wine lessons, adapted from my book *Great Wine Made Simple,* that will let you do exactly that. You're probably thinking, Will there be a test? In a way, every pulled cork is a test, but for the *wine:* Are you happy with what you got for the price you paid, and would you buy it again? This mini-course will teach you to pick wines that pass muster by helping you learn what styles and tastes you like in a wine and how to use the label to help you find them.

If you want, you can complete each lesson in a matter of minutes. As with food, tasting impressions form quickly with wine. Then you can get dinner on the table, accompanied by your wine picks. Start by doing the first lesson, "White Wine Made Simple," one evening, and then Lesson 2, "Red Wine Made Simple," another time. Or you can invite friends over and make it a party. Everyone will learn a little bit about wine, while having fun.

Setup

Glassware: You will need three glasses per taster. A simple all-purpose wineglass is ideal, but clear disposables are fine, too.

Pouring: Start with a tasting portion (about an ounce of each wine). Tasters can repour more of their favorite to enjoy with hors d'oeuvres or dinner.

Flights: Taste the Lesson 1 whites first and then the Lesson 2 reds (pros call each sequence of wine a *flight*). There is no need to wash or rinse the glasses.

To Taste It Is to Know It

Tasting is the fastest way to learn about wine. My restaurant guests tell me this all the time: they know what wines they like when they try them. The trick is in understanding the style and knowing how to ask for it and get it again: "I'd like a Chardonnay with lots of buttery, toasty oak and gobs of creamy, tropical fruit flavors." If you don't know what it means, you might feel silly offering a description like that when wine shopping. But those words really are in the glass, and these easy-to-follow tasting lessons will help you recognize the styles and learn which ones are your favorites.

The Lessons

What You'll Do:

For Lesson 1, "White Wine Made Simple," you will comparison-taste three major white wine grapes: Riesling, Sauvignon Blancs and Chardonnay. For Lesson 2, "Red Wine Made Simple," you will compare three major reds: Pinot Noir, Merlot, and Cabernet Sauvignon. Follow these easy steps:

1. Buy your wines. Make your choice from the varietal sections of this book. It's best to choose wines in the same price category—for example, all one-dollar-sign wines. To make the most of the lesson, choose wines from the region(s) suggested in each grape's "tasting notes."
2. Chill (whites only), pour, and taste the wines in the order of body, light to full, as shown in the tasting notes.
3. Use these tasting notes below as a guide, and record your own if you want.

What You'll Learn:

Body styles of the major grapes—light, medium, or full. You'll see that Riesling is lighter (less heavy) than

Chardonnay, in the same way that, for example, skim milk is lighter than heavy cream.

What the major grapes taste like—When tasted side by side, the grapes are quite distinctive, just as a pear tastes different from an apple, a strawberry tastes different from a blueberry, and so on.

What other wine flavor words taste like—Specifically, you'll experience these tastes: oaky, tannic, crisp, and fruity. Knowing them is helpful because they're used a lot in this book, on wine bottle labels, and by sellers of wine—merchants, waiters, and so on.

Getting comfortable with these basics will equip you to describe the wine styles you like to a waiter or wine merchant and to use the information on a bottle label to find those styles on your own. In the "Buying Lingo" section that follows, I've defined lots of other style words and listed some wine types you can try to experience them.

Tasting Lesson 1
WHITE WINE MADE SIMPLE

Instructions: Taste the wines in numbered order. Note your impressions of:

Color: Which is lightest and which is darkest? Whites can range from pale straw to deep yellow-gold. The darker the color, the fuller the body.

Scent: While they all smell like white wine, the aromas differ, from delicate and tangy to rich and fruity.

Taste and Body: In the same way that fruits range from crisp and tart (like apples) to ripe and lush (like mangoes), the wine tastes will vary along with the body styles of the grapes, from light to full.

Which grape and style do you like best? If you like more than one style, that's OK, too!

The White Wines

Grape 1: Riesling (any region)—Light-bodied

Description: Crisp and refreshing, with vibrant fruit flavor ranging from apple to peach.

Brand Name: _____

Your notes: _____

_____

Grape 2: Sauvignon Blanc (France or New Zealand)—Medium-bodied

Description: Very distinctive! The smell is exotically pungent, the taste tangy and mouthwatering, like citrus fruit (lime and grapefruit).

Brand Name: _____

Your notes: _____

_____

Grape 3: Chardonnay (California)—Full-bodied

Description: The richest scent and taste, with fruit flavor ranging from ripe apples to peaches to tropical fruits. You can feel the full-bodied texture, too. "Oaky" scents come through as a sweet, buttery, or toasty impression.

Brand Name: _____

Your notes: _____

_____

Tasting Lesson 2
RED WINE MADE SIMPLE

Instructions: Again, taste the wines in numbered order and note your impressions.

Color: Red wines range in color from transparent ruby, like the Pinot Noir, to inky dark purple—the darker the color, the fuller the body.

Scent: In addition to the smell of "red wine," you'll get the cherrylike smell of Pinot Noir, perhaps plum character in the Merlot, and a rich dark berry smell in the Cabernet. There are other scents, too, so enjoy them. You can also compare your impressions with those included in the reviews section of the book.

Taste and Body: Like white wines, red wines range from light and delicate to rich and intense. You'll note the differences in body from light to full and the distinctive taste character of each grape. As you can see, tasting them side by side makes it easy to detect and compare the differences.

The Red Wines

Grape 1: Pinot Noir (any region)—Light-bodied

Description: Delicate cherrylike fruit flavor, silky-smooth texture, mouthwatering acidity, all of which make Pinot Noir a versatile wine for most types of food.

Brand Name: _____

Your notes: _____

_____

Grape 2: Merlot (California, Chile, or Washington)—Medium-bodied

Description: More intense than Pinot Noir: rich "red wine" flavor, yet not too heavy. That's probably why it's the red grape of the moment!

Brand Name: _____

Your notes: _____

_____

Grape 3: Cabernet Sauvignon (France or California)—Full-bodied

Description: The fullest-bodied, most intense taste. Notice the drying sensation it leaves on your tongue? That's tannin, a natural grape component that, like color, comes from the skin. As you can see, more color and more tannin come together. Tasting high-tannin wines with fat or protein counters that drying sensation (that's why Cabernet and red meat are considered classic partners). In reds, an "oaky" character comes through as one or more of these scents: spice, cedar, smoke, toastiness, vanilla, and coconut. No wonder buyers love it!

Brand Name: _____

Your notes: _____

_____

Buying Lingo

Here are the meanings of other major wine style words that you see in this book and on wine bottles.

Acidity—The tangy, tart, crisp, mouthwatering component in wine. It's a prominent characteristic of Riesling, Sauvignon Blanc, and Pinot Grigio whites and Pinot Noir and Chianti/Sangiovese reds.

Bag-in-a-Box—A box with a wine-filled plastic bag inside that deflates as the wine is consumed.

Balance—The harmony of all the wine's main components: fruit, alcohol, and acidity, plus sweetness (if any), oak (if used in the winemaking), and tannin (in reds). As with food, balance in the wine is important to your enjoyment, and a sign of quality. But it's also a matter of taste—the dish may taste "too salty" and the wine "too oaky" for one person but be fine to another.

Barrel aged—The wine was fermented or aged (or both) in oak barrels. The barrels give fuller body, as well as an "oaky" character to the wine's scent and flavor, making it seem richer. "Oaky" scents are often in the sweet family—but *not* sugary. Rather, *toasty, spicy, vanilla, buttery,* and *coconut* are the common wine words to describe "oaky" character. Other label signals that mean "oaky": Barrel Fermented, Barrel Select, Barrel Cuvée, Cask Fermented.

Bouquet—All of the wine's scents, which come from the grape(s) used, the techniques (like oak aging), the age of the wine, and the vineyard characteristics (like soil and climate).

Bright—Vivid and vibrant. Usually used as a modifier, like "bright fruit" or "bright acidity."

Buttery—Literally, the creamy-sweet smell of butter. One by-product of fermentation is an ester that mimics the butter smell, so you may well notice this in some wines, especially barrel-fermented Chardonnays.

Creamy—Can mean a smell similar to fresh cream or a smooth and lush texture. In sparkling wines, it's a textural delicacy and smoothness of the bubbles.

Crisp—See Acidity.

Dry—A wine without sweetness (though not without fruit; see Fruity for more on this).

Earthy—As with cheeses, potatoes, mushrooms, and other good consumables, wines can have scents and flavors reminiscent of, or owed to, the soil. The "earth" terms commonly attributed to wine include *mushrooms, truffles, flint, dusty, gravely, wet leaves,* and even *barnyard.*

Exotic—Just as it applies to other things, this description suggests unusual and alluring characteristics in wine. Quite often refers to wines with a floral or spicy style or flavors beyond your typical fruit bowl, such as tropical fruits or rare berries.

Floral—Having scents that mimic flower scents, whether fresh (as in the honeysuckle scent of some Rieslings) or dried (as in the wilted rose petal scent of some Gewürztraminers).

Food-friendly—Food-friendly wines have taste characteristics that pair well with a wide variety of foods without clashing or overpowering— namely, good acidity and moderate (not too heavy) body. The food-friendly whites include Riesling and Sauvignon Blanc; the reds include Chianti, Spanish Rioja, red Rhône, and Pinot Noir wines.

Fruity—Marked by a prominent smell and taste of fruit. In whites the fruit tastes can range from lean and tangy (like lemons and crisp apples) to medium (like melons and peaches) to lush (like mangoes and pineapples). In reds, think cranberries and cherries, plums and blueberries, figs and prunes. Note that *fruity* doesn't mean "sweet." The taste and smell of ripe fruit are perceived as sweet, but they're not sugary. Most wines on the market are at once dry (meaning not sweet) and fruity, with lots of fruit flavor.

Grassy—Describes a wine marked with scents of fresh-cut grass or herbs or even green vegetables (like green pepper and asparagus). It's a signature of Sauvignon Blanc wines, especially those grown in New Zealand and France. *Herbal* and *herbaceous* are close synonyms.

Herbal, herbaceous—See Grassy.

Legs—The drips running down the inside of the wineglass after you swirl it. Not a sign of quality (as in "good legs") but of viscosity. Fast-running legs indicate a low-viscosity wine and slow legs a high-viscosity wine. The higher the viscosity, the richer and fuller the wine feels in your mouth.

Nose—The smell of the wine. Isn't it interesting how wines have a nose, legs, and body? As you've no doubt discovered, they have personalities, too!

Oaky—See Barrel aged.

Off-dry—A lightly sweet wine.

Old vines—Refers to wine from vines significantly older than average, usually at least thirty years old and sometimes far older. Older vines yield a smaller, but often more intensely flavored, crop of grapes.

Regional wine—A wine named for the region where the grapes are grown, such as Champagne, Chianti, Pouilly-Fuissé, etc.

Spicy—A wine with scents and flavors reminiscent of spices, both sweet (cinnamon, ginger, cardamom, clove) and savory (pepper, cumin, curry).

Sweet—A wine that has perceptible sugar, called *residual sugar* because it is left over from fermentation and not converted to alcohol. A wine can be lightly sweet like a Moscato or very sweet like a Port or Sauternes.

Tannic—A red wine whose tannin is noticeable— a little or a lot—as a drying sensation on your tongue ranging from gentle (lightly tannic) to velvety (richly tannic) to harsh (too tannic).

Terroir—The distinctive flavors, scents, and character of a wine owed to its vineyard source. For example, the terroir of French red Burgundies is sometimes described as *earthy.*

Toasty—Wines with a toasty, roasted, caramelized, or smoky scent reminiscent of coffee beans, toasted nuts or spices, or burnt sugar.

Unfiltered—A wine that has not been filtered before bottling (which is common practice). Some say filtering the wine strips out flavor, but not everyone agrees. I think most tasters cannot tell the difference.

Varietal wine—A wine named for the grape used to make it, such as Chardonnay or Merlot.

Handling Wine Leftovers

I developed the Kitchen Countertop Survivor™ and Kitchen Fridge Survivor™ grades to give you an idea of how long each wine stays in good drinking condition if you don't finish the bottle. In the same way that resealing the cereal box or wrapping and refrigerating leftovers will extend their freshness window, you can do the same for wine by handling the leftovers as follows:

Still Wines

Recork—At a minimum, close the bottle with its original cork. Most wines will stay fresh a day or two. To extend that freshness window, purchase a vacuum-sealer (available in kitchenware shops and wine shops). You simply cork the bottle with the purchased rubber stopper, which has a one-way valve. The accompanying plastic vacuum pump is then placed on top of the stopper; you pump the handle repeatedly until the resistance tightens, indicating the air has been pumped out of the bottle. (Note: A few wine experts don't think rubber stoppers work, but I have used them for years. In my restaurants, I have found they extended the life of bottles opened for by-the-glass service two days longer than just sealing with the original cork.)

Refrigerate stoppered (and vacuum-sealed) bottles, whether white, pink, or red. Refrigeration of anything slows the spoilage, and your red wine, once removed from the fridge and poured in the glass, will quickly come to serving temperature.

For even longer shelf-life, you can preserve partial bottles with inert gas. I recommend this especially for more expensive wines. Wine Life and Private Preserve are two brands that I have used (sold in wine shops and accessories catalogs). They come in a can that feels light, as if it's empty. Inside is an inert gas mixture that is heavier than air. The can's spray nozzle is inserted into the bottle. A one-second sprays fills the empty bottle space with the inert gas, displacing the air inside, which is the key because no air in contact with the wine means no oxidation. Then you quickly replace the cork (make sure the fit is tight). My experience in restaurants using gas systems for very upscale wines by the glass is that they keep well for a week or more.

Sparkling Wines

Your best bet is to purchase "clam shell" Champagne stoppers, with one or two hinged metal clamps attached to a stopper top that has a rubber or plastic gasket for a tight seal. You place the stopper on top, press down, and then anchor the clamps to the bottle lip. If you open your sparkler carefully and don't "pop" the cork, losing precious carbonation, a stoppered partial bottle will keep its effervescence for at least a few days, and sometimes much longer.

SAVVY SHOPPER: RETAIL WINE BUYING

Supermarkets, pharmacies, price clubs, catalogs, state stores, megastores, dot.coms, and boutiques . . . where you shop for wine depends a lot on the state where you live, because selling wine requires a state license. What many people don't realize is how much the wine laws vary from one state to the next.

In most states, the regulations affect the prices you pay for wine, what wines are available, and how you get your hands on them (ideally, they are delivered to your door or poured at your table, but this isn't always legal). Here is a quick summary of the retail scene to help you make the most of your buying power wherever you live.

Wine Availability The single biggest frustration for every wine buyer and winery is bureaucracy. To ensure the collection of excise taxes, in nearly all states every single wine must be registered and approved in some way before it can be sold. If a wine you're seeking isn't available in your area, this is probably the reason. For many small boutique wineries, it just isn't worth the bother and expense to get legal approval for the few cases of wine they would sell in a particular state. One extreme example is Pennsylvania, a "control state" where wine is sold exclusively by a state-run monopoly that, without competition, has little incentive to source a lot of boutique wines. By contrast, California, New York, and Chicago, with high demand and competition, are good markets for wine availability.

Wine Prices and Discounts Wine prices can vary from one state to the next due to different tax rates. And in general, prices are lower in competitive markets, where stores can use discounts, sale prices, and so on to vie for your business.

Where they are legal, case discounts of 10 to 15 percent are a great way to get the best possible prices for your favorite wines. On the more expensive wines, many people I know coordinate their buying with friends and family so they can buy full cases and get these discounts.

Delivery and Wine-by-Mail In many states, it is not legal for stores or other retailers to deliver wine to the purchaser.

Many catalogs and websites sell wine by mail. Some are affiliated with retail stores or wineries, while others are strictly virtual stores. The conveniences include shopping on your own time and terms, from home or office, helpful buying recommendations and information, and usually home delivery. But the laws governing such shipping are complex, and vary from state to state (in some states it is completely prohibited). When you add in shipping costs, there may not be a price advantage to shopping online, but many people swear by the convenience and buying advice it offers. It is also an easy way to send wine gifts.

Where Should I Shop? That depends on what you're buying. If you know what you want, then price is your main consideration, and you'll get your best deals at venues that concentrate on volume sales— discount stores, price clubs, and so on. If you want buying advice, or are buying rare wines, you're better off in a wine shop or merchant specializing in fine wines. These stores have trained buyers who taste and know their inventory well; they can help you with your decision. The better stores also have temperature-controlled storage for their rare wines, which is critical to ensure you get a product in good condition. There are also web-based fine and rare wine specialists, but that is a fairly new market. I suggest you purchase fine and rare wines only through sources with a good track record of customer service. In that way, if you have problems with a shipment, you will have some recourse.

Can I Take That Bottle on the Wine List Home with Me? In most states, restaurants' wine licenses allow for sale and consumption "on-premise" only, meaning they cannot sell you a bottle to take home.

Burgundy Buyers, Beware With the exception of volume categories such as Beaujolais, Macon, and Pouilly-Fuissé, buyers of French white and red Burgundy should shop only at fine wine merchants, preferably those that specialize in Burgundy, for two reasons. First, Burgundy is simply too fragile to handle the storage conditions in most stores. Burgundy specialists ensure temperature-controlled storage. Second, selection is a major factor, because quality varies a lot from one winery to the next, and from one vintage to the next. Specialist stores have the needed buying expertise to ensure the quality of their offerings.

Is That a Deal or a Disaster? Floor stacks, "end caps," private labels, and bin ends can be a boon for the buyer, or a bust, depending on where you are shopping. Here's what you need to know about them:

"Floor Stacks" of large-volume categories and brands (e.g., branded varietal wines)—These are a best bet in supermarkets and other volume-based venues, where they're used to draw your attention to a price markdown. Take advantage of it to stock up for everyday or party wines.

"End Cap" wine displays featured at the ends of aisles—A good bet, especially in fine wine shops. You may not have heard of the wine, but they're usually "hidden gems" that the buyer discovered and bought in volume, to offer you quality and uniqueness at a savings.

"Bin Ends"—Retailers often clear out the last few bottles of something by discounting the price. In reputable retail stores, they are usually still good quality, and thus a good bet. Otherwise, steer clear.

Private labels—These are wines blended and bottled exclusively for the retailer—again, good bets in reputable stores, who stake their reputation on your satisfaction with their private labels.

"Shelf-talkers"—Written signs, reviews, and ratings. Good shops offer their own recommendations in lieu of, or along with, critics' scores. If the only information is a critic's score, check to be sure that the vintage being sold matches that of the wine that was reviewed.

Buying Wine in Restaurants

Wine List Strategy Session

A lot of us have a love-hate relationship with the wine list. On the one hand, we know it holds the potential to enhance the evening, impress the date or client, broaden our horizons, or all three. But it also makes us feel intimidated, inadequate, overwhelmed, and . . .

Panicked by prices—That goes for both the cheapest wines *and* the most expensive ones; we're leery of extremes.

Pressured by pairing—Will this wine "go with" our food?

Overwhelmed by options—Can this wine I've never heard of possibly be any good? Does my selection measure up? (Remember, the restaurant is supposed to impress *you,* not the other way around.) This "phone book" wine list makes me want to dial 911.

Stumped by Styles—Food menus are easy because we understand the key terms: appetizer, entree, dessert, salad, soup, fish, meat, and so on. But after *white* and *red,* most of us get lost pretty quickly with wine categories. (Burgundy . . . is that a style, a color, a place, or all three?)

Let's deal with the first three above. For the lowdown on wine list terms, use the decoder that follows to pinpoint the grapes and styles behind all the major wine names.

Wine List Prices
The prices on wine lists reflect three things:

- *The dining-out experience*—The restaurant wine markup is higher than in retail stores because the decor is (usually) nicer, and you get to stay awhile, during which time they open the wine, serve it in a nice glass, and clean up afterward. They also invested in the cost and expertise to select and store the wine properly. Consequently those who enjoy drinking wine in restaurants, are accustomed to being charged more for the wine than you would pay to drink the same bottle at home. That said, exorbitant markups are, in my opinion, the biggest deterrent to more guests enjoying wine in restaurants (which is both good for the guests and good for business). You can always vote with your wallet and dine in restaurants with guest-friendly wine pricing.

- *Location*—Restaurants in exclusive resorts, in urban centers with a business clientele, or with a star chef behind them, tend toward higher wine markups, because they can get away with it. The logic, so to speak, is that if you're on vacation, it's on the company, or it's just the "in" place, high markups (on everything) are part of the price of admission. However, I don't really think that's right, and I do think these places would sell more wine with lower markups.

- *The rarity of the wine*—Often, the rarer the wine (either because it's in high demand due to critics' hype or because it's old and just a few bottles remain), the higher the markup. It's a form of rationing in the face of high demand/low supply. Food can be the same way (lobsters, truffles, caviar, etc.).

Getting the Most Restaurant Wine for Your Money

Seeking value doesn't make you a cheapskate. Here are the best strategies to keep in mind:

1. Take the road less traveled—Chardonnay and Cabernet Sauvignon are what I call "comfort wines" because they're so well known. But their prices often reflect a "comfort premium" (in the same way that a name-brand toothpaste costs more than the store brand). These spectacular wine styles often give better value for the money, because they're less widely known:

Whites

Sauvignon Blanc and Fumé Blanc

Sancerre (a French Loire Valley wine made
   from the Sauvignon Blanc grape)

Anything from Washington State or New
   Zealand

Reds

Côtes-du-Rhône and other French Rhône
   Valley reds

Red Zinfandel from California

Spanish Rioja and other reds from Spain

Cabernet Sauvignon from Chile

2. Savvy Splurging—There's no doubt about it:
nothing commemorates, celebrates, or impresses better than a special wine. Since splurging on wine in a restaurant can mean especially
big bucks, here are the "trophy" wine styles
that give you the most for your money on wine
lists:

> French Champagne—I think that Cham-
> pagne (the real stuff from France's Cham-
> pagne region) is among the most affordable
> luxuries on the planet, and its wine list
> prices are often among the best of all the
> "badge" wine categories (such as French
> Bordeaux and Burgundy, cult California
> Cabernets, and boutique Italian wines).

> California's Blue Chip Cabernets—I don't
> mean the tiny-production cult-movement
> Cabernets but rather the classics that have
> been around for decades, and still make
> world-class wine at a fair price. Names like
> Beringer, BV, Cakebread, Jordan, Mt.
> Veeder, Robert Mondavi, Silver Oak, Simi,
> and Stag's Leap all made the survey, and for
> good reason: they're excellent and available.

> Italian Chianti Classico Riserva—This
> recommendation may surprise you, but I
> include it because the quality for the price
> is better than ever, and recent vintages
> have been great. I also think that across the
> country a lot of people celebrate and do

business in steak houses and Italian restaurants, which tend to carry this wine category because it complements their food.

3. The Midprice/Midstyle "Safety Zone"—This is a strategy I first developed not for dining guests but for our *waiters* trying to help diners choose a bottle, usually with very little to go on (many people aren't comfortable describing their taste preference, and they rarely broadcast their budget for fear of looking cheap). The midprice/midstyle strategy is this: in any wine list category (e.g., Chardonnays, Italian reds, and so on), if you go for the midprice range in that section, odds are good the wine will be midstyle. Midstyle is my shorthand for the most typical, crowd-pleasing version, likely to satisfy a high proportion of guests and to be sticker shock free. The fact is that the more expensive the wine is, the more distinctive and even unusual its style is likely to be. If it's not to your taste *and* you've spent a lot, you're doubly disappointed.

4. Ask—With wine more popular than ever, restaurants are the most proactive they've ever been in seeking to put quality and value on their wine lists. So ask for it: "What's the best red wine deal on your list right now?" Or, if you have a style preference, say something like "We want to spend $XX. Which of these Chardonnays do you think is the best for the money?"

Pairing Wine and Food

Worrying a lot about this is a big waste of time, because most wines complement most foods, regardless of wine color, center-of-the-plate protein, and all that other stuff. How well? Their affinity can range from "fine" to "Omigod." You can pretty much expect at least a nice combination every time you have wine with food and great matches from time to time (of course, frequent experimentation ups your odds). The point is, your style preference is a lot more important than the pairing, per se, because if you hate the dish or the wine, you're hardly likely to enjoy the pairing. That said, here is a list of wine styles that are especially favored by sommeliers and chefs for their exceptional food affinity and versatility, along with a few best-bet food recommendations:

Favorite "Food Wines" White	Best-Bet Food Matches
Champagne and Sparkling Wine—So many people save bubbly just for toasts, but it's an amazing "food wine"	Sushi All shellfish Cheeses (even stinky ones) Omelets and other egg dishes Mushroom sauces (on risotto, pasta or whatever)
Riesling from Germany, Alsace (France), America, Australia	Mexican, southwestern, and other spicy foods Shellfish Cured meats and sausages
Alsace (France) White Wines—Riesling, Pinot Gris, and Gewürztraminer	Pacific Rim foods—Japanese, Thai, Korean, Chinese Indian food Smoked meats and charcuterie Meat stews (really!)
Sauvignon Blanc and wines made from it (French Sancerre, Pouilly-Fumé, and white Bordeaux)	Goat cheese Salads Herbed sauces (like pesto) Tomato dishes (salads, soups, sauces)

Red	
Beaujolais (from France)	Mushroom dishes
Pinot Noir	Fish (especially rich ones like tuna, salmon, and cod) Smoked meats Grilled vegetables Duck
Chianti, Rosso di Montalcino, and other Italian reds made from the Sangiovese grape	Pizza, eggplant parmigiana (and other Italian-American–inspired tastes) Cheesy dishes Spicy sausages
Rioja from Spain	Roasted and grilled meats

Choosing from the Wine List

You've got the wine list. Unless you know a lot about wine, you now face at least one of these dilemmas:

- You've never heard of any of the wines listed or at least none of those in your price range (OK, maybe you've heard of Dom Pérignon, but let's be real). Or the names you do recognize don't interest you.

- You have no idea how much a decent selection should cost. But you *do* know you want to keep to your budget, without broadcasting it to your guests and the entire dining room.
- The wine list is so huge you don't even want to open it.

Wine List Playbook

Remember, you're the buyer. Good restaurants want you to enjoy wine and to feel comfortable with the list, your budget, and so on. As far as the wine-snobby ones go, what are you doing there anyway? (OK, if you took a gamble on a new place or somebody else picked it, the strategies here can help.)

The basics:

1. *Don't worry if you haven't heard of the names.* There are literally thousands of worthy wines beyond the big brand names, and many restaurants feature them to spice up their selection.
2. *Determine what you want to spend.* I think most people want the best deal they can get. With that in mind, here are some price/value rules of thumb. In most restaurants the wine prices tend to relate to the food prices, as follows:
   - Wines by-the-glass. The price window for good-quality wines that please a high percentage of diners usually parallels the restaurant's mid- to top-priced appetizers. So if the Caesar salad (or wings or whatever) is $5.95, expect to spend that, plus or minus a dollar or two, for a good glass of wine. This goes for dessert wine, too. Champagne and sparkling wines can be more, due to the cost of the product and greater waste because it goes flat.
   - Bottles: This is far more variable, but in general most restaurants try to offer an ample selection of good-quality bottles priced in what I call a "selling zone" that's benchmarked to their highest entree price, plus a

margin. That's the variable part. It can range from $5–10 on average in national chain restaurants and their peers to at least $10–20 in luxury and destination restaurants. So if the casual chain's steak-and-shrimp-scampi combo costs $17.95, the $20–30 zone on their wine list will likely hold plenty of good bottle choices. In an urban restaurant where the star chef's signature herb-crusted lamb costs $28, you could expect a cluster of worthy bottles in the $35–55 range.

We in the trade find it funny, and nearly universal, that guests shy away from the least expensive wines on our lists, suspicious that there's something "wrong" with the wine. But any restaurant that's committed to wine, whether casual chain or destination eatery, puts extra effort into finding top-quality wines at the lowest price points. They may come from grapes or regions you don't know, but my advice is to muster your sense of adventure and try them. In the worst-case scenario, you'll be underwhelmed, but since tastes vary, this can happen with wine at any price. I think the odds are better that you'll enjoy one of the best deals on the wine list.

The wine list transaction: You've set your budget. Now it's time to zero in on a selection. You've got two choices—go it alone or ask for help. In either case, here's what to do:

1. Ask for the wine list right away. It's a pet peeve of mine that guests even *need* to ask (rather than getting the list automatically with the food menus), because that can cause both service delays and anxiety. Many people are scared to request the list for fear it "commits" them to a purchase, before they can determine whether they'll be comfortable with the prices and choices available. As you're being handed the menus, say "We'll take a look at the wine list, too" to indicate you want a copy to review, not a pushy sales job. Tip: I always ask that the wine-by-the-glass list be brought, too. Since many places change them often, they may be

on a separate card or a specials board. (I think verbal listings are the worst, because often key information, like the price or winery, can get lost in translation.)

2. Determine any style particulars you're in the mood for:
   - White or red?
   - A particular grape, region, or body style?

   If the table can't reach a consensus, look at wine-by-the-glass and half-bottle options. This can happen when preferences differ or food choices are all over the map ("I'm having the oysters, he's having the wild boar, we want one wine . . ." is a stumper I've actually faced!).

3. Find your style zone in the list. Turn to the section that represents your chosen category—e.g., whites, the wine-by-the-glass section, Chardonnays, Italian reds, or whatever—or let the server know what style particulars you have in mind.

4. Match your budget. Pick a wine priced accordingly, keeping in mind these "safety zones":
   - The wines recommended in this book
   - Winery or region names that you remember liking or hearing good things about (e.g., Chianti in Italy or a different offering from your favorite white Zinfandel producer)
   - The midprice/midstyle zone (as I explained earlier, many lists have this "sweet spot" of well-made, moderately priced offerings)
   - Featured wine specials, if they meet your price parameters

   You can communicate your budget while keeping your dignity with this easy trick I teach waiters:
   - Find your style zone—e.g., Pinot Grigios—in the wine list.
   - With both you and the server looking at the list, *point to the price* of a wine that's close to what you want to spend and then say, "We were looking at this one. What do you think?"
   - Keep pointing long enough for the server to see the price, and you'll be understood

without having to say (in front of your date or client), "No more than thirty bucks, OK?"

I ask my waiters to point to the price, starting at a moderate level, with their first wine suggestion. From there the guest's reaction shows his or her intentions, without the embarrassment of having to talk price.

There's no formula, but the bottom line is this: whether glass or bottle, it's hard to go wrong with popular grapes and styles, moderate prices, the "signature" or featured wine(s) of the restaurant, and/or the waiter's enthusiastic recommendation. If you don't like it, chalk it up to experience—the same could happen with a first-time food choice, right? Most of the time, experimentation pays off. So enjoy!

Wine List Decoder

Wine is like food—it's easy to choose from among the styles with which you're familiar. That's why wines like Pinot Grigio, Chardonnay, Chianti, and Merlot are such big sellers. But when navigating other parts of the list, namely less-common grape varieties and the classic European regional wines, I think many of us get lost pretty quickly. And yet these are major players in the wine world, without which buyers miss out on a whole array of delicious options, from classic to cutting edge.

This decoder will give you the tools you need to explore them. It reveals:

The grapes used to make the classic wines—If it's a grape you've tried, then you'll have an idea of what the wine tastes like.

The body styles from light to full of every major wine category—The waiters and wine students with whom I work always find this extremely helpful, because it breaks up the wine world into broad, logical categories that are easy to understand and similar to the way we classify other things. With food, for example, we have vegetables, meat, fish, and so on.

The taste profile, in simple terms—The exact taste of any wine is subjective (I say apple, you say pear), but knowing how the tastes *compare* is a great tool to help you identify your preferred style.

The names are set up just as you might see them on a wine list, under the key country and region headings, and in each section they are arranged by body style from light to full. (For whites, Italy comes before France in body style, overall. Their order is reversed for reds.) Finally, where applicable I've highlighted the major grapes in italics in the column on the left to help you quickly see just how widely used these grapes are and thus how much you already know about these heretofore mystifying wine names.

Sparkling Wines

- ### Italy

Asti Spumante	Muscat (Moscato)	Light; floral, hint of sweetness
Prosecco	Prosecco	Delicate; crisp, tangy, the wine used in Bellini cocktails

- ### Spain

Cava	Locals: Xarel-lo, Parellada, Macabeo plus Chardonnay	Light; crisp, refreshing

- ### France

Champagne	The red (yes!) grapes Pinot Noir and Pinot Meunier, plus Chardonnay	To me, all are heavenly, but check the style on the label: Blanc de Blancs—delicate and tangy Brut NV, vintage and luxury—range from soft and creamy to rich and toasty

White Wines

- ### Italy

Frascati	Trebbiano, Malvasia	As you've noticed, mostly local grapes are used in Italy's whites. But the style of all these is easy to remember: light, tangy, and refreshing. Pinot Grigio, the best known, is also more distinctive—pleasant pear and lemon flavors, tasty but not heavy. The less common Pinot Bianco is similar.
Soave	Garganega, Trebbiano	
Orvieto	Grechetto, Procanico, and many others	
Gavi	Cortese	
Vernaccia	Vernaccia	
Pinot Grigio		

- **Germany**
  Riesling

	Riesling rules Germany's quality wine scene	Feather-light but flavor-packed: fruit salad in a glass

- **France**
  - **Alsace—Grape names are on the label:**

	Pinot Blanc	Light; tangy, pleasant
Riesling	Riesling	Fuller than German Riesling but not heavy; citrus, apples, subtle but layered
	Pinot Gris	Smooth, richer texture; fruit compote flavors
	Gewürztraminer	Sweet spices, apricots, lychee fruit

  - **Loire Valley**

Vouvray	Chenin Blanc	Look for the style name: Sec—dry and tangy; Demi-sec—baked apple, hint of sweetness; Moelleux—honeyed dessert style

Sauvignon Blanc

Sancerre and Pouilly-Fumé	Sauvignon Blanc	Light to medium; subtle fruit, racy acidity

  - **White Bordeaux**

Sauvignon Blanc & Semillon

Entre-Deux-Mers	Sauvignon Blanc and Semillon	Tangy, crisp, light
Graves Pessac-Leognan		Medium to full; ranging from creamy lemon-lime to lush fig flavors; pricey ones are usually oaky

  - **Burgundy White**

Chardonnay

Macon St.-Veran Pouilly-Fuissé	Every Chardonnay in the world is modeled on white French Burgundy	Light; refreshing, citrus-apple flavors
Chablis		Subtle, mineral, green apple

St. Aubin

Meursault		Medium; pear, dried apple, nutty; complexity ranging from simple to sublime
Puligny-Montrachet		
Chassagne-Montrachet		
Corton-Charlemagne		

Red Wines

- **France**
  - *Red Burgundy*

Beaujolais	Gamay	Uncomplicated, light; fruity, pleasant
Beaujolais-Villages		
Beaujolais Cru: Morgon, Moulin-à-Vent, etc.		More complex, plum-berry taste, smooth (the wines are named for their village)

Pinot Noir

Côte de Beaune	Pinot Noir	Ranging from light body, pretty cherry taste to extraordinary complexity: captivating spice, berry and earth scents, silky texture, berries and plums flavor
Santenay		
Volnay		
Pommard		
Nuits-St.-Georges		
Vosne-Romanée		
Gevrey-Chambertin		
Clos de Vougeot, etc.		

  - *Red Bordeaux*

Merlot

Pomerol	Merlot, plus Cabernet Franc and Cabernet Sauvignon	Medium to full; oaky-vanilla scent, plum flavor
St. Emilion		

Cabernet Sauvignon

Médoc	Cabernet Sauvignon, plus Merlot, Cabernet Franc, and Petit Verdot	Full; chunky-velvety texture; cedar-spice-toasty scent; dark berry flavor
Margaux		
Pauillac		
St-Estèphe		

- **Rhône Red**

Syrah, aka Shiraz

Côtes-du-Rhône	Mainly Grenache, Syrah, Cinsault, Mourvedre	Medium to full; juicy texture; spicy raspberry scent and taste
Côte-Rôtie	Syrah, plus a splash of white Viognier	Full; brawny texture; peppery scent; plum and dark berry taste
Hermitage	Syrah, plus a touch of the white grapes Marsanne and Roussane	Similar to Côte-Rôtie
Châteauneuf-du-Pape	Mainly Syrah, Grenache, Cinsault, Mourvedre	Full; exotic leathery-spicy scent; spiced fig and berry compote taste

(Red Zinfandel is here in the light-to-full body spectrum)

- **Spain**
  - **Rioja**

Rioja Crianza, Reserva and Gran Reserva	Tempranillo, plus Garnacha, aka Grenache, and other local grapes	Ranging from soft and smooth, juicy strawberry character (Crianza); to full, caramel-leather scent, spicy-dried fruit taste (Reserva and Gran Reserva)

  - **Ribera del Duero**

	Mostly Tempranillo	Full; mouth-filling texture; toasty-spice scent; anise and plum taste

  - **Priorat**

Sometimes Cabernet Sauvignon

Priorat	Varied blends may include Cabernet Sauvignon, Garnacha, and other local grapes	Full; gripping texture; meaty-leathery-fig scent; superconcentrated plum and dark berry taste

- **Italy**

As you'll notice from the left column, Italy's classic regions mostly march to their own *belissimo* beat.

  - **Veneto**

Valpolicella	Corvina plus other local grapes	Light; mouthwatering, tangy cherry taste and scent

Amarone della Valpolicella	Corvina; same vineyards as Valpolicella	Full; rich, velvety texture; toasted almond/prune scent; intense dark raisin and dried fig taste (think Fig Newtons)

- ### *Piedmont*

Dolcetto d'Alba (the best known of the Dolcettos, but others are good, too)	Dolcetto	Light; zesty, spicy, cranberry-sour cherry taste
Barbera d'Alba (look for Barbera d'Asti and others)	Barbera	Medium; licorice-spice-berry scent; earth and berry taste
Barolo Barbaresco	Nebbiolo	Full; "chewy" texture; exotic earth, licorice, tar scent; strawberry-spice taste

- ### *Tuscany*

Chianti/ Chianti Classico	Sangiovese	Ranges from light, easy, lip-smacking strawberry-spice character to intense, gripping texture; plum, licorice, and earth scent and taste
Vino Nobile di Monte-pulciano	Prugnolo (a type of Sangiovese)	Medium-to-full; velvety texture, earth-spice, stewed plum taste
Brunello di Montalcino	Brunello (a type of Sangiovese)	Very full; "chewy" in the mouth; powerful dark-fruit flavor

Sometimes Cabernet Sauvignon

"Super Tuscans"— not a region but an important category	Usually a blend of Sangiovese and Cabernet Sauvignon	Modeled to be a classy cross between French red Bordeaux and Italian Chianti; usually full, spicy, and intense, with deep plum and berry flavors

The bottom line on restaurant wine lists: In my opinion, it's not the size of the list that matters but rather the restaurant's effort to make enjoying wine as easy as possible for its guests. How? As always, it comes down to the basics:

Top Ten Tip-Offs You're in a Wine-Wise Restaurant

1. You're *never* made to feel you have to spend a lot to get something good.
2. Wine by the glass is taken as seriously as bottles, with a good range of styles and prices, listed prominently so you don't have to "hunt" to find them.
3. The wine list is presented automatically, so you don't have to ask for it (and wait while the waiter searches for a copy).
4. There are lots of quality bottle choices in the moderate price zone.
5. Wine service, whether glass or bottle, is helpful, speedy, and proficient.
6. Waiters draw your attention to "great values" rather than just the expensive stuff.
7. *Affordable* wine pairings are offered for the signature dishes—either on the menu or by servers.
8. You can ask for a taste before you choose a wine by the glass if you're not sure which you want.
9. It's no problem to split a glass, or get just a half-glass, of by-the-glass offerings. (Great for situations when you want only a little wine or want to try a range of different wines.)
10. There's no such thing as no-name "house white and red." (House-featured wines are fine, but they, and you, merit a name or grape and a region.)

IMMER BEST BETS

Sometimes you just need quick recommendations for the buying occasion at hand. Here are my picks.

Best Restaurant Wineries

The following list of wineries probably includes some names that are familiar to you. These wineries are what we in the restaurant wine list business call *anchors*—the core names around which to build a well-balanced, high-quality wine list that pleases a lot of people. It's not a comprehensive anchor list. Rather, it is my personal list of the benchmark names that I've featured on wine lists for years because, in addition to name recognition with guests, they consistently deliver quality and value across their product line and are generally priced at a relative value compared to the competition in their categories. You can choose your favorite grape or style with extra confidence when it's made by one of these producers.

Beringer, California
Cakebread, California
Calera, California
Cambria, California
Château St. Jean, California
Estancia, California
Ferrari-Carano, California
Hugel, France
Jolivet, France
Jordan, California
Joseph Phelps, California
Kendall-Jackson, California
King Estate, Oregon
Moët & Chandon, France
Morgan, California
Penfolds, Australia

Ridge, California
Robert Mondavi, California
Rosemount Estates, Australia
Ruffino, Italy
Silverado, California
St. Francis, California
Taittinger, France
Trimbach, France
Veuve Clicquot, France

Best Wine List Values

Although wine list pricing varies widely, I regularly see these wines well priced in restaurants around the country and thus offering great value for the money.

White	Red
Bonny Doon Pacific Rim Riesling, USA/Germany	Firesteed Pinot Noir, Oregon
Alois Lageder Pinot Grigio, Italy	Cambria Julia's Vineyard Pinot Noir, California
King Estate Pinot Gris, Oregon	Casa Lapostolle Classic Merlot, Chile
Jolivet Sancerre, France	Franciscan Oakville Estate Merlot, California
Geyser Peak Sauvignon Blanc, California	Carmenet "Dynamite" Cabernet Sauvignon, California
Casa Lapostolle Sauvignon Blanc, Chile	Château Larose-Trintaudon Bordeaux, France
Estancia Pinnacles Chardonnay, California	Guenoc Cabernet Sauvignon, California
Gallo of Sonoma Chardonnay, California	Penfolds Bin 389 Cabernet/ Shiraz, Australia
Simi Chardonnay, California	Cline Zinfandel, California
Château St. Jean Chardonnay, California	J. Lohr 7 Oaks Cabernet Sauvignon, California

Best "House" Wines for Every Day— Sparkling, White, and Red

(*House* means *your* house.) These are great go-to wines to keep around for every day and company too, because they're tasty, *very* inexpensive, and go with everything from takeout to Sunday dinner. They're also wines that got high Kitchen Countertop/Fridge Survivor™ grades, so you don't have to worry if you don't finish the bottle right away. (Selections are listed by body style—lightest to fullest.)

Sparkling

(It is disappointing but true: very few sparklers made the ranks of top-selling wines—check the Top 50 Wines You're Not Drinking section for more "house" bubbly recommendations.)

Domaine Ste. Michelle Cuvée Brut Sparkling,
  Washington

House Whites

Columbia Winery Cellarmaster's Reserve Riesling,
  Washington
Miguel Torres Viña Sol, Spain
Beringer Founders' Estate Sauvignon Blanc,
  California
Penfolds Semillon Chardonnay, Australia
Lindemans Bin 65 Chardonnay, Australia
Gallo of Sonoma Chardonnay, California

Reds

Kendall-Jackson Vintner's Reserve Pinot Noir,
  California
Duboeuf (Georges) Côtes-du-Rhône, France
Marqués de Cáceres Rioja Crianza, Spain
Columbia Crest Merlot, Washington
Rosemount Estates Cabernet/Merlot, Australia
Casa Lapostolle Classic Cabernet Sauvignon, Chile

Impress the Date—Hip Wines

White

Bonny Doon Pacific Rim Riesling, USA/Germany
Frog's Leap Sauvignon Blanc, California
Brancott Reserve Sauvignon Blanc, New Zealand
Didier Dagueneau Silex Pouilly-Fumé, France
R.H. Phillips Toasted Head Chardonnay, California

Red

Coppola (Francis) Presents Rosso, California
Firesteed Pinot Noir, Oregon
Monteviña Amador Zinfandel, California
Penfolds Cabernet/Shiraz Bin 389, Australia

Impress the Client—Blue Chip Wines

Sparkling/White

Veuve Clicquot Yellow Label NV Champagne, France

Cloudy Bay Sauvignon Blanc, New Zealand

Ferrari-Carano Fumé Blanc, California

Cakebread Chardonnay, California

Talbott (Robert) Sleepy Hollow Vineyard Chardonnay, California

Red

Domaine Drouhin Pinot Noir, Oregon

Duckhorn Napa Merlot, California

Ridge Geyserville (Zinfandel), California

Stag's Leap Wine Cellars Napa Cabernet Sauvignon, California

Jordan Cabernet Sauvignon, California

You're Invited—Unimpeachable Bottles to Bring to Dinner

(You *do* still have to send a note the next day.)

Trimbach Riesling, Alsace, France

Simi Sauvignon Blanc, California

Louis Jadot Pouilly-Fuissé, France

Beringer Napa Chardonnay, California

Calera Central Coast Pinot Noir, California

Ruffino Chianti Classico Riserva Ducale Gold Label, Italy

Penfolds Cabernet/Shiraz Bin 389, Australia

St. Francis Sonoma Merlot, California

Franciscan Napa Cabernet Sauvignon, California

Robert Mondavi Napa Cabernet Sauvignon, California

Cellar Candidates

These wines have consistently proven age-worthy throughout my restaurant career. The time window shown for each is the number of years' aging in reasonably cool cellar conditions to reach peak drinking condition. But this "peak" is in terms of *my* taste—namely when the wine's texture has softened and enriched, the aromas have become more layered, but the fruit remains vibrant. You may need to adjust your cellar regimen according to your taste. Generally, longer aging gradually trades youthful fruit and acidity for a whole new spectrum of aromas, many of which you might not instantly associate with grapes or wine. In whites, aging commonly leads to softened acidity and a nutty/caramel character; in reds, softened tannins and a leathery/spicy character.

White

Trimbach Riesling, France (3–4 yrs)

Trimbach Pinot Gris, France (4–5 yrs)

Didier Dagueneau Silex Pouilly-Fumé, France (6–8 yrs)

Edna Valley Vineyard Chardonnay, California (4–5 yrs)

Grgich Hills Chardonnay, California (5–7 yrs)

Cakebread Chardonnay, California (4–5 yrs)

Château Montelena Chardonnay, California (5–7 yrs)

Leflaive (Domaine) Puligny-Montrachet, France (5–6 yrs)

Leflaive (Olivier) Puligny-Montrachet, France (2–4 yrs)

Red

Calera Central Coast Pinot Noir, California (3–4 yrs)

Etude Pinot Noir, California (5–6 yrs)

Robert Mondavi Napa Pinot Noir, California (4–5 yrs)

Felsina Chianti Classico, Italy (3–4 yrs)

Querciabella Chianti Classico Riserva, Italy (3–5 yrs)

Frescobaldi Chianti Rufina Riserva, Italy (3–5 yrs)

Ruffino Chianti Classico Riserva Ducale Gold Label, Italy (5–7 yrs)

Selvapiana Chianti Rufina, Italy (3–5 yrs)

Banfi Brunello di Montalcino, Italy (6–8 yrs)

Duckhorn Napa Merlot, California (5–7 yrs)

Shafer Merlot, California (4–5 yrs)

Château Greysac Bordeaux, France (3–4 yrs)

Cakebread Napa Cabernet Sauvignon, California (4–5 yrs)

Château Gruaud-Larose Bordeaux, France (6–8 yrs)

Groth Napa Cabernet Sauvignon, California (4–5 yrs)

Heitz Napa Cabernet Sauvignon, California
(5–6 yrs)

Mt. Veeder Cabernet Sauvignon, California
(5–7 yrs)

Penfolds Bin 389 Cabernet/Shiraz, Australia
(6–8 yrs)

Silver Oak Alexander Valley Cabernet Sauvignon,
California (6–8 yrs)

Stag's Leap Wine Cellars Napa Cabernet Sauvignon,
California (4–5 yrs)

Muga Rioja Reserva, Spain (7–9 yrs)

Pesquera Ribera del Duero, Spain (7–9 yrs)

Château de Beaucastel Châteauneuf-du-Pape,
France (6–8 yrs)

Grgich Hills Sonoma Zinfandel, California (4–5 yrs)

Ridge Geyserville (Zinfandel), California (5–7 yrs)

Would You Drink It on a Plane?

Disregard the package (screw-capped splits)—if you
see these wineries on the beverage cart, you can take
heart. They won't be the greatest wine you ever
drank, but they are often the only redeeming feature
of flying coach.

Glen Ellen Proprietor's Reserve
Sutter Home
Georges Duboeuf
CK Mondavi

CUISINE COMPLEMENTS

Whether you're dining out, ordering in, or whipping it up yourself, the following wine recommendations will help you choose a wine to flatter the food in question. If your store doesn't carry that specific wine bottle, ask for a similar selection.

Thanksgiving Wines

More than any other meal, the traditional Thanksgiving lineup features a pretty schizo range of flavors—from gooey-sweet yams to spicy stuffing to tangy cranberry sauce and everything in between. These wines are like a group hug for all the flavors at the table and the guests around it. My tip: choose a white and a red, put them on the table, and let everyone taste and help themselves to whichever they care to drink. (Selections are listed by body style—lightest to fullest.)

	White	Red
S T E A L	MezzaCorona Pinot Grigio, Italy Hogue Fruit Forward Johannisberg Riesling, Washington Geyser Peak Sauvignon Blanc, California Marqués de Riscal White Rueda, Spain Fetzer Echo Ridge Gewürztraminer, California Gallo of Sonoma Chardonnay, California	Louis Jadot Beaujolais-Villages, France Coppola (Francis) Presents Rosso, California E & M Guigal Côtes-du-Rhône, France Marqués de Cáceres Rioja Crianza, Spain Cline Zinfandel, California Rosemount Diamond Label Shiraz, Australia
S P L U R G E	Martin Codax Albariño, Spain Trimbach Riesling, France Robert Mondavi Napa Fumé Blanc, California Hugel Gewürztraminer, France Kendall-Jackson Grand Reserve Chardonnay, California	Morgan Pinot Noir, California Château de Beaucastel Châteauneuf-du-Pape, France Penfolds Bin 389 Cabernet/Shiraz, Australia Pesquera Ribera del Duero, Spain Ridge Geyserville (Zinfandel), California

Barbecue

Penfolds Semillon Chardonnay, Australia
Dry Creek Fumé Blanc, California
Black Opal Shiraz, Australia
Coppola (Francis) Presents Rosso, California
Jaboulet Côtes-du-Rhône, France
Monteviña Amador Zinfandel, California

Chinese Food

Hugel Pinot Blanc, France
Jolivet Sancerre, France
Fetzer Echo Ridge Gewürztraminer, California
Firesteed Pinot Noir, Oregon
Marqués de Cáceres Rioja Crianza, Spain
Louis Jadot Beaujolais-Villages, France
Allegrini Valpolicella, Italy

Nuevo Latino (Cuban, Caribbean, South American)

Miguel Torres Viña Sol, Spain
Ecco Domani Pinot Grigio, Italy
Marqués de Riscal White Rueda, Spain
Concha y Toro Frontera Merlot, Chile
Santa Rita 120 Cabernet Sauvignon, Chile
Los Vascos Cabernet Sauvignon, Chile
Vega Sindoa Tempranillo/Merlot Navarra Tinto,
  Spain
Woodbridge (Robert Mondavi) Zinfandel,
  California

Picnics

CAVIT Pinot Grigio, Italy
Domaine Ste. Michelle Cuvée Brut Sparkling,
  Washington
Beringer White Zinfandel, California
Fetzer Sundial Chardonnay, California
Riunite Lambrusco, Italy
Citra Montepulciano d'Abruzzo, Italy
Duboeuf (Georges) Beaujolais-Villages, France

Sushi

Moët & Chandon White Star Champagne, France
Trimbach Riesling, France
Martin Codax Albariño, Spain
Jolivet Sancerre, France
Brancott Reserve Sauvignon Blanc, New Zealand
Frog's Leap Sauvignon Blanc, California

Louis Jadot Pouilly-Fuissé, France
B&G Beaujolais-Villages, France
Firesteed Pinot Noir, Oregon
Calera Central Coast Pinot Noir, California

Clambake
Kendall-Jackson Vintner's Reserve Sauvignon Blanc,
    California
Murphy-Goode Fumé Blanc, California
Gallo of Sonoma Chardonnay, California
Beringer Napa Chardonnay, California
Sterling North Coast Chardonnay, California
Coppola (Francis) Presents Rosso, California
Beaulieu (BV) Coastal Zinfandel, California

Mexican Food
Livio Felluga Pinot Grigio, Italy
King Estate Pinot Gris, Oregon
Meridian Sauvignon Blanc, New Zealand
Hugel Gewürztraminer, France
Buena Vista Sauvignon Blanc, California
Beringer White Zinfandel, California
Dry Creek Fumé Blanc, California
Duboeuf (Georges) Côtes-du-Rhône, France
Cline Zinfandel, California
Ravenswood Vintners Blend Zinfandel, California

Pizza
Citra Montepulciano d'Abruzzo, Italy
Santa Cristina Sangiovese, Antinori, Italy
Montecillo Rioja Crianza, Spain
Viña Carmen Cabernet Sauvignon, Chile
Monteviña Amador Zinfandel, California
Gallo of Sonoma Dry Creek Valley Zinfandel,
    California
Jacob's Creek Shiraz/Cabernet Sauvignon, Australia

The Cheese Course
Frescobaldi Chianti Rufina Riserva, Italy
Penfolds Bin 389 Cabernet/Shiraz, Australia
Château de Beaucastel Châteauneuf-du-Pape,
    France
Muga Rioja Reserva, Spain
Pesquera Ribera del Duero, Spain
St. Francis Sonoma Zinfandel, California
Ridge Geyserville (Zinfandel), California
Grgich Hills Sonoma Zinfandel, California

Mt. Veeder Cabernet Sauvignon, California
Château Gruaud-Larose Bordeaux, France
Banfi Brunello di Montalcino, Italy
Alvaro Palacios Les Terrasses Priorat, Spain

Steak
Talbott (Robert) Sleepy Hollow Vineyard
  Chardonnay, California
Morgan Pinot Noir, Oregon
Domaine Drouhin Pinot Noir, Oregon
Ruffino Chianti Classico Riserva Ducale Gold
  Label, Italy
Banfi Brunello di Montalcino, Italy
Shafer Merlot, California
Cakebread Napa Cabernet Sauvignon, California
Beringer Knights Valley Cabernet Sauvignon,
  California
Robert Mondavi Napa Cabernet Sauvignon,
  California
Groth Napa Cabernet Sauvignon, California
Stag's Leap Wine Cellars Napa Cabernet Sauvignon,
  California
Joseph Phelps Napa Cabernet Sauvignon, California
St. Francis Sonoma Zinfandel, California

Salad
Ruffino Orvieto, Italy
Hugel Pinot Blanc, France
Trimbach Riesling, France
Lucien Crochet Sancerre, France
Henri Bourgeois Pouilly-Fumé, France
Fetzer Echo Ridge Sauvignon Blanc, California
Louis Jadot Mâcon-Villages Chardonnay, France
Allegrini Valpolicella, Italy
Calera Central Coast Pinot Noir, California

Vegetarian
Folonari Pinot Grigio, Italy
Trimbach Pinot Gris, France
Rodney Strong Charlotte's Home Sauvignon Blanc,
  California
Callaway Coastal Chardonnay, California
Hess Select Chardonnay, California
Estancia Pinnacles Pinot Noir, California
Gabbiano Chianti, Italy
Jaboulet Côtes-du-Rhône, France

Winery Index

Coastal Chardonnay **$** 79
Coastal Merlot **$** 134
Coastal Sauvignon Blanc **$** 62
Coastal Zinfandel **$** 186
Rutherford Cabernet Sauvignon **$$$** 150

Benziger, California
Chardonnay **$$** 80
Sonoma Fumé Blanc **$$** 62

Beringer, California
Founders' Estate Cabernet Sauvignon **$** 150
Founders' Estate Chardonnay **$** 80
Founders' Estate Merlot **$** 134
Founders' Estate Pinot Noir **$** 118
Founders' Estate Sauvignon Blanc **$** 63
Johannisberg Riesling **$** 56
Knights Valley Cabernet Sauvignon **$$$** 150
Napa Chardonnay **$$** 80
Napa Sauvignon Blanc **$$** 63
North Coast Zinfandel **$$** 187
White Zinfandel **$** 111

Bernardus, California
Chardonnay **$$$** 81

Black Opal, Australia
Cabernet Sauvignon **$** 151
Cabernet/Merlot **$** 151
Shiraz **$** 181

Blackstone, California
Merlot **$$** 134

Blandy's, Portugal
10-Year-Old Malmsey Madeira **$$$** 194

Blue Nun, Germany
Liebfraumilch **$** 104

Bogle, California
Merlot **$$** 135

Bolla, Italy
Merlot **$** 135
Pinot Grigio **$** 52
Soave **$** 104
Valpolicella **$** 178

Bonny Doon, California
Pacific Rim Riesling (USA/Germany) **$** 56
Vin Gris de Cigare Pink Wine **$** 112

Bouvet, Loire Valley, France
Brut NV **$$** 44

Brancott, New Zealand
Reserve Sauvignon Blanc **$$** 64

Buehler, California
White Zinfandel **$** 112

Columbia Crest, Washington
Cabernet Sauvignon **\$** 155
Chardonnay **\$** 86
Johannisberg Riesling **\$** 57
Merlot **\$** 138
Sauvignon Blanc **\$** 66
Semillon/Chardonnay **\$** 105

Columbia Winery, Washington
Cellarmaster's Reserve Riesling **\$** 57

Concannon, California
Petite Syrah **\$** 176

Concha y Toro, Chile
Casillero del Diablo Sauvignon Blanc **\$** 67
Frontera Merlot **\$** 138
Sunrise Cabernet Sauvignon/Merlot **\$** 156
Sunrise Chardonnay **\$** 86
Terrunyo Carmenere **\$\$** 176

Coppola (Francis), California
Rosso **\$** 176

Corbett Canyon, California
Cabernet Sauvignon **\$** 156
Merlot **\$** 138
Sauvignon Blanc **\$** 67

Covey Run, Washington
Fumé Blanc **\$** 67
Riesling **\$** 58

Cristom, Oregon
Willamette Pinot Noir **\$\$\$** 120

Crochet (Lucien)
Sancerre **\$\$** 73

David Bruce, California
Central Coast Pinot Noir **\$\$** 120

DeLoach, California
Chardonnay **\$\$** 86

Didier Dagueneau, France
Silex Pouilly-Fumé **\$\$\$** 68

Domaine Carneros, California
Brut Sparkling **\$\$\$** 44

Domaine Chandon, Argentina
Brut Fresco Sparkling NV **\$** 45

Domaine Chandon, California
Extra Brut Classic Sparkling **\$\$** 45

Domaine Drouhin, Oregon
Willamette Valley Pinot Noir **\$\$\$\$** 121

Domaine Ste. Michelle, Washington
Cuvée Brut Sparkling **\$** 45

Frescobaldi, Italy
Chianti Rufina Riserva **$$$** 130

Frog's Leap, California
Merlot **$$$** 140
Sauvignon Blanc **$$$** 70

Gabbiano
Chianti **$** 129
Chianti Classico Riserva **$$** 129

Gallo of Sonoma, California
Cabernet Sauvignon **$** 158
Chardonnay **$** 88
Dry Creek Valley Zinfandel **$$** 188
Merlot **$** 141
Pinot Noir **$** 122

Georges Duboeuf, France
Côtes-du-Rhône **$** 182
Beaujolais Nouveau **$** 115
Beaujolais-Villages **$** 116

Geyser Peak, California
Chardonnay **$$** 89
Sauvignon Blanc **$** 70

Glen Ellen, California
Proprietor's Reserve Cabernet Sauvignon **$** 158
Proprietor's Reserve Chardonnay **$** 89
Proprietor's Reserve Merlot **$** 141
Proprietor's Reserve Sauvignon Blanc **$** 70

Gossamer Bay, California
Cabernet Sauvignon **$** 159
Chardonnay **$** 89
Merlot **$** 141

Gosset, France
Brut Rosé Champagne NV **$$$$** 46

Greg Norman, Australia
Cabernet/Merlot **$$** 159

Grgich Hills, California
Chardonnay **$$$** 90
Fumé Blanc **$$$** 70
Sonoma Zinfandel **$$$** 188

Groth, California
Napa Cabernet Sauvignon **$$$$** 159

Guenoc, California
Cabernet Sauvignon **$$** 160
Sauvignon Blanc **$$** 71

Guigal (E&M), Rhône, France
Côtes-du-Rhône **$** 182

Gunderloch, Germany
Riesling Kabinett Jean Baptiste **$$** 58

Trimbach, Alsace, France
Pinot Gris $$ 54
Riesling $$ 60

Turning Leaf, California
Cabernet Sauvignon $ 169
Chardonnay $ 101
Merlot $ 146
Pinot Grigio $ 55
Pinot Noir $ 126
Zinfandel $ 192

Vega Sindoa Navarra, Spain
Tempranillo/Merlot Tinto $ 174

Vendange, California
Cabernet Sauvignon $ 169
Merlot $ 147
White Zinfandel $ 114
Zinfandel $ 192

Veramonte, Chile
Cabernet Sauvignon $ 169
Primus $$ 178

Veuve Clicquot, Champagne, France
Yellow Label NV $$$$ 50

Villa Maria, New Zealand
Private Bin Sauvignon Blanc $ 77

Viña Carmen, Chile
Cabernet Sauvignon $ 169

Viña Santa Carolina, Chile
Chardonnay/Sauvignon Blanc $ 102

Walnut Crest, Chile
Cabernet Sauvignon $ 170
Merlot $ 147

Wente, California
Riesling $ 61

Weingärtner, Austria
Gruner Veltliner Federspiel $ 110

Wild Horse, California
Pinot Noir $$ 126

Willakenzie, Oregon
Willamette Valley Pinot Noir $$$ 127

Willamette Valley Vineyards, Oregon
Pinot Noir $$ 127

Woodbridge (Robert Mondavi), California
Cabernet Sauvignon $ 170
Chardonnay $ 102
Merlot $ 147
Sauvignon Blanc $ 77
Zinfandel $ 192

THANKS TO . . .

The tasting panel! You've made buying and drinking wine better and more fun for everyone who picks up this book. Thanks for sharing your hidden gems, and for telling it like it is. Keep tasting!

The trade insiders, for their view of the wines leading the market—especially Brian Yost at Marriott, Annette Alvarez and David Andrew at Costco, Super-Target and Marshall-Field's, Darden Restaurants, Morton's Steakhouse, and the Master Sommeliers.

Cindy Renzi, Chris Goodhart, and Maria Kline, who made the survey happen; and Michael Preis, for MBA and wine pro skills right when I needed them most.

Angela Miller and Broadway Books, especially Jennifer Josephy and Steve Rubin, for believing in the book.

DEDICATED TO . . .

My family.

In loving tribute to the memory of the missing from Windows on the World, where wine really was for everyone.

PLEASE JOIN MY TASTING PANEL

To share your comments on wines you like (or dislike), visit www.greatwinemadesimple.com or e-mail andrea@greatwinemadesimple.com. Or to request a paper survey by mail, please fill out and return this card.

☐ Mr.   ☐ Mrs.   ☐ Ms.

_____
Your Name (and company if applicable)

_____
Street Address   Apt./Suite #

_____
City   State   Zip

Optional

_____
E-mail address

_____
Occupation

To order *Andrea Immer's Wine Buying Guide for Everyone,* check all that apply, and we will contact you by e-mail, mail, or phone:

☐ Customized copies
☐ Bulk order
☐ Signed copies
☐ Single copies/small quantities (help me find a store in my area)

Please contact me by (choose one):

☐ Phone (   ) _____-_____
☐ E-mail
☐ Mail } Please fill in the above form.